The Use of Punishment

The Use of Punishment

edited by

Seán McConville

WILLAN
PUBLISHING

Published by

Willan Publishing
Culmcott House
Mill Street, Uffculme
Cullompton, Devon
EX15 3AT, UK
Tel: +44(0)1884 840337
Fax: +44(0)1884 840251
e-mail: info@willanpublishing.co.uk
website: www.willanpublishing.co.uk

Published simultaneously in the USA and Canada by

Willan Publishing
c/o ISBS, 920 NE 58th Ave, Suite 300
Portland, Oregon 97213-3644, USA
Tel: +001(0)503 287 3093
Fax: +001(0)503 280 8832
website: www.isbs.com

First published 2003

ISBN 1-84392-033-6 (paperback)
ISBN 1-84392-034-4 (hardback)

British Library Cataloguing-in-Publication Data
A catalogue record for this book is available from the British Library

Project management by Deer Park Productions, Tavistock, Devon
Typeset by GCS, Leighton Buzzard, Beds
Printed and bound by T.J. International, Padstow, Cornwall

Contents

Acknowledgements

The Harry Frank Guggenheim Foundation initiated and generously supported the work on which this volume is based. Contributors were given opportunities to meet undisturbed in pleasant locations, initially to discuss approaches to their topics and in due course to submit their penultimate drafts for discussion. All of this took a deal of organising and we are indebted to the Foundation and to Karen Colvard and her colleagues for their thoughtfulness and care. Academics are not always the easiest people with whom to work, but the Foundation's blend of encouragement, involvement and patience made the task of putting this book together as pleasant and free from friction as could be. All contributors are also grateful to those in the somewhat wider group who attended meetings and who offered their suggestions and comments on approaches and papers.

I must express warm thanks to my co-contributors who responded so positively to editorial notes and who happily undertook meticulous revisions through the somewhat extended gestation period for this project. The consequent updatings gave us an opportunity to make further improvements. Three contributors joined us at a later stage, and while they were spared the frustrations of delays, had to familiarise themselves with all the work undertaken by contributors to that point. Re-orienting the collection in the light of continuing discussions meant that some completed essays would not be included in the book. We thank those authors for their participation, understanding and support.

Linda Cox, my secretary at Queen Mary, has provided her customary support unstintingly, loyally and efficiently, repeatedly saving great trouble and time. Susan Hemp, also at Queen Mary, gave much assistance in the concluding phases of the project and as always, responded positively and cheerfully to all my requests.

Seán McConville
Department of Law
Queen Mary, University of London

Notes on contributors

Marcellus Andrews is Professor of Economics in the School of Public Affairs at Baruch College, City University of New York. He is the author of *The Political Economy of Hope and Fear: Capitalism and the Black Condition in America* (New York University Press, 2001).

Alan Duce is a priest and Canon of the Church of England. He has been a full-time prison chaplain for 28 years and editor of *New Life* (the Prison Service chaplaincy review) for some 20 years.

Mark Fleisher is the Dr Semi J. and Ruth W. Begun Professor and Director of the Begun Center for Violence Prevention Research and Education, Mandel School of Applied Social Sciences, Case Western Reserve University, Cleveland, Ohio. He is editor of the refereed book series, *Violence Research and Policy*, AltaMira Publications, Walnut Creek: California.

Carolyn Hoyle is Lecturer in Criminology at the Centre for Criminological Research, University of Oxford, and a Fellow of Green College. She is the author of *Negotiating Domestic Violence* (OUP, 1997) and co-editor of *New Visions of Crime Victims* (Hart, 2002). She is currently directing a project on the use of restorative justice within the police complaints process.

L. Rowell Huesmann is Professor of Psychology and Communication Studies at the University of Michigan and a Senior Research Scientist at the Institute for Social Research where he directs the Aggression

Research Program. He previously had been a faculty member at Yale University and the University of Illinois at Chicago.

Nicola Lacey is Professor of Criminal Law at the London School of Economics and Adjunct Professor of Social and Political Theory at the Research School of Social Sciences of the Australian National University. She is the author of *State Punishment* (Routledge, 1988) and a number of related books. She is a Fellow of the British Academy.

Cheryl-Lynn Podolski is a PhD candidate in clinical psychology at Michigan State University. She received her BA in Psychology from the University of Michigan in 1991 and has co-authored a number of publications on the development of aggressive behaviour.

Seán McConville is Professor of Criminal Justice and Professorial Research Fellow in the Department of Law, Queen Mary, University of London. He has published widely on punishment and related topics and has advised government bodies and legislatures on both sides of the Atlantic. His most recent book is *Irish Political Prisoners 1848-1922: Theatres of War* (Routledge, 2003).

Richard Sparks is Professor of Criminology at Keele University. His main research interests are in the sociology of punishment (especially imprisonment), penal politics and public responses to crime and punishment. He is the author or editor of a number of books on these topics, the latest being (with Tim Newburn, eds.) *Criminal Justice and Political Cultures* (Willan).

Richard Young is Reader in Criminal Justice and Assistant Director of the Centre for Criminological Research, University of Oxford. He has written widely on criminal justice and restorative justice and conducted a number of empirical studies in these areas. Full details of these projects and publications can be found on www.crim.ox.ac.uk

Introduction

I first went to prison in the autumn of 1967, and can still vividly recall that confused sequence of impressions as the season progressed into winter. I had fleetingly visited prisons before and had come away convinced that they were a different part of the planet from any I had previously seen. Some of the surroundings had been exotic for a newcomer: sombre buildings, bars, gates, high walls and the continuous noise of locks turning and doors banging; perhaps imagined, but everywhere I went, high social tension. The little world of the cell had an enormous impact. In the Victorian prisons these were 8 feet wide, 12 in length, 9-foot ceilings (frequently vaulted) and a high, barred window – dirty or opaque glass restricting the view, and a cleverly sloping sill to prevent the prisoner drawing himself up to look out. This was indeed a strange and awful habitation in which to pass the greater part of each day and the passing of the months and years. The sight of a young man of my own age in parti-coloured clothing walking alone around the exercise ring in one of these prisons – a high-security prisoner at the start of a life sentence, I was told – kept me awake that night and was in my mind for weeks.

As it happened, my 'own' prison was not of the jailhouse type. It was a decommissioned US Army hospital, dating back to the Second World War: long rows of Nissen huts simply laid out on the fields and linked together by walkways. This was an open (minimum-security) prison. The low walls that marked out the estate were no more formidable than those with which any property owner would protect his holdings; the intention was to keep would-be lovers and traffickers (and the merely curious) out rather than keep the prisoners in. Here the apparatus of captivity was in the mind rather than the buildings.

The inmates fell into two main categories: minor offenders whose sentences showed them to have impressed the courts as nuisances rather than threats, and those who had almost completed long sentences in closed prisons and were now being tested, re-socialised and 'decompressed', preparatory to release. The categories could be misleading. Among the ostensibly minor offenders in those years there lurked incognito a man who had already committed murder, and who would go on to become one of the most notorious serial killers in criminal history. And among the known murderers (and there were many) there was a large group who were non-criminal in the sense that neither before nor after their terrible deed had they broken or would break the law. Chance, a combination of circumstances and, sometimes, an episode of passion, had propelled them into the criminal process. They were ordinary, civil and often deeply remorseful and conscience-torn, and it was difficult not to see them as instances of the fate of many, but for the grace of God.

In two instalments I was to spend the better part of a year at this prison and was thereafter committed to a life of punishment – that is to say, a life spent studying, writing, lobbying, consulting and litigating – all in connection with the penal process. Hardy had perhaps got it right – the course of our lives can be determined by a chance meeting, or indeed a failure to meet. In my case a fascination was born which has scarcely waned in the intervening years, and which still grips and constantly stimulates.

The setting, as I have indicated, was prosaic – unremarkable if somewhat dilapidated buildings in an inappropriately bucolic setting. The magnetism of the place and the ineradicability of the experience lay in the life that was lived there, the penal portion of our times. Men had come by many different paths to be prisoners, uniformed officers, clerical or trade staff, or administrators. For some, the personality was penetrated to the core; for others, the prison may have been no more than a passing episode, and that one of many. But for all, for a time at least, this was life in an extremity of conditions.

Imprisonment is loss of freedom. This is an obvious enough statement, but it must be given meaning either by experience or study. The most minute decisions are denied the prisoner – his clothing, food, work, study, correspondence, visitors and daily routine are all governed by detailed rules and these are interpreted by others. (At the time to which I refer, prisoners were denied access to any but a handful of the rules – lest they manipulate them to their own advantage, it was contended.) Privacy is removed and one loses the ability to control personal space and choice of companions. Personal security acquires a centrality it never previously had: companionship and mutual support become extremely important – sometimes literally vital. Always there is the corrosive contemplation of the outside world – past, present and to come – and consignment to what at times must seem the fate of the spectre: present, seeing and hearing, full of regrets and longings, but without substance and unable to act. In prison, it is said, those who learn to live in the present are, if not the happiest, those most able to minimise suffering.

On the other side of the counter, officers and administrators are similarly cast adrift from the ordinary world. Although theirs is not a pariah occupation, it is one that produces unease in outsiders, sometimes mixed with a morbid curiosity. Fairly strict rules and a fear of being compromised prevent discussion of the prison with civilians and this adds to a sense of oddness, both for those who work within it and those who meet them socially. Patterns of shift-work, staff housing policies and sometimes the out-of-the-way location of the prison increase distance from the everyday world and make for a degree of introspectiveness. After-hours socialising in the staff club, where conversation centres on institutional life, compounds all of this. Some staff count off the months and years to the release of retirement and pension. As at any prison, it was well-known but referred to only guardedly, that the pressures of this life could have unhappy effects on some families.

As the years passed, I visited and sometimes worked in other prisons in many different countries. The basic patterns were to be found almost everywhere. Some effects were diluted, others intensified. Staff who lived in their own houses and were dispersed through an urban community, for example, were less inclined to be prisonised. Prisoners who lived in one of the gang-ridden penitentiaries of Illinois, Indiana, or California were forced into intense relations of dependence and exploitation with each other and were understandably preoccupied with personal security. Even without the textbooks, I would have understood immediately that the women's prisons I visited were ordered in a very different way, with most women far more strongly attached than men to life beyond the walls, and with little violence and much less regimentation in their institutional experience.

One of the mysteries of that autumn of 1967 waited some years for its resolution. What was supposed to be happening in prison? Were the men there for punishment? If so, what form did it take? That question was apparently resolved by an aphorism formulated in the 1930s by a great figure in British penal history, Sir Alexander Paterson: 'Men go to prison *as* punishment, not *for* punishment'. Initially satisfying, closer examination suggested that this was no answer – or at least not a full one. If they were in prison as punishment, what was supposed to be happening to them there? Were they simply supposed to be in a kind of civic suspended animation? Another answer was offered – Rule 1 of the Prison Rules: 'The purpose of the treatment and training of prisoners is to fit them to lead a good and useful life.' Looking around, weighing the routine of each day, I wondered further: by which official actions were the treatment and training provided? I saw men leading a life shaped by the necessities of a residential institution – a daily routine of rising, eating, washing, limited trade-training and workshops, interviews, housekeeping work and rules: a mass of details and a tangle of wishes and frustrations managed only by a great deal of uniformity in clothing, possessions, entitlements and treatment, and a hierarchy of authority of which the prisoners comprised the bottom layer. Despite a significant amount of goodwill and co-operation, life was a kind of crippled existence, permeated with stigma, shame and loss of position and social freedom.

I could not see in institutional life itself the basis of that reconstruction that was supposed to lead to a good and useful life. There was provided a form of conversation therapy. At one level this was practical, useful and problem-solving, addressing the mess that many of the prisoners had made of their lives and that went well beyond their brush with justice – marital discord, divorce, child access and custody, disputes, alcoholism (these were the blessed pre-drugs days), poor work skills, illiteracy, unemployment, homelessness, mental and physical health problems and so on. A truly impressive amount of good was done in tackling those obstacles to a good and useful life. But was this 'treatment and training'; did it address the mental and emotional problems that perhaps had generated many of the more practical difficulties?

There was at that time a deal of awareness about the psychological background to many of the men's crimes. But what to do about it? With a population of several hundred and maybe three or four members of staff at all equipped to carry out psychologically based casework, and those involved in numerous other duties besides, this was a hopeless endeavour. (Ignoring the questions about the efficacy of such inter-ventions, even when carried out in optimum conditions.) In truth, sympathetic members of the uniformed and civilian staff, and others such as the chaplain, listened to prisoners' accounts of these deeper problems, and did what they could to understand and advise. Some no doubt accumulated experience and wisdom over the years, but there seemed to be very little difference between these informal counsels of the prison – and one must not omit prisoners themselves from this list of counsellors – and what might be available through the confidants and confidences of the average workplace.

At the end of my spell in prison, therefore, I was little wiser as to what the institution was supposed to be *doing*: mere existence hardly seemed enough. Some years later, conducting research on penal history, I came across part of the explanation of the 'treatment and training' that was so central to imprisonment that it occupied Rule 1 of the English prison rules, yet was so elusive, vague and hard to identify. (And the open prison at which I had worked would have most certainly been the optimum habitat for Rule 1 – in the overcrowded, under-funded and increasingly dilapidated local prisons of the time, Rule 1 could scarcely have had a meaning even as an aspiration.)

From my research it appeared that the last time that most English prisons had been precise instruments of punishment – routine specifically tied to objectives – was prior to 1898. From the 1860s until the turn of the twentieth century, the purpose of English local prisons (a rough equivalent to the American jail) had been to inflict a known and measured deterrent experience on the convicted offender and to stand *in terrorem* to the general population. This was done through remorseless isolation, discomfort, exertion, cold and deprivation – working to the limits of physical and mental endurance and systematically on all the senses. Public sentiment and political thought shifted, and at the beginning of the twentieth century the Victorian pain and discomfort machine that was imprisonment was set aside in favour of something more vaguely punitive. The staff remained the same, the conditions as bleak, sordid and unpromising as before, but pain and discomfort were not actively sought through the regime. That they necessarily occurred was acknowledged, a form of deterrence in the twilight.

In the late 1890s Evelyn Ruggles Brise, the head of the English prison service – young, new in post and carrying on his shoulders some great reformatory expectations – confronted a public-relations difficulty: how was he to explain to Parliament and the taxpayer what was happening in their prisons now that the crank (a friction machine to enforce useless hard labour in solitude) and the treadwheel were gone? He came up with an answer that has served until our own times. Unlike foreign experimental methods (he was referring to the European Continent and the United States of America) the English penal method was 'quiet and unostentatious … orderly government'. This was no military-like system that dealt with men by numbers, ignoring their humanity. Instead it insisted on 'order and obedience and cleanliness and industry, as a primary and essential condition of imprisonment'. These qualities (incidental, one might observe, to any institutional routine) gave English imprisonment its distinctive and ever-so-convenient reformatory power. Just being in prison, in other words, was a reformatory experience.

In this way was the public relations problem solved in 1898, and without much comment this remained the position for most of the twentieth century in the majority of English prisons (there were a few notable exceptions). When I went looking for treatment and training in my open prison in the autumn of 1967, I should have realised that it was all around me – in the rising and setting of the sun and the routine that filled the time in between. What was prison for? Reformation. And how is reformation achieved? Being in prison.

It was an undoubted nonsense, yet over the decades and within its folds and vagueness there were many attempts to find a rational and defensible regime and to use imprisonment as a positive means of reducing re-offending. Some of these experiments hung on gossamer; others were demonstrably practical. From the late 1960s, however, the penal wind shifted and new-old purposes were given to imprisonment: those crystallised around retribution and public protection. These remain with us at the top of the public agenda despite their manifold imperfections. As shall be seen elsewhere in this book (and in many of the critical sources cited in the bibliographies) retribution is an objective consisting of rather more metaphysics than its greatly assorted proponents might care to recognise, a range of problems in its calculation and calibration and a deal of uncertainty in its administration. (Yet in 1991 – at least in theory – it became the basis of English sentencing.) Public protection is nothing new in penal policy and, although banished to the background in more sanguine times, has always been a major requirement of the penal process. The English prison population has almost doubled in the last decade, and politicians of both main parties seem to be set on the American path and imagine they can build themselves out of crime.

I hope I may be acquitted of egoism in inserting my own penal experiences and collections into this account. The point that I have wished to make could have perhaps been more compressed, but that would not fully convey the vagueness of penal policy, the uneven ground on which it is based and the tides and swells that carry it here and there.

This is not a book about imprisonment or indeed about the specifics of penal policy, but is much more generally about punishment. These preliminary observations are intended only to underline the dramatic elements in punishment and some of the distinctive characteristics of the institutions that administer it. That I should turn to the prison for examples is not simply a matter of personal experience, but of the defining nature of imprisonment in our times. In Western societies (with the exception of the United States) prison is the state's ultimate expression of power over the citizen. But its purposes are diffuse as well as precise: many would argue that it is the sanction and the fallback that makes more lenient punishments possible. While the shadow of the prison looms very faintly over the law-abiding, it is unquestionably the threat that compels payment of fines and compliance with the requirements of non-custodial punishment. Indeed, no matter how inventive we are with words, we come back to 'non-custodial' to describe fines, probation and community service in all their various forms and combinations. Prison is the penal gold-standard.

The common element across the range of punishments, custodial and non-custodial, seems to be a loss of autonomy, adulthood even. The errant employee receiving a formal verbal warning is in some way cast back to childhood. The motorist rebuked by traffic police must be polite and submissive or risk stronger sanctions. Those on probation must keep appointments, are asked to account for themselves and must follow directions. Community service also obliges one to turn up on time and to carry out the designated task: rebelliousness, truculence or non-compliance will be further punished. Punishment at this end of the spectrum shades off into the deference, compliance and orderliness that we all must show in everyday life; it starts with a mother's displeasure with her infant and follows us into education and then the world of work.

So is punishment a universal experience and, if it is, is that a good thing? Is there an amount of punishment in a person's life that is necessary to civilise him or her? Contrarywise, is punishment a distorting and mutilating experience? Is it the antithesis of civilisation and will our progress, as Churchill suggested, be marked by a decline in its severity? Or is punishment the inevitable consequence of the way we choose to live, confirmation that we are inhabitants of an unjust society? Attempts to answer these questions could fill many paragraphs and pages, and certainly take us to the heart of several key psychological, political and philosophical disputes. These conundrums will never be settled or stilled, but from time to time a consensus emerges and may even become an orthodoxy and a test of intellectual respectability. Inevitably that will be the source of a heterodoxy, and so on. Exploring this ground, this collection makes no claim other than the projection of some freeze-frames from an endlessly shifting and developing debate.

This is not to say that exactly the same arguments are rehearsed each time the topics are considered: over time the area of contention moves around a larger landscape of uncertain size and delineation. For most of the twentieth century the explicit consensus was that decent societies were non-punitive. The prevailing view (certainly in political circles) has not swung around to the opposite, but to an acceptance of the apparently productive and positive nature of punishment and a willingness to increase its use in pursuit of order and social engineering. Looking no further than 25 years into the future, it is hard to see what direction a new consensus will take, or around what propositions it will form, or when, or how.

This collection was not conceived as a review of particular aspects of penal policy, although it should be of interest to anyone who wishes to cast penal policies in a wider and more reflective context. No one line of approach has been taken, and it will be found that the authors differ in backgrounds and disciplines and also in philosophical and political stances. All the essays have attended to the complexity of the various arguments, have a cautiousness about contradictions in penal thought and a reluctance to draw apparently straightforward and facile conclusions. All are aware of the volatility of penal thought and its susceptibility to be influenced by and employed in the see-saws of party politics.

The book gets under way with a contribution from Alan Duce, an Anglican clergyman and prison chaplain of many years' standing. It is a commonplace that many of the core elements in criminal law derive from religious teaching. At one level it should be easier for a person with strong and clear religious beliefs to deal with punishment and its variety of issues. An unchanging moral code – even though interpretation may shift somewhat with the times – takes one past some of the preliminary difficulties of the secularist, particularly the justifications for criminal law. A voice that speaks from revealed doctrine can be much more confident than one that proceeds on the basis of present usefulness or even tradition. That is not to say that all religious interpretations can be equally confident and certain, or that the believer can ignore a clash of values, with religious doctrine taking one strong line and social and political consensus another. The havoc caused in the various Christian denominations by changing sexual mores demonstrates the intensity of those conflicts.

Alan Duce, however, looks not so much to debates about the origins of laws as to Christian thinking about punishment. A particularly interesting aspect of his contribution is that he is a working Christian who must every day find an approach to his institutional duties which is compatible with the doctrines of church and conscience: *can* one serve Caesar and God, Duce asks. Anyone who has spent any time in prison and who is at all reflective, will agree that the conscientious chaplain's tasks is one of the most vulnerable and difficult in the institution, but at the same time is possessed of enormous potential.

How can a religious approach maintain its integrity within a state-ordered and politically determined system of punishment? Obliged to make judgements, how can a religious person reconcile that duty with his understanding that all human judgement is imperfect? And given that one must minister to the offender, who is often in emotional, psychological and spiritual distress, what can and should be done to bring him a personal accounting for the harm that has been done to his victim, to society and indeed to himself? Central to all the monotheistic religions is the doctrine that man has been created by God, and that all share in the fellowship of that common creation. How then can punishment be conceived and administered, judging without excluding, condemning without extinguishing hope? Is there a danger that the teaching that all are sinners will simply dwindle into an empty and rather ridiculous unwillingness to denounce crime and uphold moral virtues? And in this connection, is everyone *entitled* to forgiveness? Are there crimes that are beyond our capacity to forgive? Must a notorious and wicked criminal remain only that or are we all in the process of becoming, until we die? What has Christian theology to say about repentance? And what of vengeance and retribution? In the turmoil of these questions, what is truth?

From the outset, all contributors agreed that the variety of our disciplinary backgrounds would enrich the project not simply because of the different perspectives, but also because we would need a common language and this would oblige us to climb over the various boundary walls of our intellectual neighbourhood. Academic psychology has perhaps pushed those walls higher than most, as it has become ever more specialised and fragmented. (Though, on reflection, this has been the fate of many if not most branches of the social sciences: a depressing development.) I owe a particular debt of gratitude to Rowell Huesmann and Cheryl-Lynn Podolski, who worked and reworked their essay on the psychology of punishment in order to make it more accessible to the non-specialist.

Anyone who follows a trade for a while must pick up the shortcuts, and the academic trade is no exception. There are various ways of starting lectures, and the first few minutes in a series can be critical. At the risk of (undoubtedly justified) accusations of hamming it up, I must reveal an opening line I sometimes use when meeting a new class or seminar group to discuss punishment. I look around the assemblage and remark 'Everyone here, myself included, has been punished.' I go on to outline the range of actions or inactions that constitute punishment from, say, a mother's unhappy frown or a partner's silence, to the heaviest of state punishments. Punishment, thus defined, is unavoidable in the course of our lives – even among the meekest, most conformist and law-abiding.

Belonging to a generation that witnessed (and experienced) corporal punishment in schools, and was angered and revolted by it, I cannot be sanguine about the ubiquity of punishment. It is a matter of some consequence that we should know, as parents, persons in authority or simply as citizens, the effects of punishment. Some retributionists would see the punishment of wrong as an end in itself, but for those who feel that the principal penal objective is a change of behaviour, it is important to know what scientific studies have to say about effectiveness. Strange indeed, that in the face of all the obvious costs of punishment to the person, family, community and state, there is little to show that legislators attend to this kind of evidence. The abundance of research material and the nature of a range of findings are examined by Huesmann and Podolski.

Starting with the combination of genetic, physiological and environmental factors that contribute to aggressive and antisocial acts, Huesmann and Podolski outline major theories of the learning process and relate these to punishment. This is a critical linkage, since unless one is a sadist or a particularly metaphysical retributionist, one must consider punishment as a type of learning. That being so, if a form of punishment does not educate or socialise in the way one expects, or if it produces results contrary to those which are sought, one must make changes. The punishment in question must be modified, or inflicted in a different way, or take place at a different point in the offending-behaviour/punishment sequence, or be dropped altogether. As the authors show, existing scientific knowledge gives important guidance on these matters.

I have never actually heard that classic humbug 'This hurts me more than it hurts you', but it certainly was an implied part of the situation in some schools and institutions. It would scarcely have been *respectable* for a grown-up to beat a child were that simply a venting of anger, rage or frustration. Yet we know that this is precisely what happens in many of those punitive encounters. What does punishment do to the inflictor and to the person being punished who sees the behaviour and grasps the motivation of the inflictor? And what happens when punishment is ritualistically carried out in front of a class of immature and suggestive children? Contrarywise, is a punishment which is seen to fit the offence, which is proportionate and connected with some immediacy or directness to that offence, not an important and constructive part of civil life? How can penal policy be informed by studies of the learning process and the effects of childhood punishment?

This is precisely the topic taken up by Mark Fleisher, an ethnographer who has studied one of the groups prominent in virtually all discussions of crime and punishment – the youth gang. On any consideration, it is an oddity that those who shape, make and apply criminal policy can speak in confident terms about who they would like to see punished and the condign effects that punishment would have. Are they not sometimes thinking about of their own imagined reaction to punishment, rather than that of the target group? Yet anyone who attends the criminal courts regularly, or works with delinquents, knows how misleading this assumption might be. There are persons whose ties to society are so weak or misdirected, or who are so damaged, inadequate or degraded, that they are manifestly beyond the effects of punishment. Others, more shrewd and cunning, have taken a calculated risk and often accept their punishment stoically. More rarely, there comes before the court the adherent of a political, social or religious cause, for whom punishment is an apotheosis.

Mark Fleisher approaches the place of punishment in the life of a youth gang in the only way that can be sensible – an understanding of the daily life and world-view of the members. Relevant matters include the physical territory controlled by the gang, their criminal activities, their interactions with each other and with the 'straight' world. The last comprises school, adults (though some of these are far from straight), police, courts and custody. Given the great importance of early socialisation, it is no revelation that hardcore youth gang members come overwhelmingly from neglectful and abusive families and go on themselves to early parenthood. Such facts are repeated so often that we seemingly cease to listen to them.

How can punishment reach such young people? Even should they calculate the risks of being caught and dealt with, many are beyond the basic restraints of shame and fear and thus apparently the deterrent effects of punishment. When these teenagers are locked up, their reactions are not as might be expected by respectable society. Fleisher points out that they are made apathetic rather than devastated by loss of freedom. In prison the gang member does not miss the major institutions that shape other lives – these have at best been peripheral. Indeed, incarceration creates new opportunities. Behind the bars they encounter delinquents from other gangs and areas and, in a real sense, broaden their criminal education. The supposed benefits of imprisonment – academic and vocational training, drug treatment and psychological counselling, appear to be far outweighed by the near-indelible stigma of imprisonment and the barrier this constitutes for employment. The marketplace is bleak and unforgiving for these minimum-skill and tainted youngsters. Fleisher argues that juvenile justice policy 'sets the stage for failure'. He proposes instead comprehensive intervention and prevention programmes.

One of the most remarkable phenomena of modern times has been the vast and rapid expansion of imprisonment in the United States. The incarcerated population – federal, state and county, prison and jail, has risen beyond two million. Nor is this simply a reflection of an increase in the general population. Between the 1920s and 1970s the *rate* of imprisonment stayed stable in the US (i.e. as a proportion of the population). In the last 30 years, however, it has increased by several hundred per cent. The costs are enormous, but there are many politicians and analysts who insist that every penny budgeted for incarceration is well spent: society benefits by removing offenders from circulation and by the deterrent effects of incarceration. This is a topic that has driven liberal and conservative thinkers into opposing camps where a generation ago there was a surprisingly strong consensus that imprisonment is an expensive means of making bad people worse. Electorates, however, are willing to back this modern shift in penal policy and there are few politicians willing to criticise or oppose it (whatever their private reservations).

But it is certainly a major deployment of a nation's resources and America's penal policy is the subject of Marcellus Andrews' economic analysis. Social analyses of punishment must fairly quickly come to the realisation that penal policy is hard to separate from social, urban and educational policy and that employment structure and levels, the fiscal regime and even international economic relations all have consequences for crime and punishment. With the tools of the economist, Andrews covers this ground, starting with a discussion of the nature of choice and therefore of deterrence. Just as lawyers, when driven into a corner, will turn to the concept of the 'reasonable man' (who coincidentally is likely to be on their side), so economists approach choice with the rational man or woman in mind. Calculations of the costs and benefits of punishment are heaped upon this somewhat improbable figure, even though the realities of criminal justice, on even the most superficial acquaintance, indicate that the rational decision-maker may be more elusive than the unicorn, or at least the salamander.

And quite apart from criminal irrationality, it may not be too wise to assume that public policy is shaped by rational decision-making. Andrews sets out a cost–benefit analysis looking not only at money but also opportunity cost: 'if I do this to what extent am I prevented from doing that?' And then there are accountancy-type calculations. Given that an offender commits crime at such and such rate and that I can convert that into a money cost, I can calculate how much saving there will be to society should I lock him up. One theorist computes the annual net saving from the incarceration of a convicted person – the social benefit – to be around US$16,700. In this sense imprisonment pays and it is rational to seek to build our way out of crime.

But 'crime' is heterogeneous, ranging from income-tax evasion to aggravated homicide and treason. Does the calculation of benefit hold across the board? Does society benefit to the same extent from the incarceration of all categories of criminals? Is the criminal such a lost cause that removing him or her from society (or rather to a different part of society) is wholly beneficial? Andrews poses some difficult questions here, particularly about the impact of imprisonment upon particular communities.

Is there an even more intractable problem to be addressed? In a society that has grown fabulously wealthy, there has emerged a greater degree of class polarity than any would have expected 50 years ago. A substantial group – unskilled, uneducated and poorly socialised – seems to be excluded from the world of work and consumption by the imperatives of a high-investment, high-skill economy. The prospects of unskilled work becoming available on its previous scale seem remote. What are we to do with this group on the margins of our society, a disproportionate section of which belongs to ethnic minorities? And if we cannot offer a solution to the economic problems of these groups, are we not condemning them – and ourselves – to an increasingly divided, security-conscious, high-incarceration society? Is there any way out?

With these questions we move into the form of meta-analysis that is attempted by Richard Sparks. The treatment of persons under punishment has long been taken by observers of the political structure as an important index of its values. With this as a starting-point, Sparks asks what the changes in penal policy of the last generation or so tell us about how we live, and where our society might be going. That we live in a different world – startlingly different, in many ways – cannot be gainsaid. Fifty years ago the Cold War dominated international relations at every level. In the West, wealth and well-being were based on heavy industries that in many respects had changed little since Queen Victoria's death. The social order had certainly been shaken and in part demolished by the two great wars, but although empires had fallen the structures and mores of earlier times were still a powerful presence. Nations sat behind their frontiers, as did the social classes, and travel across either kind of border was for the lucky minority. Technological innovations of many kinds, globalisation and one of its consequences – mass migration – the dissolution of old social structures and modification or abandonment of a range of key values, all amount to change, large-scale and profound. What connections can we make between these sweeping developments and modern penal thinking and policy?

Sparks points out that the penal system used to be identified with social welfare – education, social work and mental health. Whereas penal thinking and policy have not totally broken away from welfare, the attitude towards the 'normal' adult offender has significantly shifted. One of the consequences of developing special policies for groups such as the mentally ill or afflicted, drug-addicted and drug-driven and juvenile offenders, is that the remaining majority may be more directly and severely held to account. This 'normal' group has been the focus of a good deal of political debate, and that in turn has had a significant party-political component. Sparks analyses both the nature of this attention and the language and tone of debates. He surely makes a telling point when he refers to the 'emergency' posture that governments have adopted in these deliberations.

The security of its citizens is a cardinal task of the state. An intriguing part of Sparks' essay deals with the management of risk. He draws our attention to the fact that risk is at the centre of the 'new' economy and its political structures – risk assessment and management have spawned a number of new legal, organisational and financial arrangements. The transfer of private-sector approaches into the public sector has gone well beyond language and management styles, and many functions long thought to be definitively within the public sphere have been sold, contracted or delegated to private-sector organisations. These transfers frequently focus on risk and the consequent private profits are justified by the transfer of risk. The shift from one sector to the other is the outcome of some degree of fragmentation of state operations and has significant implications for criminal and penal policy. The control of risk leads us beyond deterrence, reformation and retribution to incapacitation in one form or another. Sparks, with others, argues that risk – or at least thinking and talking about risk – has become a pervasive part of public life.

It is essential to acknowledge the realities that lie behind the intrusion of a consciousness of risk into everyday life and its consequent projection onto the political agenda. We may note that the way we live and the political-economic choices that have been made (and one may question the extent to which they have consciously been made or fully understood) have had a number of outcomes, including a rise in crime. It is quite another and much less defensible position to imply that concern about risk is unreasonable. Statistics, both from police reports and victim surveys, show levels of theft (including burglary) and offences against the person that are unacceptably high and that, although spread across a number of social groups, particularly blight the lives of the most vulnerable – the urban poor and many ethnic minorities. Fear of victimisation, however, can be unreasonable and it certainly can also be an unproductive part of political life. As in many other approaches to policy, finding the point of balance is a delicate and sometimes hit-or-miss affair, especially given the rough and tumble of party politics, the impact of sensational cases, and the constantly shifting locus of the balance.

A consequence of the rise of social democracy in Western countries has been the erosion of class structures and the promulgation of an egalitarian agenda. While social justice has been advanced by many of these changes, it is still uncertain where the new style of politics is going. As noted above, in some respects there has been an increase in social polarisation. Freed from class anchors and, to an extent, from party disciplines and structures, politics are necessarily more volatile than before. Authority has been challenged in many ways and there is certainly far less deference to professions and other elite groups. The media and its creations – celebrities – have a place in national life that requires a more subtle analysis than we usually see. The authority of these groups appears to be new, both in strength and persuasiveness. This is the background to a number of observations that Sparks makes about populism. It is not appropriate to summarise these here – they are wide-ranging and reasonable, if polemical. Are we now living in political doldrums caught between two tidal pulls, social democracy and a new type of individualism?

One reaction to the individualism of Western society, and to the politics and state action that accompany and express it, is a lamentation for the loss of community. There are several distinct voices in this chorus. One need not greatly detain us for it is simply nostalgic. It looks back to the post-war period (and beyond) and seeks a restoration of what was a settled social order. The family was strong, fathers worked in a well-established occupational structure, mothers stayed at home – and both parents stayed together. All kinds of agencies, from church and school to the neighbourhood, assisted in promulgating and upholding moral standards. Esteem mattered, anonymity was difficult and shame was devastating. There is a high degree of rose-tinted nostalgia in this account of course, but its veracity or otherwise need not detain us: there is no going back.

15

If this is conservative nostalgia, what of the left? There remain many advocates of big-state social intervention, but for all that they are a corralled minority, mainly talking to each other. Although democratic socialists were among the most steadfast opponents of Leninism in its several varieties, the collapse of the Soviet empire has lessons for many types of statism, democratic and undemocratic alike. Its proponents might (or might not) demur, but communitarianism is an attempt to defend some key values of the old left without having to defend its baggage. Some varieties of this doctrine have claimed to be the 'third way'.

This is the territory explored by Nicola Lacey, who examines punishment as an expression of 'shared values and commitments'. She points to the much-discussed weaknesses in retributive and utilitarian approaches to punishment; she also argues that mixed (more pragmatic) positions also have drawbacks and may in particular not be able sufficiently to integrate, or even reconcile, their several components. Lacey attempts to go to the heart of the issue by asking us to consider how punishment affects the social good, which she sees in broad and shifting terms.

Over the last two and a half centuries there have been repeated attempts to systematise our thinking about penal philosophy and policy and to clear the ground for a more certain and justifiable approach. Looking to the twentieth century, Lacey reviews the rise and decline of the rehabilitative school. The reformatory movement arose from an appreciation of the many factors that contribute to criminal behaviour, including both inherited characteristics and the effects of the social environment. For a number of reasons this approach failed to deliver promised reductions in re-offending. As this failure became more manifest and attracted criticisms about its vagueness, lack of accountability and intrusiveness, the rehabilitative programme was modified or abandoned. It would be fair to say that in this essay Nicola Lacey treats these developments as though they were fairly autonomous. It is not in any way that she is unaware of political and economic dimensions, but rather that she does not seek to address the linkages in the limited space available.

The vogue penal doctrine from the 1970s and 1980s has been retributivism. This satisfied conservative thinkers by emphasising individual responsibility and making the offender more clearly accountable – he or she had committed the crime, not their environment. Those on the liberal left were also attracted to retributivism because it appeared to limit punishment to harm done, as distinct from deterrence or reformation, which were not so constrained. In the event, retributive calculations on the quantum of harm of a particular offence were hard to agree: even harder to compare the harms of different offences and harder still to justify scales of punishment. Garnering both conservative and liberal support, retributivism offered a vocabulary and grammar attractive to politicians and was widely adopted as a basis for criminal legislation and sentencing scales. It remains the dominant element in British sentencing policy, for example, despite its many imponderabilities and implausibilities. Apparent simplicity masks a thicket of complexities.

How might we proceed, asks Nicola Lacey. She sets out the communitarian conception of the person as 'one which recognises human identity as a fundamentally social construction'. That being so, she goes on to argue, 'personal autonomy and welfare can only be realised in a social context'. The principal purpose of punishment according to this doctrine would not be deterrence, reformation or incapacitation, but rather to ensure that the community's values are taken seriously. The *symbolic* property of punishment would therefore be central. Lacey uses this point of departure to criticise the use and administration of imprisonment in Britain and the United States.

Those who have noted in recent years the reports of pathetic but potentially dangerous groups of vigilantes rampaging around British council estates (public housing) as they seek out supposed paedophiles (reportedly turning on one occasion on a paediatrician) must have cause to think twice or thrice about 'community values': far rather, some would insist, the values of an educated elite than the imaginings and ignorant passions of the mob. But where does this leave the communitarian? For the purposes of argument, leave aside the mob and consider only the vote-hungry, office-hungry politician who claims to be the authentic voice of the people. Lacey does not duck these issues and sets out the dangers inherent in some communitarian positions.

It does not arise directly from communitarian thinking, but restorative justice shares many of its concerns and values. The conventional criminal justice process is expensive, bureaucratic, not particularly satisfying to victims and has a poor record of effectiveness. Even community penalties, some would argue, all too easily become formalities – official process with little substance or human effect. Imprisonment is costly and however well administered, has the negative effect of further sundering ties between offender and community. Popular dissatisfaction with criminal justice is a compound of feeling that here, as elsewhere, things are not working, that elite groups evade criticism and are not accountable, and that ordinary people are excluded from important decisions that affect the quality of their lives.

Into this complex of disputes and concerns comes the notion of restorative justice. As the name clearly proposes, the objective is a form of restoration – directly in the sense of restoring stolen property, making reparation or (more difficult) re-establishing a sense of security or tranquillity; indirectly in the sense of healing the wound that the crime has inflicted or the victim and the community: There are besides a number of other goals, including a reduction of re-offending and fear of crime. The restorative process is seen as engendering or strengthening a sense of community, which in itself has productive effects and may reduce criminality. The key methodology is a meeting or series of meetings which require the participation of the victim, the offender and a community representative.

One might relatively easily get support for the use of this procedure to deal with and divert away from the formal justice system minor and less hardened offenders. Indeed, shorn of its terminology, it would appear to be no more than the type of informal procedure that has been followed in certain neighbourhoods, communities and jurisdictions for many years. Richard Young and Carolyn Hoyle, while approaching the restorative justice movement in a questioning manner, suggest that it has far more potential than an apology to a neighbour in the presence of a police officer. They trace its modern origins to Canada and, significantly, to the 'sentencing circles' which drew on indigenous Canadian peace-making processes. Adoption and adaptation seem to have gone furthest in New Zealand, where 'family group conferencing' is the standard response to serious youth crime. In England and Wales, by contrast, restorative justice projects are mainly used for minor offences by young people.

Restorative justice is widely discussed in criminal justice circles and has caught the eye of government and the judiciary in a number of countries. For the method to have a practical impact, however, it would need to be able to take on adults convicted of more serious offences. Some such programmes are now in train and are being evaluated. Much will turn on their effectiveness and economy. Positive evaluations in turn may affect public perceptions and willingness to countenance this form of complementary justice. Among other considerations, however, Young and Hoyle point out an inherent conflict between governments' desire for speedy justice and the inevitably protracted business of arranging restorative justice conferences to accommodate the various parties.

The hard case for most people when considering restorative justice is the violent or sexual offence. Some argue that bringing the victim of a sexual or other violent assault into the presence of the criminal adds one trauma to another. And even if there is not a meeting, a horribly painful and haunting episode is re-opened. (This of course is also a criticism made of the conventional trial.) On the other hand, were such a victim to *choose* a restorative justice conference format and provided they were given sufficient emotional and practical support, might this not open new possibilities for all involved?

For restorative justice to become a significant part of the criminal process, the state has to take a hand. At what point should state agencies become involved – pre-trial, sentencing or post-sentence – and who should be the lead officials? The division over the last issue seems to boil down to a choice between police or social workers. There are obvious differences in training, work experience and orientation here, but is it possible for these two sets of functionaries to work together – or does that simply add further complication and delay and shift the focus from the victim and the offender?

We have become a pronouncedly rights-conscious society. When added to the confrontational nature of Anglo-American and common-law jurisprudence, even the most respectable and conformist among us are extremely wary about making admissions. (Our car-insurance companies constantly insist on the point to their customers.) Yet restorative justice requires admissions and acceptance and one cannot imagine a productive meeting or conference conducted along adversarial lines. One of the appealing points of the method, surely, is the learning that takes place when culpability is admitted and fully assumed. Yet there may be conflicts of interest, and the possibility of injustice: what part therefore should legal advice play in these proceedings? Would it be possible to avoid a restorative justice process being offered as an inducement to admit guilt? What safeguards do we have against a manipulative use of this prospect by police or prosecutors, and would such use not devalue and inevitably destroy the process?

An essential function of state justice is to provide a set of procedures that help remove emotion from an examination of deeds and circumstances that are fraught with it. I have already noted how some writers on the communitarian theories of justice are bothered by what could degenerate into mob justice. Do similar problems exist for restorative justice? Is not the dispassionate tariff of punishments provided by the state safer? Might the state allow the restorative process to run but provide a backstop to prevent excesses? How do retribution and just deserts fit in when reparation and penalty are considered?

Some of the most interesting information provided by Young and Hoyle concerns victims' reactions. Opinion polls consistently show public dissatisfaction with what is seen to be over-lenient sentencing. Media reports and comments on cases frequently do not set out all the facts and circumstances which are made known to the sentencing courts. When that is done and members of the public are asked to sentence hypothetical cases, their sentences apparently turn out to be in general agreement with court practice. Does this open the way for more public acceptance of restorative justice procedure? Possibly, with careful education, media goodwill and with no sentencing disasters (a restorative justice procedure followed perhaps by a horrible crime). Chance plays a much greater part in public policy than many imagine or the textbooks allow.

An editor who carries his or her own contribution in a collection of essays faces a small but delicate point of arrangement: where should that essay go in the sequence? Put it first, and readers might imagine it is a claim to set the tone; last, and the vain editor is claiming a final word. In truth, I had no such difficulty. Placement came quite naturally, since my piece is an attempt to defend the moral element in punishment and the place of the responsible individual in penal doctrine. It follows three essays that certainly have a different emphasis in their analysis of crime, the individual and society. Its place in the sequence is intended to be some kind of answer or at least alternative to these different perspectives, but it is certainly not the last word in a difficult and elusive discussion.

One of the chief sources of criminology was the investigation of the regularities of crime. Age, sex, domicile, parents' education and occupation all proved powerful predictors of crime. From the time of the first collation of national criminal statistics, what had previously been anecdotal evidence was confirmed: criminal behaviour was not randomly distributed throughout the population. It followed that crime was greatly influenced by social factors and that therefore (some held) individual culpability was diluted. Criminologists discussed and investigated the form and extent of this dilution. But the social approach to criminology was not the only one. Building on Darwinian biology, attempts were made by the Italian criminologist Cesare Lombroso and his followers to construct a different kind of determinism – that of the 'born criminal'. And if there were a significant heritable element in crime, where did that leave culpability? For the last 50 years and more, the biological contribution to criminology has been neglected, tainted by its association with Nazi ideology and crimes. Remarkable advances in genetics have changed that, and we now have to consider the possible impact of that science on the criminal process and our thinking about punishment.

Rubashov, Koestler's Old Bolshevik protagonist in *Darkness at Noon*, had spent 40 years in the service of his party, an organisation that doctrinally denied the existence of the autonomous individual: 'The definition of the individual was: a multitude of one million divided by one million.' Rubashov himself called 'I' 'the grammatical fiction'. In the days, hours and minutes before his party-decreed death, Rubashov speculates on the nature of the individual and traces the monstrous course of his party, and his own life, to an inability to acknowledge the full existence of the individual, and the willingness only to embrace the aggregate.

Stalinism was an extreme doctrine of social determinism which produced unspeakably cruel results. Far less sinister are those doctrines that draw attention to the aggregate to give a compassionate context to individual wrongdoing. In a universe of causes, those theorists argue, the doctrine of free will must be seen as metaphysical, and without free will there can be no absolute culpability; culpability indeed must always be primarily a matter for social determination. Here, although the background is far from Stalin's Russia or Rubashov's regrets, the critical issue is the weight placed upon the individual. I contend that some social theory approaches to punishment have moved too far towards the aggregate, ironically in the interests of a humane criminology and penology.

Absolute doctrines of social determinism now find adherents only in tiny anachronistic sects and cells. But what if a new and scientific form of *biological* determinism were to gain acceptance? I consider some of the implications of the new biology, and the possibilities of genetical testing, against the background of a criminal process which, as we have noted, in the last decade or more has shifted from the traditional objectives to risk assessment and control, and which seems to be willing to advance yet further to social defence in the form of long periods of incarceration. Given those strategic objectives, is it not extremely likely that the possibilities of the new technologies will be harnessed to the criminal process?

For more than a century we have downplayed the role of the autonomous individual in the criminal process: do we now have the will to resist calls to identify the 'born criminal'? And once identified, must we not subject him or her to measures of social protection – custody, semi-custody, direction, exclusion – all determined not by guilt or harm done, but by our assessment of the risk of future behaviour? The saving grace of a dynamic ontology, a constant 'coming to be' would be unacceptable; the notion that a person might change would be irrelevant. Those who future-gaze usually find themselves in embarrassed retractions or *post hoc* rationalisations. Perhaps these ruminations on the application of the new biology and its technologies will in ten years' time leave me red-faced and nonplussed: I hope they will.

But whether or not the new biology and criminal justice take the course I anticipate and fear, my essay is a plea for the individual to remain as the defining object of criminal justice and the penal process. By 'individual' I mean a person endowed with moral capacity and entitled to be treated by the state as a moral agent. This means that we have got to accept, at least as a doctrine, the notion of free will, to conduct ourselves 'as if'. Any other course is problematic for criminal law and punishment. I do not place the same emphasis as some of my colleagues on the social dimension of crime and the criminal. I cannot of course avoid a full recognition of the inequities and inequalities of life: we are called upon to do justice in an unjust world. Rather than seek a wider equitable balance or at least a substantial measure of compensatory adjustment in the administration of criminal justices, I contend that the chances of life must be accepted as inseparable from our human condition. That acceptance, combined with a belief in moral capacity, lends dignity, grace and even heroism to our lives.

This introduction, and the book, have been completed close to a midsummer's day. It would be reassuring to be able to join with Shakespeare and declaim:

> If we shadows have offended,
> Think but this, and all is mended,
> That you have but slumber'd here
> While these visions did appear.

If the essays are up to the mark they will certainly provoke discussion; none, we hope, will offend. We had best not go into their soporific properties, but again we take a positive view. The issues that 'we shadows' bring before you will not, however, easily be mended. Rather, they will continue to occupy a central place in moral philosophy and in public policy, and in the working out of democratic politics.

Chapter 1

A Christian approach to punishment

Alan R. Duce

In *The Tempest*, Prospero refers to Caliban as 'this thing of darkness, which I acknowledge mine', a phrase sometimes taken as referring to a wider social and psychological darkness engulfing everyone. Prospero could have been referring to prisons because every prison is a 'thing of darkness' and 'mine' in the sense that it is owned by society.

Many believe that questions associated with the 'darkness' of imprisonment can be interpreted through the insights of religious faith. This chapter explores some of these possibilities, considering them in terms of the work of a prison chaplain, of the history of Christian involvement in prisons, of theological concepts relevant to criminality and victimisation, and in terms of a religious critique of classic theories of punishment.

People sometimes find it strange that I should believe it worthwhile to have worked full-time as a minister of religion in a prison – a 'thing of darkness'. They may not immediately appreciate the extent to which insights associated with my training enable me to talk about relatively abstract topics in more vivid and human terms. Writing about these insights, concentrating on theological and ethical issues, involves a personal selection from a wide range of concepts, the development of which over the centuries, has shaped penal policy.

Background to chaplaincy

A chaplain usually receives accreditation from state and church. The governing connection, however, is the church, which trains clergy in the traditions of the faith. It is in the expectation of its traditional help that prisoners turn to the church. The chaplain's work derives from the continuing commitment by Christian denominations to compassionate work among prisoners, from the contribution of the churches to the underpinning of a common morality in Western countries, notably the United Kingdom and the United States, and from the churches' emphasis on upholding the intrinsic worth of men and women. These commitments demonstrate that Christians do not just subscribe to being law-abiding as a criterion for moral conduct, nor do they simply believe that better laws or more vigorous enforcement will by themselves create a more moral society. Christians claim to have something to say about punishment in prison because of 'truth' conveyed in their faith.

The chaplain works at the punitive end of the criminal justice system. He or she is expected to listen to prisoners, sometimes able to absorb only the pathos of a damaged person's situation or mediating meaning and hopefulness in the light of spiritual truths. All human characteristics are displayed in exaggerated form in prisons, places where superficialities are swept aside. Prisons are crucibles testing the strength and significance of Christian theology.

Misunderstandings about prison chaplaincy

The chaplaincy occasionally becomes controversial. In prisons attitudes and social stances can be divisive. Misunderstandings that might be faced by a chaplain illustrate problems encountered by anyone attempting to present an objective analysis of a place in which flourish scepticism and cynicism about personal and professional motives. Equally, a subjective opinion must be tempered by honesty and fairness, constantly puncturing one's own pieties and preconceptions as well as stripping away the cant of others.

Compromise

In a prison's strained atmosphere, questions of identity and allegiance are omnipresent. Chaplains appear to be conspicuously linked to the state: by receiving a salary from the prison authorities, carrying keys, appearing to collude with methods of control, signing forms of allegiance to the state and, possibly, appearing to benefit from the status associated with their profession. Misunderstandings raised by the possibility of compromise cannot be ignored by Christians wishing to work with integrity.

It is difficult to imagine how a minister can sustain access to prisoners without acceding to compromise and its attached weight of criticism. The principle of the Incarnation and the general 'down to earthness' of the activity of God revealed in the Bible suggest that Christians are not always called to seek 'pure' ways of serving God, free from ambiguity or compromise. The purposes of God are often furthered by risky and open involvement in realities and institutions. The church becomes a fraud only if it forgets that an essential strand in its existence should be 'godly independence'.

Two sets of theological models mirror these tensions. The one, a model of the transcendent God who 'stands out' but to whom one can relate, is counterbalanced by the other, a model of the immanent God who 'fits in' and with whom one can also commune. The first is demonstrated in the prophetic model with its 'confrontational' pattern, mirroring the moral critic or denouncer; the second is demonstrated in the incarnational model with an 'involvement-and-suffering-with' pattern, like the feet-washing servant. Most of the time chaplains follow the 'incarnational' and the 'involvement-and-suffering-with' pattern. This way their duties open innumerable opportunities for Christian presence and witness, despite the possibility of inappropriate compromise.

Making judgements

The possibility that chaplains might be perceived as people who pass judgement on others is brought home to me whenever I visit the early nineteenth-century prison chapel in the grounds of the medieval Lincoln Castle. It is the only place in England where one can still see original Victorian segregated, upright, coffin-like pews out of which only the heads of prisoners appeared during sermons preached by my predecessors from a pulpit near the ceiling. The place is now a macabre tourist attraction where a recorded sermon, delivered every few minutes, caricatures a judgemental prison chaplain denouncing a poacher, a timeless figure amid rural poverty in Lincolnshire. The building closed to prisoners in 1874 when the prison where I work was opened. Expectations of the public about what the chaplain should preach did not close with the old prison.

There are many reasons for the expectation that chaplains will make judgements. Prisons are places of judgement, holding people labelled guilty and culpable. Some prisoners are unwilling to admit guilt; others find the church moralistic or alien. George Bernard Shaw once described the prison chaplain as 'a moral snob with no time for anything but the distribution of unreadable books'. Prison staff may give the impression that they expect the chaplain to collude with their attitudes.

Karl Barth, the Swiss theologian, recognised the likelihood of judgement on prisoners. He served in the German trenches in the First World War and later witnessed destructive individualism and secularism after the Second World War. At the end of his life he showed interest in the work of a prison chaplain. Preaching his last 28 sermons in Basel Prison, he demonstrated belief that a prison is one of the most moving places left in today's world to proclaim the Gospel. Almost all the sermons were based upon unusual texts reflecting the mercy of God. One sermon was preached on Isaiah 54:10 which has a poignant relevance to prisoners:

> For the mountains shall depart and the hills be removed, but my kindness shall not depart from you, neither shall the covenant of my peace be removed, says the Lord who has mercy on you.

Karl Barth felt that the purpose of ministry in a prison was to convince prisoners that God loved them, believing that everything else important would follow.

One-sidedness

Some think that prison chaplains can be affected by the adversarial nature of the criminal justice process, which has a tendency to implant and foster entirely divergent thinking in the minds of those who participate.

Victims have no say in framing criminal charges, nor are their needs taken into account in the disposition of the case. A crime that might have dramatically affected them becomes the property of the state. If victims are alive, they are heard as witnesses, but not officially told what happens to the offender. This absence of any semblance of personal power can exacerbate their sense of injury.

The accused rather than victims are the major focus of attention. Yet many offenders feel they have been treated vindictively. This makes them focus on their own plight and see their future as a vendetta in which to retaliate, acting out the character that society has given them. Offenders often construct elaborate rationalisations for their offences. Imprisonment gives them time to do this, and the judicial process feeds them with defensive arguments. The majority of prisoners insulate themselves from thinking about their victims.

The chaplain represents the church's interest in the offender. There is no comparable figure in the church representing care for the victim. There may not be much a chaplain can do to heal the wounds of victims because it is not usual practice for victims to visit prisons. The position of a chaplain highlights the difficulties of maintaining a fair balance in the consideration of all questions of punishment and searching for a just resolution.

Theology and punishment

It might seem logical to look for roots of prison chaplaincy and Christian attitudes towards crime in Jesus' command to visit prisoners (Matthew 25: 31–46) or in the exhortation in the Epistle to the Hebrews (10: 34) that Christians should sympathise with and minister to those in prison. This would be misleading because in the New Testament imprisonment was not regarded as a necessary element in a penal system. A prisoner was essentially no different from a prisoner-of-war. The word used in Greek for military, political and judicial prisoners was *desmios*, which described a person in chains or captivity. It did not have associations implicit in our word 'convict'.

Some elements of early Christian thought on crime, however, set important standards. There was concern to foster a spirit of peaceful resignation toward offences and offenders, as opposed to one of zealous righteousness. Attention was given to the spiritual implications of offences against the community rather than social cost. There was also emphasis on the offender's reconciliation with the community and with God. Tertullian, for instance, explained than certain acts performed by magistrates were inadmissible. He wrote:

As to the duties of civil power the Christian must not decide on anyone's life or honour – about money it is permissible: but he must bind no one, nor imprison or torture any.

Constantine legalised Christian worship and he initiated a policy of penal reform. He forbade the infliction of capital punishment, except when the accused confessed his crime or when the testimony of witnesses was unanimous. He laid down that criminals were no longer to be branded on the face, that debtors were not to be scourged, and that prisoners must not be kept in dark dungeons or unnecessarily loaded with chains.

The church has moved a long way from early Christian communities struggling to survive in a hostile world. In the later Roman Empire a church–state alliance developed. The result was not to consecrate human institutions to the service of God, but to identify God with the maintenance of human institutions. The alliance became an important feature and blunted the Christian's critical attitude towards the state. Although Christianity became allied with an often repressive social order, in its best moments it identified with the powerless and oppressed, serving as a protector and a sign of a new order to come. We retain something of the medieval heritage of Christian thought on law, crime and punishment. Fundamental issues, especially concerning the concept of blame, have remained as medieval Christianity defined them. Theological understanding of God, the world and human life has advanced; basic Christian reflection on crime and punishment has not changed.

Modern imprisonment traces certain of its characteristics back to feudal punishment and Canon Law. The feudal state was, essentially, theocratic. There was deep penetration of ecclesiastical power into medieval political life. Sanctions, like sequestration and cellular confinement, were first imposed on clergy for confession and penance. The supposed therapeutic nature of these practices later combined with an enforced period of time away. These followed a transition from private dealing with matters of conscience to the appearance of sequestration in institutional seclusion. Penance, in particular, had a corrective character because it upheld values. This was transformed into confinement in a monastery. Separation gave a chance for examination and expiation of guilt through meditation. Thus monastic organisation had a special influence on the prison ethos. Projection of the original sacramental rite of penance onto secular institutions developed in part from the Eastern monastic tradition of contemplation and asceticism; thus prisons have some monastic characteristics, such as 'cells'.

About 200 years ago the medieval roots of imprisonment were adapted to the ideas of the Enlightenment. There was reaction to the caprice and savagery of existing punishments, and some revulsion at the widespread use of capital punishment. Difficulties arose with the penal transportation of felons overseas and there was growing belief that humanitarian understanding about the causes of human misbehaviour could lead to the induced alteration of behaviour. Prisons built at the end of the eighteenth century reflected the belief that architectural design, secular organisation and Christian principles could produce beneficial outcomes.

Christian theology and the church have been a source of inspiration and support for many traditions of penology and the criminal law in the Western world. This has contributed to the development of imprisonment in its prominent and extremely controversial position, especially in the United States and, to some extent, certain countries in Western Europe.

Well-intentioned beliefs and practices of an age of more widespread religious faith have become distorted and their ethos has been incorporated into institutions. The Christian roots of the legal and penal system are still accepted as a form of validation. Although the church is no longer involved in the administration of criminal justice, the status of criminal law as an extension of God's law has survived. Criminal law continues to be seen as a weapon in the fight between Good and Evil. Some church leaders are perceived as unquestioningly upholding the status quo, and the church has appeared to encourage popular belief in the right of the state to punish, and accept the ultimate justness of punishment, as well as endorse imprisonment.

Contemporary theology and punishment

Theology offers a perspective within which to interpret controversial contemporary social problems. At the beginning of the twenty-first century, thinking about punishment, and particularly imprisonment, was confused. This is symptomatic of wider social confusion. Some confusion in public policy and debate may not be a bad thing. Certainty and apparent clarity could demonstrate incompetence, over-simplification or even naivety.

Society seems trapped in a set of false expectations about progress based on popular acceptance of liberal humanism, scientific advances and the value of continual political reorganisation. The popular ethos has led to seemingly endless debates and confusion. An exploration of theological responses to this uncertainty is timely.

Contention is unavoidable when one lists the consequences of imprisonment. The penalty is meant to be only the deprivation of freedom, but many associated practices seem to be based on repression and restraint. Imprisonment is isolating. It removes from the majority a sense of personal power and self-worth and gives prisoners a 'mass identity'. It is associated with work that is often repetitive and unconstructive. It is degrading and sometimes a place of bullying as well as suicide. It is disproportionate. It is affected by social and racial prejudice, does not produce a reduction in crime, is enormously expensive and leads many to substance abuse and addiction. Imprisonment compounds problems that the offender had before sentence and is nearly always detrimental to family life. For many women, imprisonment leads to a separation from children at a crucial time of maternal nurturing. For men, deprivation of choice, as of liberty, can be felt as an attack upon manhood, an attack made all the more severe by anxieties about masculinity which arise in an all-male society.

These observations are associated with several contemporary tensions. Popular fury and disquiet demand authoritative action but at the same time generate suspicions of authority. There is ambivalence towards those in authority, who are either seen as 'hard' retributivists fanning the fear of crime, or they seem to offer 'soft', easy-going alternatives to imprisonment. In general, less deference to authority in the present generation has led to widespread questioning about the work of public residential institutions, which has strengthened the trend away from confining people towards supervising them in the community. The low-tax, high-efficiency politics of the last two decades have emphasised the need to run institutions with as little trouble and cost as possible. It is not fashionable, where the media in particular can easily blame one person for failure, to enable responsibility to be readily owned by the community. Amid these political sensitivities, 'truth' is an elusive concept.

Confusion is increased by the ability of the media and political forces to stereotype offenders, distorting the significance of actions deemed morally inferior, and raising the level of fear and contempt. Stereotyping sells newspapers, sustains political parties and exploits our innate tendencies to find scapegoats. It sometimes distorts stories in a worrying way. Take the response to a 14-year-old delinquent who took to hiding in ventilation shafts when police were looking for him. He was dubbed 'Ratboy' by the British press. Only his mother, it seemed, could hang on to who he really was: 'He's not a rat. He's my son.'

The rejection of social concerns often arises from a failure to face up to understanding the requirements and the opportunities of a healthy community. This poses difficulties for theology and is a constant theme in Scripture. Jesus levelled this accusation against the Pharisees:

> You pay tithes of mint and rue and every garden-herb, but have no care for justice and the love of God. It is these you should have practised, without neglecting the others.
>
> (Luke 11: 42)

Most people today would say that accountability means punitive consequences. This is a limited and abstract understanding of accountability. True accountability exists only when there is an intrinsic link between the act and its consequences. As long as consequences are decided only for offenders, accountability will not involve responsibility. Genuine accountability would include an opportunity to understand the consequences of one's acts, to face up to the 'truth' of what one has done and to whom one has done it. Several theological themes address this problem; all the themes are relevant to pastoral work among people undergoing punishment.

A Christian understanding may be better able to connect those protected by the law, those who frame the law and those punished by the law. The state represents not only the injured party: it acts for the whole community, including the offender. This is a fundamental principle of far-reaching importance which can become obscured by the fact that those who frame laws are, for the most part, reputable citizens not expected to fall under the operation of laws they enact. It can appear to offenders that one group of citizens enacts laws for the control of another, or, in the extreme, that the respectable are inflicting vengeance on vagabonds.

It may not be without significance that one of the most enlightened British Home Secretaries this century was Winston Churchill, the only holder of that office known to have served time as a prisoner. His experience as a prisoner-of-war in South Africa deeply affected his feeling for, and articulation of, the situation of a prisoner. At the end of a speech in the House of Commons on 20 July 1910, he said that: 'We must not forget that when every material improvement has been effected in prisons … the convict stands deprived of everything a free man calls life.'

Soon after his election, Pope John XXIII went to see prisoners in the chapel in the large Regina Coeli Prison. He said he had come 'as Joseph, your brother'. He told them that two of his cousins had been inside and not come to any lasting harm. More significantly, he departed from his text with the words: 'I want my heart to be close to yours. I want to see the world through your eyes'.

The experience of both these people is reflected in the witness of the prophet Ezekiel, who worked among Jewish exiles imprisoned in Babylon:

> Then I came to them of the captivity at Tel-abib, that dwelt by the river of Chebar, and I sat where they sat and remained there astonished among them seven days.
>
> (Ezekiel 3: 15)

Polarised perceptions of offenders and victims can obscure the reality that laws are enacted by all members of a community acting through their representatives. The essence of punishment is that it is the reaction of a community against a member, not one member or one group of members acting against another. The community has three interests to hold together: maintenance of its own life and order; the interest of individual members generally; and the interest of the offending member. Of these William Temple, Archbishop of Canterbury, once said:

> I believe that this is the true, indeed the necessary, order of priority. But wrong is done if any of the three is neglected. In particular it is to be noticed that though the interest of the offender comes last, yet if this is neglected, the action taken loses its quality of punishment and deteriorates into vengeance; for the offender is then no longer treated as within the society that takes penal action, but over against it and therefore outside it.

Biblical doctrines and punishment themes

Everyone has to be realistic about the state of mankind. They must avoid being facile or fatalistic. That biblical writers take crime seriously is illustrated by some of the harsh punishments prescribed by Old Testament society.

A theology of punishment might usefully be elucidated by considering it in terms of biblical themes combining an optimistic and a pessimistic interpretation about the state of humanity. It is important to place an initial emphasis on the role of optimism because all Christian endeavour must start from the possibility that there is a way forward in difficulties. Pessimism, on the other hand, points to regrettable characteristics in mankind. These are relevant matters connected with punishment. The insights are timeless and truthful.

Fostering optimism – the pilgrimage perspective

A 'pilgrimage perspective' is a theologically based communal concept linking theology and the moral basis of social processes such as punishment. Crime, observed Emile Durkheim, was not just a crisis but also an opportunity; it could be a focus and stimulus for the creation of new rules and thus for the socialisation and reintegration of society. The character in Chinese for a 'crisis' contains a sign for a 'danger' and a sign for a 'chance'. A pilgrimage perspective can inspire similar opportunities for change which emerge from the Judaeo-Christian tradition.

This theological response is suggested by the stories and symbols of passing through the wilderness, being on a journey, maintaining a pilgrimage, going out like Abraham, 'not knowing whither he went', having 'no permanent city ... but looking for the city that was to come' (Hebrews 11: 8–10). Such a 'pilgrimage' can be seen as a shared way forward for God and man, a collaborative exploration in the midst of uncertainty and a journey towards the solution of problems. This perspective is also implicit in the reference to God as 'a Spirit that will lead you into all truth' (John 16: 13). A pilgrimage perspective also fits in with Christian ideas of eschatology.

The metaphor also implies pressure to move on in a difficult situation, preventing uncritical acceptance of the existing order of things. It encourages hard questions about state actions and emphasises communal interest rather than self-interest. The perspective combines a commitment to the demands of the present with a readiness for detachment in the interest of moving to where there might be less inhumanity. This could apply to offenders and prison inmates as much as to those who have to administer the criminal justice system or to those who suffer as victims.

Theological insight is a device for disturbing the water rather than providing blueprints for change. It provides material for creative responses and critical judgements when directed towards contemporary problems. This can lead to redrawing boundaries giving a sense of exploration, progress and optimism. Many people feel that optimism is dying in our society – not least because of the growth of crime and the current essentially static punitive response.

Facing pessimism – legal and moral order

By nature, people seem to be obsessively in conflict and competition; there is constant possibility of disintegration. Crime, a manifestation of this disintegration, often desecrates the self-confidence, beliefs and precious personal domain of individuals. It provokes a 'crisis'. The word 'crime' comes from the Greek *krinein*, to decide in a crisis or dispute. Crime can upset the fundamental assumption on which all life is based – that the world is an orderly and meaningful place. Current concerns about crime undermine the fragile relationship between classes, and especially in the United States between races, and attack the whole sense of social order. So much that is 'good' in life, like civility, beauty and truth, can flourish only within a context of order, in the context of the right balance between authority and autonomy. Theology accepts punishment because it recognises the fundamental need for order.

Biblical theology gives a prominent place to the concept of order in the universe and the legal authority of the state. The link between these concepts reveals closeness of thought between Bible writers and those wrestling with contemporary problems. The Book of Genesis portrays God's original intention to bring 'order' out of chaos in the way the Spirit of God moves over the primordial waters, which symbolised chaos, to begin the ordered stages of creation. God is depicted as despairing of his original creation because the world had become perverted and 'full of violence of man's making' (Genesis 6: 11). God sent the flood to wipe out all that had been built, preserving the carefully ordered remnant of the ark and its inhabitants which became the foundation of the 'new covenant'.

Similarly, 'order' is portrayed as the first law of society. The New Testament emphasises the need for respect for those exercising legal authority in the state. Stability and balance are vital to the functioning of all political endeavour. Coercion is necessary because some human beings lack ability to control their independence, and failure to punish criminal offenders would mean that those complying with the law voluntarily would be penalised. Attention has been paid to the famous saying 'Render unto Caesar that which is Caesar's' (Matthew 22: 21) or to Paul's admonition to obey the powers that be (Romans 13: 1–5). A major problem for theology is to press for fairness in the administration of criminal justice.

It is said that punishment should be witness to, or expressive of, the order that follows from moral obligations. This assumes that such a moral judgement is accepted by the community for which the law is prescribed. Traditional thinking argues that the law should have a fundamental connection with morality, reinforcing moral judgements and providing training in the rudiments of moral behaviour. Because of the complicated nature of society it is necessary that the majority of people feel that they should be under obligation to obey the law. Others say that the diverse moral and cultural society at the end of the twentieth century has moved the basis of formulating law more towards a relativistic and utilitarian justification.

Were law and morality to be separated it would be necessary to have some other sort of public behaviour to confirm adherence to an ordered moral consensus or to display moral disapproval, such as the boycott, the march, the sit-down protest and the pressure group. Neither law nor morality can sustain themselves, from generation to generation, without the threat of punishment. If the law gets out of step with morality, people lose respect for it. Since morality and theology are historically closely connected it is important to appreciate theological approaches, especially in situations involving punishment, where theological and moral thinking can harmonise.

More punishment is not the answer to the problem of crime. The law should be an educating institution, sharpening its effect through its pedagogical or moral influence. Habit keeps people law-abiding. When this is the case, the abiding majority is likely to exert social pressure toward conformity on those who may not themselves accept a moral code. Behaviour that emanates from respect for the law is different from behaviour that reflects a fear of punishment; to ignore the distinction is to confuse authority with coercion. Coercion may reinforce respect for the law, but in the last analysis, respect for authority depends on people's willingness to obey the law because it is the law. Thus the moral-pedagogical role of the law, in which theological insights have an important place, is central to the functioning of society.

Biblical doctrines and individual life

Biblical doctrines connected with punishment might usefully be considered in relation to individual and to corporate life; theologically both interconnect. Disadvantages associated with the contemporary emphasis on individualism have dominated philosophy and juris-prudence since the eighteenth century. Pervasive individualism, and at the same time the disappearance of the individual in the impersonal mass, cause many to feel cut off from their fellows. The result, especially for those associated with crime, has been individual self-fulfilment rather than contribution to a genuine community. Individualism has thus resulted in a 'fortress mentality' where those excluded from material advantages are controlled by surveillance cameras, electronic tagging and prison walls.

Another disadvantage of the contemporary emphasis on the person is a widespread belief that everything is relative. Something can be accepted as true by one person but not another. It is also fashionable to say that tolerance of the beliefs of others is the only real virtue and that concentration on looking after 'number one' is of foremost importance. This problem is compounded by a disillusionment with organised religion and a relative decline in one common morality. A life of faith can so enhance human living, coping, forgiving and trying again that humanity can be encouraged to replace excesses of individualism with an enhanced sense of corporate life.

Image of God

This metaphor implies that human life must be placed in a wider context than that dictated by immediate problems. Taken seriously in relation to punishment, this symbolic phrase suggests that people are moral agents. That is they have free will and are not wholly determined beings. It also implies that everyone is endowed with some reflection of divine characteristics, which counters cynicism about the apparent hopelessness of some offenders.

The original reference to the 'image of God' comes from the creation story. To describe men and women as 'in the image of God' emphasises the transcendent status of life; although everyone is finite, everyone is portrayed as dependent on a reality beyond human existence. The doctrine also suggests that human beings are social rather than individual entities; it was the human couple, male and female, that were made in the image and the likeness of God (Genesis 1: 27). This phrase describes the human condition as it is commonly understood by Christianity, Islam and Judaism.

Discouraging compartmentalised understandings about the place of the human person, the doctrine suggests limits to coerciveness in changing an individual's outlook. It implies that institutions in which people live should not set out to break down anyone's sense of active responsibility and encourages the idea that everyone is meant to take the work of creation further in making a difference to their lives and surroundings. The doctrine should not be understood as concentrating on individual and static characteristics – so neglecting other important aspects of human createdness – such as the social and the material.

A former director general of the English Prison Service, Joe Pilling, said, 'There is more than one way to close a prison door', referring to the fact that prison doors have deep symbolic significance as pointers to the recognition of human dignity. Prisoners who have been locked up describe themselves as 'banged up'. Cell doors are open or shut, reflecting status as guilty or not guilty. They are stigmatising frontier posts between freedom and captivity, but also entry points into the only place inmates can call home. They present opportunities for personal greeting as well as a means of security, secret surveillance, separation or, when slammed, rejection.

Recognition of the 'image of God' is in part conveyed by the modern use of the word 'respect'. Although the word is not frequently used in the Bible, it is a biblical concept. A judge should ensure that a guilty person is not given more than 40 lashes (Deuteronomy 25: 1–3) because if they are flogged more than that they will be degraded. Similarly, James (2: 1–4) taught that, contrary to the custom of his day, it is not good to treat differently a man who comes to a meeting wearing shabby clothes and put him in a place inferior to one wearing a gold ring and fine clothes. Unfortunately, for many prisoners the respect they ought to pay to others is often lacking, and the respect that they desire for themselves is often based on an appetite for power and popularity rather than on kindness and love. In theological terms, the word 'respect' means that they are being treated with the respect that God has for all people because they are in his image.

The 'image of God' doctrine points to potential 'non-disposable' characteristics in men and women, indicating that they have an active rather than passive role. Where there is structural pressure to be passive, the image of God can be clouded over. This is generally true when people have no way of changing the conditions in which they live; this is one of the raw 'truths' about prison life. The idea of the 'image of God' suggests that inherent qualities in all human beings enable them to reach to infinite levels in their relationship with God. People should never accept themselves or be viewed as 'finished' or complete.

Archbishop William Temple concluded his Clarke Hall Fellowship Lecture in 1934:

> No character is fully formed till death, and there is always place for remedial and reformative treatment. But the more established the character is, the more completely may the man who has committed a crime be treated merely as a criminal. Where, through immaturity of age or through lack of opportunity to develop some side of nature, the character is unstable, it is good to think more of what the man may become than of what he is. For in such a case the potentialities are actually greater than the actualities; and to treat the character as what it may be is to treat it as what it actually is: for it is chiefly potentiality. Sympathy and justice are here coincident.

Sin

Any organisation responsible for making decisions about offenders faces questions connected with the negative potential in humanity. Sin is the exclusively theological concept describing the state of 'fallen human nature', as portrayed in the creation story. It refers to unproductive patterns of life in which humans have become trapped by ignoring the environment and its limits, and the restrictions that other realities, including the needs of other human beings, impose on human wants. The doctrine of sin has, at one extreme, been equated with moral death and damnation, but at the other can be understood as attempting to locate what is wrong and face it constructively. The wisest response to sin has always been associated with searching the conscience for 'truth', as is inferred in the sentiments expressed in Psalm 51: 6: 'Behold, thou requirest truth in the inward parts.'

Individually, sin is pictured as falling short of the expectations of God by making selfish choices. Humans can, in the words of the Lord's Prayer, be lead 'into temptation' by the 'unruly wills and affections of sinful men' (1662 Prayer Book). Theologically, a sinner is understood as having responsibility before God for developing the potential to find release from his or her situation. Sin is part of an understanding about humanity which combines a readiness to face the worst, but assists in moving on towards the best. Collectively, sin can be viewed as embodied in the structures of society. The Old Testament has frequent references to God's wrath being directed against society and its corporate wickedness because of the ways the poor are left to their fate.

The notion of sin also raises the question of wickedness. People have a choice when they deliberately promote evil. The doctrine of sin has been used to magnify the problems of evil. This exploitation serves as a warning against underestimating what one is up against in coming to terms with innate reactions against human and social wrongs.

The Christian understanding of sin suggests that there is no absolute distinction between problem-solvers and those who are problems. There is a sense in which all are sinful – all have fallen short of the glory of God (Romans 3: 23). There is, therefore, a solidarity in sinfulness for everyone. All human beings are linked with offenders; all are part of one society and are all part of the problem. Distinctions have to be made and maintained in practice, but in the search for more creative responses the status of everyone needs to be acknowledged. Inmates may not be familiar with George Bernard Shaw, but they have absorbed his thesis in 'The Crime of Imprisonment' that 'the thief who is in prison is not necessarily more dishonest than his fellows at large'. A phrase from the *Alternative Service Book* of the Church of England makes the same point in a more gentle way, echoing Luke 15: 20, 'while we were still far off, you met us in your Son...'

Forgiveness, guilt and repentance

In Christian terms forgiveness has traditionally been viewed as a virtue. Christians are called to forgive their enemies because God has forgiven them. They believe that people cannot be free while dominated by enmity. From a practical and experiential point of view this is possible only in relatively unusual circumstances. Forgiveness applies to parties who often cannot meet, like victim and victimiser. It is the mutual recognition that the repentance of either or both parties is genuine and that right relationships have been restored or achieved. Forgiveness cannot be willed or forced; it must come in its own time. It is helpful if victims are able to forgive because a sense of having been forgiven is one way in which an offender may achieve a sense of self-worth.

The concept of forgiveness is often misunderstood. On the victim's side, forgiveness is not forgetting, writing off the crime, letting the victimiser off the hook. It is not bland benevolence, especially as it is impossible to forget. Nor does it mean devaluing the offence by rationalising it away. Forgiveness means releasing the power of the offence and hence the power of the offender over the victim. It allows the offence to become part of a person's life story in an important but non-controlling way. An expression of responsibility, regret and repentance by the offender can help release the powerful hold a criminal act has on the life of the victim.

Many people feel that forgiveness is not possible for some offenders. They might have in mind child molesters or serial murderers. The thought of forgiving such people does not come easily because Christian teaching can appear to offer an easy way out of evil, a way which in itself appears evil. The Christian approach to forgiveness can be represented as enabling offenders not to take seriously consequences or responsibility for what has been done in crime. Those who believe in the traditional Christian virtue of forgiveness can only defend the possibility of wholeness and growth in anyone who feels forgiven by pointing to the dimension of a hurting God at the centre of things, manifested in a person on a cross.

All offenders need some experience of forgiveness, to ease, if not always to resolve, their guilt, to move on to a new life developing a more healthy identity and a sense of self-worth. They often feel guilty and personally worthless. Some say guilt can be resolved by punishment, but it must be felt as legitimate and deserved. Because their alleged crime is depicted as against society, which for them is an abstract concept, they feel little identification with the offence. Society has rituals for condemnation in court and the enforcement of exclusion, but lacks parallel rituals which acknowledge that the debt has been paid. In practice, society administers punishment in ways that seem damaging and then denies opportunity for forgiveness and social re-acceptance. To think in terms, not just of punishing, but also of forgiving, opens up a radical and disturbing set of issues for modern penal policy.

It is difficult to see whether an offender can ever cease to feel some guilt and self-reproach. One paradox is that the more perspective the offender achieves of himself and his offence, the less likely he is to cease from self-condemnation and reproach. Some might say that this is a sign of growing maturity. The way in which a prisoner talks about inner perceptions can reveal a measure of the realism and stability shown in other ways. This raises many open-ended questions.

Many offenders can feel guilty but avoid admitting it in order to maintain their sense of self-worth. Guilt is important in the criminal justice process, but rather than being a positive emotion helping to prevent the repetition of offences, is seen in prison as a destructive force. Howard Zehr points out in his book *Changing Lenses* that guilt which is accepted can become anger at oneself, sometimes leading to suicide, while equally destructive guilt which is denied can become anger directed at others. In many cases prisoners swing between the two emotions. Punishment as administered in our society denies opportunities for forgiveness.

I often ponder how best a prisoner might be helped to assimilate the past, to recognise what has been done, to imagine it from another standpoint, particularly the victim's, and then to face living in a stable way with the recollection. Many people, both victims and offenders, need constant permission to speak their rage, hurts and fears. It is important to help other people make the imaginary leap into looking at problems in a larger world than just that of their own needs. This is the essence of repentance. Again, it raises the theme of 'truth', echoed in a similar sense in John 8: 32:

> … ye shall know the truth, and the truth shall make you free.

In the face of these needs the business of the church is not to say something good but to help people see the truth about their situations. Sometimes the only truth is that the memory hurts and that it is right to give air to the wound. A significant contribution of churches towards these difficulties is to offer constant support for ex-offenders to live with the truth.

Biblical doctrines and corporate life

Fellowship

Christians are urged to seek communal ways in which to be creative. The

Law in the Old Testament envisages a community where this is taking place. According to the New Testament, the possibility of such a community existing depends on the shared certainty that everyone is an object of the unrestricted love of God. This is emphasised in the injunction to 'love one's neighbour as oneself' and is the focal point of many of Jesus' parables, supremely the parable of the Good Samaritan. Jesus spent much of his time with the weak and vulnerable often enabling the seemingly weak to emerge as the heroes, like the prostitute, Mary Magdalen. God's love is also spelt out in the life, death and resurrection of Jesus Christ, through which people are set free to establish an all-embracing community in which no one's welfare is to be pursued at the expense of someone else.

The doctrine of the Trinity, developed in the early church, has proved to be a time-honoured way for Christians to think about the nature of God, His manifestation in the world in the person of Jesus and His omnipresence through the power of the Holy Spirit. Explored afresh in recent years, an understanding of this doctrine can bring a new emphasis to contemporary questions like the meaning of personhood, society and justice. Any attempt to express the reality of a triune God, Father, Son and Holy Spirit, puts 'persons' before concepts. Within this understanding of God one can observe the experience of love in freedom. Trinitarian doctrines emphasise the openness of God to the world and humankind as well as the openness of the world to the future that God holds for it, and reveal God as a communion consisting of unbroken personal relationships: 'God is love' (1 John 2: 8). In Trinitarian theology the concept of the person is social or communitarian. Karl Barth developed a Trinitarian anthropology in which relations of reciprocity in the being of God were used to throw light on the human condition. Human beings are those who look each other in the eye, mutually speak to and hear each other, render mutual assistance to each other and do all these things 'with gladness'. No one is excluded from personhood.

This point can be practically illustrated in the design of new prisons. Prisoners eat alone in their cells, which is cheaper than having a communal dining hall. There is little concern in this conceptual framework for consideration of the long-term mental health, communication skills or impact on a prisoner's ability to relate to others. Michael Schluter of the Jubilee Centre in Cambridge said: 'There is a real danger that prisons could become, in effect, down-market, fenced-in hotels or perhaps, in the future, zoos.'

The point can also be illustrated in the way that crime, justice and punishment are divorced from the local community and handed over to the state. Offenders are often tried in courts with no community support and if sent to prison may be held hundreds of miles from home. This reinforces the idea that the community is not responsible for its members.

Punishment must make it possible for individuals to feel valued and affirmed. It should ensure that the community works for the good of its members. People mature when they learn how to act and hope in relation to each other and not as self-sufficient entities. If crime is a failure in the mutuality and the interdependence of a healthy community, it is worth asking about the wider causes of such a failure, and the messages society sends out about its values.

The consequences of this failure are illustrated in the way the Bible portrays crime. Consider David's murder of Bathsheba's husband. Bathsheba was widowed, Uriah lost his life, the Israelite army lost a good general and David and Bathsheba lost a child as punishment from God. (2 Samuel: 11–12). In more recent times Professor Leopold Kohr, burgled dozens of times over the past ten years, commented:

> There is no community here. We need translucent communities where everyone knows each other, where everyone knows the police, where thieves can be confronted. These crimes were committed in the darkness of mass society.

Mending the web of human relationships damaged by crime should be seen as a primary concern of the criminal justice system.

Justice

Christians have inherited from the Old Testament a concern for justice. Jesus offered a radical extension of this in his criticism of the working and the interpretation of the law in his own time. The biblical message is that legislators and judiciary cannot be relied upon to maintain conditions in which justice will always prevail. An objective standard alongside which to measure procedures is needed. Christians relate their standards of human justice to their understanding of the justice of God. These standards are mainly shared with the majority of their fellow citizens. The distinctive standard of the church is to challenge, in the name of God and His justice, all human institutions and procedures falling short of these standards. Consider Jesus' rather uncomplimentary descriptions of the Pharisees as 'whitewashed tombs' (Matthew 25: 27) or his comments about the rich and their problems in entering the kingdom of heaven (Matthew 19: 24). Christians can never cease asking serious questions of a society whose prisons contain a disproportionate number of black people or members of the less-endowed social classes.

A sense of justice also requires that attention is paid to the other side of the coin. Consideration should be given to what is currently called 'tough love', which requires justice be applied to the long-term welfare of a person, even when this may conflict with short-term happiness. In Scripture this notion is described primarily in terms of discipline and is illustrated by the love that good parents have for children. Biblical teaching frequently emphasises that it is only when there is discipline that people know that they are God's children. Despite extensive criticism of imprisonment, some prisoners would say that, although they found the experience 'tough', they were treated with a fairness equating with justice. It is interesting that the concept of 'discipline' has a constructive connection with the word 'disciple' and yet in prison has more negative connotations.

Commenting on justice is impossible without referring to victims. Tragedies encountered by victims can too easily be abstracted in a courtroom drama. Instead of a tragic confrontation between two individuals, the legal process and the media transform it into a crime involving a criminal and, as a secondary consideration, a victim, a drama between two abstractions. The event becomes a story, a news-bite, a myth, in which victims can feel frightened, vulnerable and blameworthy. It is not uncommon for them to struggle to regain trust in others. Many experience intense anger. In describing their experiences, victims of burglary often sound much like victims of rape.

Classic theories of punishment

The chaplain's theological and ethical reasoning can equally be applied to an assessment of classic theories of punishment which are used as day-by-day yardsticks in the application of justice. Not all the secular theories of punishment are theologically important, but several matters of interest do arise. A consideration of some issues raised by these theories in the light of the Christian heritage illustrates the versatility of theology in moving from the abstract to the practical. Theology has an important function when people realise that criminal justice theories deal with ethical considerations as a matter of abstract and intellectual interest. When they are viewed in this way, theology can raise important issues of moral and practical concern. Punishment always needs careful controlling because it is a peculiarly human phenomenon closely connected with the instinctive nature of mankind; concern about this instinctive characteristic is the mainspring for the articulation theological ideas.

Retribution

Retributive punishment has been championed by major philosophers of modern times, especially Kant and Bradley. It argues for the infliction of punishment as a physical evil deserved as a result of moral evil. This understanding of punishment rests on a formal, rule-bound foundation and is the oldest and most frequently used justification for punishment. Religions that acknowledge Abraham as a prophet, namely Judaism, Islam and Christianity, attach a special kind of guilt to sins that can be expiated only by sacrifice or suffering. Consequently, religious practices are related to the retributive tradition.

· Retribution is based upon the premise that the offender is a moral agent, possessed of free will. It insists that he or she is not a person to be used as an example to deter others by the infliction of punishment. Revival of interest in the retributive justification for punishment is due to a reaction against the utilitarian approach, which has become unpopular partly because of excessive prison terms in the United States and partly because of discouraging evidence about the efficacy of sentences designed to reform or deter.

Francis Bacon said: 'Revenge is a wild kind of justice.' Retributive philosophy refines this 'wild' element and distinguishes punishment from revenge based upon an instinctual and emotional response. When a higher degree of social organisation developed, responses to crime became less focused on individuals and more on the concern of recognised group authority. This is still the case with Islam. The Babylonian Code of Hamurabi and the Hebrew Mosaic Law were the products of such developments. Both sought to limit personal vengeance in favour of prescribed, institutionalised punishment administered in proportion to the seriousness of the crime. Retributivists stress that the function of their view of punishment, the so called *lex talionis*, is to soften harshness and base the sanction on proportionality rather than allowing purely vengeful reaction. It is regrettable that the use of the *lex talionis*, has sometimes been interpreted as an apparent divine endorsement of disproportionate retaliation against criminals.

Retributionists hold that an offender must have been responsible for the crime; this means that there is moral choice. Pure retributionists believe that severity of the penalty should match the offender's culpability: this can be an elusive calculation. They are also concerned with motive, and hold that it would be unjust to punish an individual who is not freely responsible for his actions. On such grounds the mentally ill and juvenile offenders have been excluded from being treated as criminals. Under the substantial influence of Christian theology classical penology and criminal justice systems have reflected the belief that offenders act as free moral agents. Retribution can be regarded as fair by criminals only if they view it as being deserved.

Retributive punishment has also been perceived as a sacred or ritualistic obligation dependent on a divinely ordained code of right and wrong. The 1662 Prayer Book of the Church of England conveys the influence of this idea in 'The Prayer for the Church Militant' with the words 'that those who are put in authority ... may truly and impartially minister justice, to the punishment of wickedness and vice, and to the maintenance of true religion and virtue'. The bald expression of such sentiments has not been repeated in modern versions of the service.

The idea that pain should be inflicted on a person because he or she has committed an earlier wrong seems indefensible when the person inflicting the pain is human, not divine. The notion that the moral order can be restored by human action may not be appropriate and raises troubling questions about the role of the state. Vast differences exist in moral guilt, but crimes are culturally determined and not all acts worthy of moral blame attract criminal punishment.

Christianity has incorporated much of the Old Testament thinking out of which it sprang. Christian minds have been coloured by the language of the Psalms and references to righteous rejoicing when they see vengeance being heaped on evildoers, and where the conception of God as a Judge is common. This language supports a fundamentalist outlook. No allowance is made for the fact that it was originally used in a context where the law held together a cult as well as a nation. Some have argued that biblical writers are speaking anthropomorphically about divine punishment. They claim God no more punishes than he walks in the Garden of Eden in the cool of the day. To suggest that God punishes, attributes to God reactions and ways of behaviour more appropriate to human beings than their Maker. It is not God who punishes, they say, but man who punishes himself. As a moral being, man cannot do evil without becoming evil. As a free creature, he cannot reject the offer of a relationship with God without losing that relationship. If his rejection is final, then so is his loss.

The view that an offender chose to violate the law and was aware of the consequences came under attack in the nineteenth century when environmental factors were accepted as contributory causes; it was argued that 'determinism' provided a more accurate account of human actions. Retributionists responded to this argument by insisting that their position respects human personality and moral capacity. Respecting responsibility means respecting the right of offenders to be punished for their offences. According to G.W.F. Hegel retributive punishment honours criminals as rational beings, gives them the right to be treated with dignity as people, and acknowledges their moral potential common to all humankind. The Christian theologian, C.S. Lewis, also argued that retribution acknowledges human capacity and dignity and was thus a form of empowerment.

The recent revival of retributive thinking about punishment is connected with the revival of market economics, characterised by a surfeit of choice over obligation. Contemporary attractiveness of 'cut and thrust' choice in the marketplace has led to competitive and production-measured expectations sustaining the retributivist urge. Such a view seems particularly influential in the United States. It is assumed that individuals progress in society by ensuring that no competitor is given an unfair advantage. The American understanding of retribution is linked to the Protestant work ethic, which, like much medieval Catholic piety, is inspired by the 'contract God' who rewards merit. Individuals, it is believed, should be rewarded for industrious work and punished for illicit advantage. In such a society, where the pursuit of private gain has become the organising principle, there is fertile ground for the growth of crime and for a retributive response.

The greatest failure of retributive theory is its lack of attention to the social dimension. It deals with offence against the law rather than injury to the community, and with the individual acting alone rather than in society. The retributive view might offer some vindictive satisfaction to victims and help avoid feuding and public turmoil; but equally, and ultimately to its detriment, retribution removes almost all opportunity from victims and their relations to make public gestures towards healing social wounds.

In place of vengeance, Jesus substituted an ethic of love. 'You have heard it said, "Love your friends and hate your enemies." But now I tell you: love your enemies, and pray for those who persecute you' (Matthew 5: 43–44). As part of that ethic, he said: 'Do not judge others, and God will not judge you; forgive others, and God will forgive you' (Luke 6: 37). Jesus emphasised that finding fault with others was a convenient means of avoiding criticism. 'Why do you look at the speck in your brother's eye, but pay no attention to the log in your own?' (Luke 6: 41). He encouraged compassion towards offenders and doing good to them even if it meant going the 'extra mile' (Matthew 5: 4). The importance of mercy is also evident in Jesus' ministry. Following the totality of this ethic from Jesus is never straightforward. Paul's famous account of love in 1 Corinthians 13 sets out similar guidelines. Christian love is supposed to be kind and patient, and continued whether or not it is returned.

When the church mistakenly came to understand itself as the kingdom of heaven on earth, the notion of human punishment with divine sanction flourished. Now that Christianity has outgrown a tendency to view itself as the earthly representative of the divine order, Christian retributive theology needs to develop a presentation more in line with its original precepts.

Utilitarianism

The utilitarian approach to punishment arose partly as a reaction to the capriciousness and savagery of seventeenth-century punishments. Beccaria was the foremost writer against brutal punishments, who in 1764 in his essay 'An Essay on Crimes and Punishments', stressed the need for certainty rather than severity in punishment. His assertion was that: 'It is better to prevent crimes than to punish them. This is the ultimate end of all good legislation ...'

Because the justification for penalising offences is that it reduces their frequency, utilitarianism is sometimes characterised as 'reductive'. This is the assumption underpinning the approaches of later utilitarians, such as Bentham, Mill and Hart. Utilitarianism refers to theories which suggest that consequences determine the morality of actions. This approach is to be found in theories of general (educative) and individual (potential) deterrence, and also in denunciation, incapacitation and reformation.

People would be impressed if utilitarianism worked but there is no conclusive evidence that threat of consequences has great effect unless the threat becomes dreadful, and even then it does not invariably prevent crime, as is evident in penal policy in China. Utilitarianism uses the criminal as a means to satisfy social purposes and not primarily as a person who has an intrinsic worth in himself or herself. The person to be punished does not necessarily have to be guilty, so long as he or she can be used as an example.

Could this philosophy suggest that it may be expedient to punish the innocent? Might it disregard justice in its elementary forms and become a tyranny needing so many qualifying principles that it forfeited the co-operation of the public? Even if the population agreed that some utilitarian laws were good social institutions, because they told people how they should behave, would it be morally right to use penalties to enforce them? This idea of vicarious punishment was put forward by

John Ruskin, who suggested that in the case of a murder an inhabitant of the area should be chosen by lot and hanged so as to encourage the whole community to keep the peace.

Bentham was concerned about these questions and stressed that expediency must be balanced by economy and frugality. Bentham's principle of successful deterrence relied upon a psychology in which human behaviour was regulated by a simple wish to avoid pain and enhance happiness; but human nature can be affected by unconscious and irrational forces as well as by love, sacrifice and longing. In *Panopticon*, Bentham developed an elaborate scheme for inducement-led reformation, but was not entirely happy about his chances ultimately to manipulate human affairs. To Christians the pleasure/pain principle is a travesty of humanity.

The deterrence of potential offenders is a traditional objective of utilitarian philosophers. In the popular mind this is often associated with severe penalties, and in particular capital punishment or long prison sentences. The association with severity has made deterrence controversial.

Deterrence, impersonal and rational, can never be more than a broad social protective. It can lose sight of the principle that punishment needs to be restricted to the offender, and appropriate to the offender's level of responsibility. The inadequacy of rational deterrence is nowhere more painfully obvious that in relation to crime driven by economic necessity, when legal deterrence can be an empty threat in the face of economic hopelessness or murderously violent peer pressure. Deterrence also seems irrelevant to the range of offences that are compulsive or self-destructive and that may even be sought by an offender through a desire to seek punishment. Fear of being detected may deter, but there are many for whom a reputation for violence has become a matter of pride; such people are also not deterred by a severe penalty.

In the infliction of a deterrent sentence the state treats the offender as a means to the good of others rather than as an end in himself. If this is all that the state has in view, it will be acting immorally because it will be going in a contrary direction to a fundamental principle of morality expressed by Kant in the maxim:

> Treat humanity, whether in your own person or in others, always as an end withal and never only as a means.

Likelihood of detection would appear to be a more effective deterrent. Most potential criminals are optimists; they assume that they are going to be among the lucky ones and ignore the severity of any sentence. The preponderance of crime is a male activity committed on the spur of the moment where the impulse to act criminally is opportunistic, often accelerated by alcohol or drugs as well as by peer encouragement.

The effect of deterrence on the punishment of young people in the United Kingdom raises further worrying questions. The number of first-time offenders continues to climb in a system where over 50 per cent of prisoners re-offend within two years. There is little evidence that for young people prison is an effective deterrent. In the United Kingdom the police are encouraged to caution rather than prosecute the young – certainly in marginal cases. This avoids a criminal record. But if the courts do not punish young offenders when they appear before them, the police and other law-enforcement agencies may take less trouble over detection and prosecution. To justify penalties as an incentive for law-enforcers rather than a disincentive for offenders may seem cynical. Cynicism is not insincerity. If the justifying aim is the prevention of as much crime as possible, the utilitarian might be led to support this within the limits of justice.

Rehabilitative ideas have often rested on muddled and questionable premises. Proponents of rehabilitation have rightly grasped that offenders do not stop being members of society and that the offender's interests are part of society's interests. They maintain that there is something to be restored after a crime. But punishment does not exist only for therapeutic reasons. Hart observed that the reason for having punishment for murder was to prevent other people from being murdered, not because people want to see murderers cured.

There is a well-worn difficulty, discussed in a famous essay by C.S. Lewis, that the rehabilitative approach seems to presuppose that no sane person would want to break the law, that it is possible to define sanity in a satisfactory way, that sanity and normality can be engineered by treatment, and, most worryingly, that treatment can be extended indefinitely until conformity is secured. Lewis exaggerated some of these menaces, but his point that a purely 'reform'-oriented theory of punishment can be a dangerous attack on the idea of human responsibility is worth pondering.

Rehabilitative ideals in a prison must always be considered in the light of general characteristics of a penal institution. One-third of people sent to prison for the first time do not re-offend. This may be due to factors unrelated to any rehabilitative policy. Of the two-thirds further sentenced, a proportion might not have re-offended if they had not been imprisoned in the first place. Some cope well with repeated visits to prison. The quality of life in a prison is not a threat to poor and marginalised people. It is merely exchanging one kind of confinement for another. In a prison population where almost 20 per cent have a reading age of ten years, and where drug and alcohol addiction are major problems, rehabilitation must be based on the acquisition of basic literary skills, and attendance at self-help groups, such as Alcoholics Anonymous.

The Christian faith continues to proclaim the infinite worth of every individual in the sight of God, and the infinity of God's forgiving love. It is, therefore, not possible for Christians to acquiesce in the abandonment of the rehabilitative ideal. Prison staff would probably find it impossible to continue their work in a humane way if they abandoned all expectation of positive response in people committed to prison. This leads to the conclusion that prisoners and those who look after them need to live in harmony with the truth.

Punishment and truth

Throughout this chapter there have been references to the connection between truth and punishment. Truth is associated with punishment because it deals with assessing openness and motivation.

Truth has an extensive historical background in language and philosophy as well as in diverse interpretations within human experience. To some people it may appear an abstract and impersonal word; others have found it useful because truth does not only consist in knowing how to reproduce facts correctly; it incorporates perceiving and expressing a straightforward association between awareness and fact. Most people would agree that truth is a corrective for deception and connects with conscience as well as with man's deepest self-awareness, influencing the integrity of all relationships and encounters. Truth sheds constructive light on human existence and is therefore relevant to the most painful of human relationships, punishment. Truth can bring light to what was described at the outset of this chapter as 'this thing of darkness' in 'you and me'.

Truth has a strong legal impress. Western philosophy has given more attention to truth as a property of statements than to the biblical sense of truth as a personal attribute. The Enlightenment brought quasi-scientific expectations for precision and proof to all questions of knowledge and truth, which led to an emphasis on objective enquiry and detached assent more than personal trust. In this Western emphasis, truth is usually defined as a correspondence of idea to object, a positive correlation between a proposition and the state of affairs to which it refers. This has caused a relative vulgarisation of 'truth' in contemporary society, where its meaning is largely confined to the legal sense. Legal truth has become the focal point in a criminal trial and has direct bearing on punishment.

Truth, nevertheless, has a deep religious meaning. In this sense it refers to a transforming experience leading to a sense of well-being, known traditionally as conversion from sin to salvation, illusion to insight, bondage to freedom, chaos to order and pessimism to optimism. If people lack a sense of ultimate truth they are too easily satisfied with short-term pleasures or short-term security. The concept of religious truth expresses various biblically based aspects of human experience which can be yardsticks in the application of punishment. These include a sense of divine reality that is permanent and effective, a personal character that is sincere and good as well as knowledge that is certain, pure, long-lasting and convincing. A person's attitude can be detected in the way he or she lives and bears witness to truth – especially to their sense of truth about God, which they believe has been revealed to them and taken them in its grip. Human life is characterised by a need to distinguish between real and unreal, powerful and powerless, clear and confused, as well as relative degrees at one extreme or the other. These are the qualities supremely needed in decisions about punishment.

At Jesus' trial Pilate asked, 'What is Truth?' (John 16: 13). One can see in this the necessary neutrality of the state when faced with the question of the reality of God. The question is unanswered by Jesus, but not by the evangelist. His answer is given in the drama of the Cross, which follows immediately. This evaluation offers mankind deeper and more thought provoking insights than the Enlightenment expectations of precision and personal detachment. Pilate spoke for law-makers of all time when he asked about truth. His situation links the pursuit of truth in law with its pursuit in religion.

Truth is a dimension universally recognised as of value on the broad political level. It has had a prominent place in resolving political crises, as, for instance, in the 'truth force' (Satyagrapha) of Mahatma Gandhi for easing tensions in India, as well as in the ideals of the Truth and Reconciliation Commission in bringing greater social harmony in post-apartheid South Africa. On the wider society level, truth is important in the presentation of crime and punishment in the media. Journalists need to avoid publishing what is irrelevant or false; their reports should not be inexpensive forms of mass entertainment which may leave the public feeling that truth is an irrelevant concept. Acceptance of truth is also influenced by broad standards of public life. Public corruption makes a contribution to disrespect for truth by providing an excuse for rationalising the existence of criminality. Thus truth becomes supremely relevant for administrators of criminal justice systems.

On a narrower level, truth has a vital place in counselling victims and offenders. Sharing truth can have a therapeutic effect in mediation processes, particularly if painful facts can be expressed sensitively, or even humourously. Truth is an ideal that is relevant to risk; in dealing with offenders it can lead to trust and hence growth in opportunity and maturity. Helping prisoners face the truth about themselves and what they have done is one of the most positive ways of disarming their denial, their hatred and their violence, enabling them to live at peace with themselves and reconciled with their neighbours.

The theologian R.C. Moberly wrote:

> There are truths of material fact, truths of abstract statement; truths of historical occurrence; truths of moral experience; truths of spiritual experience and truth that is deepest and truest, which includes and unites them all.

Truth includes all these contexts, suggesting that there is something in common to all its forms, although not everyone would accept Moberly's last claim. Practitioners of many disciplines have recognised a 'family resemblance' (Wittgenstein) among these claims and called for the recognition of the plurality of all forms of truth. In a penal environment 'truth' is a concept that has not been afforded sufficient formal recognition on the broad political level and on the narrower level of personal interaction.

Emphasising the need for truth may seem self-evident, but as George Orwell wrote 50 years ago: 'We have now sunk to a depth at which the restatement of the obvious is the first duty of intelligent men.'

Truth, particularly when interpreted in the light of theological insights, is a counterbalance to the current fashion of making decisions on the basis of prejudice, convenience or personal insecurities. It is easy to be dismissive and cynical about the obvious, but to be so denigrates the heritage of theological ideas which can be applied to punishment and underrates the human capacity for truthfully facing change.

Bibliographical review

Little has been written on prison chaplaincy. An introductory book, *Summons To Serve – The Christian Call to Prison Ministry,* by Richard Atherton (London: Geoffrey Chapman, 1978), outlines the basis of the work. An unpublished paper by R.J. Van Niekrek, 'The Prison

Chaplaincy: A Ministry in Conflict', is in library resources at Chicago, Illinois. Many articles on chaplaincy can be found in past issues of *New Life – the Prison Service Chaplaincy Review*, published annually for the last 30 years in the UK. This review has been replaced by a publication *Justice Reflections* – worldwide papers linking Christian ideas with matters of justice – publishing termly in the UK for the International Prison Chaplains' Association. Information available from the editor. The Reverend Canon Alan R. Duce, (justicereflections@hotmail.com). Other connected articles have been published as occasional papers by the Centre for Theology and Public Issues, Edinburgh. Karl Barth's last sermons to prisoners have been published in *Deliverance to the Captives*, 1961, and *Call for God*, 1967 (London: Student Christian Movement).

Topics relating to the history of imprisonment are developed in Norval Morris and David J. Rothman (eds) *Oxford History of the Prison* (Oxford: Oxford University Press, 1995). Every article is followed by extensive bibliographical notes. An overview of the American prison system is given in Charles E. Silberman's *Criminal Violence, Criminal Justice* (New York: Random House, 1978). Lee Griffith has written on prisons from a biblical point of view in *The Fall of the Prison: Biblical Perspectives* on *Prison Abolition* (Grand Rapids, MI: Eerdmans, 1999).

A wider introduction to contemporary theological questions can be found in A.E. Bottoms and R.H. Preston (eds), *The Coming Penal Crisis – A Criminological and Theological Exploration* (Edinburgh: Scottish Academic Press, 1980). This book contains a relevant chapter by David E. Jenkins. Further perspectives can be found in the Clarke Hall Lecture by Archbishop William Temple (1934) and in the Anglican booklets on 'Punishment' and 'Prisons' (Church of England, 1963 and 1978). Further theological questions are examined in *Suffering, Innocent and Guilty* by Elizabeth Moberly (London: Society for the Propagation of Christian Knowledge, 1978) and in Colin E. Gunton, *The Promise of Trinitarian Theology* (Edinburgh: T. and T. Clark, 1991), as well as in Adrian Speller, *Breaking Out: A Christian Critique of the Criminal Justice System* (London: Hodder, 1986), in D.B. Forrester's *Christian Justice and Public Policy* (Cambridge: Cambridge University Press, 1997) and in Timothy Gorringe's *God's Just Vengeance* (Cambridge: Cambridge University Press, 1996). For a listing of vocabulary and biblical references to imprisonment, see G.L. Knapp, 'Prison' in G.W. Bromiley (ed.) *The International Standard Bible Encyclopaedia* (Grand Rapids, MI: Eerdmans, 1979, pp. 973–975).

Punishment themes that connect with theological doctrines are contained in many books. Among the noteworthy ones are: Ernst van den Haag, *Punishing Criminals – Concerning a Very Old and Painful*

Question (New York: Basic Books, 1975); David Garland and Peter Young, *The Power to Punish – Contemporary Penality and Social Analysis* (London: Heinemann Educational Press, 1983); Harold E. Pepinsky and Richard Quinney, *Criminology as Peacemaking* (Bloomington: Indiana University Press, 1984); Chris Wood, *The End of Punishment – Christian Perspectives on the Crisis in Criminal Justice* (Edinburgh: St Andrew's Press, 1991); and Nils Christie, *Limits to Pain* (Oxford: Martin Roberton, 1981).

Several books explore the restorative justice perspective. Among them are Martin Wright, *Making Good – Prisons, Punishment and Beyond* (London: Burnett Books, 1982); Howard Zehr, *Changing Lenses – A New Focus* for *Crime and Justice* (Philadelphia: Herald Press, 1990); Jonathan Burnside and Nicola Baker (eds) *Relational Justice* (Winchester: Waterside Press, 1994); and C. Cordess and M. Cox, *Forensic Psychotherapy: Crime, Psychodynamics and the Offender Patient* (London: Jessica Kingsley, 1996).

There are also books on human rights and religious traditions. One is C.M. Marshall's *Crowned with Glory and Honour. Human Rights in* the *Biblical Tradition* (Telford, PA: Pandora Press, 2001). Another is P.C. Cotham (ed.) *Christian Social Ethics. Perspectives and Problems* (Grand Rapids, MI: Baker, 1979).

More information about the section on classic theories of punishment can be obtained from Nigel Walker, *Why Punish?* (Oxford: Oxford University Press, 1990); Ted Honderich, *Punishment – The Supposed Justifications* (London: Penguin, 1971); H.L.A. Hart, *Punishment and Responsibility – Essays in the Philosophy of Law* (Oxford: Clarendon Press, 1968); and Gerald Austin McHugh, *Christian Faith and Criminal Justice – Toward a Christian Response to Crime and Punishment* (New York: Paulist Press, 1978). Ethical issues are covered in Agnes Helles, *General Ethics* (Oxford: Blackwell, 1988) and in David Cayley, *The Expanding Prison: The Crisis in Crime and Punishment and the Search for Alternatives* (Toronto: Anansi Press, 1998).

Two contrasting sources of information about the concept of truth can be found in the extensive article on 'Truth' by Bultmann, in Gerhard Kitten (ed.) *Theological Dictionary of the New Testament* (Grand Rapids, MI: Eerdmans, 1964), and in Feline Fernandez-Armesto, *Truth – A History and Guide for the Perplexed* (London: Bantam Press, 1997).

Chapter 2

Punishment: a psychological perspective

L.R. Huesmann and C.L. Podolski

Punishment is a word that evokes a variety of vivid images, but these are quite different for people from different disciplines. To the lawyer, judge and human-rights activist, they may be images of imprisonment, torture and the execution of criminals; to the statesman, they may be images of war, retribution and the occupation of countries; and to the parent, they may be images of spanking or 'grounding' of children.

It is these last images that we shall address primarily in this chapter. While disciplining and punishing children has been a topic of discussion for social philosophers and humanists for centuries, the effects of punishment on children and the role of punishment in changing behaviour have only been examined from a scientific perspective since early in the twentieth century. In 1911 E.L. Thorndike first identified a role for punishment in the acquisition of behaviour with his law of effect based on animal learning. Since then punishment has developed from a topic of interest for animal behaviourists, to a topic of interest for all learning theorists, to a topic of interest for developmental psychologists, criminologists and policy-makers. And, as the role of early child rearing and early learning experiences in the development of antisocial and aggressive behaviour has become more apparent, the role of punishment in suppressing or stimulating aggressive and antisocial behaviour has become more controversial. One theme of this chapter, in fact, is that punishment often has *both* stimulating and suppressing effects on aggressive and antisocial human behaviour, and the long-term consequences of punishment may not always turn out as intended. A related theme is that many common assumptions that the public and criminal justice authorities make about the effects of punishment are not well supported by psychological analyses of punishment.

The development of antisocial behaviour

Before turning to a discussion of punishment, however, we must briefly review some conclusions from the last half-century of research on human antisocial and aggressive behaviour. Four important points need to be emphasised.

First, as evidenced in research by Len Eron in 1960, Jerome Kagen in 1988, and Richard Tremblay more recently, antisocial aggressive behaviour has been found to emerge early in life, often before age 5 or 6; and early aggressive behaviour is about the best predictor we know of later aggression and antisocial behaviour in adolescence and adulthood. Although not every aggressive child grows up to be an antisocial adult by any means, multiple longitudinal studies have shown that the more aggressive child generally grows up to be the more aggressive adult.

Second, aggression is most often a product of multiple interacting factors, including evolutionary forces and genetic predispositions, environment/genetic interactions, brain trauma and neurophysiological abnormalities, abnormal arousal or hormone levels, family violence, cultural forces, media violence, poor parenting, environmental poverty and stress, peer-group identification, social control, and other factors. One can seldom find any single factor that explains more than a small portion of the individual variation in propensity to behave aggressively. Severe aggressive and antisocial acts are most likely to occur only when there is a convergence of multiple predisposing and precipitating factors.

Third, early learning and socialisation processes play a key role in the development of habitual aggression. Aggression is most likely to develop in children who grow up in environments that reinforce aggression, provide aggressive models, frustrate and victimise them and teach them that aggression is acceptable.

Fourth, the stability of individual differences in aggressiveness over time and across situations appears to be due, to a substantial extent, to the role that cognitions – that is beliefs, attitudes, perceptions, memory and ways of thinking – play in controlling one's own social behaviour. As Rowell Huesmann and Kenneth Dodge have both argued, the empirical evidence is compelling that social behaviour, including aggressive behaviour, is mediated to a great extent by the scripts and beliefs that one acquires while growing up and by the biases in perceiving and understanding one's environment that one acquires while growing up. Contrary to the viewpoint of early social learning theorists, it is not simply how a child's environment stimulates or rewards the child that is important, it is how the child interprets and encodes what happens to the child and what the child observes others doing that has lasting effects.

Psychological theory and the learning of aggressive and antisocial behaviour

Punishment, whether delivered by parents to children or by society to adults, may have multiple purposes, but one purpose almost always is to teach the perpetrator not to engage in antisocial behaviour. Given the evidence summarised above that antisocial behaviour is to a great extent learned, it is not surprising that we should believe that antisocial behaviour can be unlearned with the right punishment. However, the theory of how behaviours are learned and unlearned is much more complex than many assume.

Most psychologists agree that there are two major ways in which behaviours are learned or unlearned: learning by doing (called *enactive learning*) and learning by imitation (called *observational learning*). Both have a part in the effects of punishment, and both must be understood if the effects of punishment are to be understood. Let us begin with enactive learning – 'learning by doing'.

There are two types of enactive learning: *classical conditioning* and *operant conditioning*. In classical conditioning a stimulus (e.g. food) that elicits a natural response (e.g. salivation) is paired repeatedly with some other stimulus (e.g. a bell) until the bell alone produces the response. Anger towards particular people or in particular situations can easily be learned this way. Suppose you have been repeatedly frustrated and irritated by your experiences with car salesmen. Then just entering a car salesroom may engender anger in you. Similarly, the sight or even smell of someone who has treated you badly may stimulate anger because of this process.

In operant conditioning, on the other hand, some behaviour that is emitted by a person becomes more or less probable in the future because of the consequences that follow. The principle of operant conditioning is that the consequences the person experiences after doing something influence the chances that the person will do it again. Thus, technically, a child who hits someone and gains nice rewards (e.g. the esteem of peers, a toy over which the child was fighting) is more likely to hit someone again in the same situation. Similarly, in theory a child who hits someone and is hit back harder and is hurt and experiences only unpleasant consequences should be less likely to hit someone again. This latter case is certainly an example of *punishment*. We will discuss the theory of punishment from a psychological perspective in much more detail below. For now, the important point is that as far as operant psychologists are concerned, punishment of a person involves either doing something aversive to the person or stopping something nice from happening to the person.

The cognitive and neurophysiological changes involved in both classical or operant conditioning are well understood, and both types of conditioning follow fairly invariant laws. Many kinds of conditioning, particularly conditioning of emotions and reflexes, occur automatically and cannot be 'resisted' very well. Over the past 30 years, however, a view has emerged among psychologists studying aggression that classical and operant conditioning are not nearly as important in the development of human aggressive behaviour as is observational learning.

The concept of observational learning of social behaviour was first specified in detail by Albert Bandura in 1977. The basic idea is that people *encode* in memory what they see others do in a particular situation, and then, in similar situations, they tend to do the same thing. Rowell Huesmann, drawing on Robert Abelson's earlier work, has outlined a detailed model of how *scripts* for social behaviour, *normative beliefs* about what is appropriate social behaviour, and *attributions* about what others intend are acquired in this way. A script is a sequence of behaviours and expected responses by others that is used as a guide for how to behave. A normative belief is a belief about what is 'OK' for the person to do. An attribution of intent is a judgement about what the intentions are of other people, e.g. hostile or benign? A key concept is that people are more likely to remember and use scripts, beliefs and attributions that are consistent with their current mood and thoughts. Consequently, an aggressive boy who finds himself in a threatening situation with peers or parents is more likely to activate schemas – sets of beliefs about a particular type of situation – that cause him to interpret non-hostile acts as hostile (e.g. looking at him as disrespect), to retrieve beliefs that aggression is normative (e.g. 'you've got to retaliate against someone who disrespects you,' and to retrieve scripts for solving the problem with aggression (e.g. 'punch him before he punches me').

Substantial evidence has accumulated over the years that observational learning is extremely important in explaining individual differences in human aggressive behaviour. The discovery of 'mirror neurons' in primates by Vittorio Gallese and Giacomo Rizzolatti has provided a neurological basis for early imitation and Andrew Metzoff has shown that it occurs in infants. A variety of research studies conducted in the past 20 years have shown that children learn aggressive scripts and beliefs from observing others behave aggressively and that they develop a hostile attributional bias (i.e. see hostility where there is none) from viewing a lot of violence. Observational learning is as fundamental and inevitable a learning process as either operant or classical conditioning, but it seems to be more important than either of them in the development of aggressive and antisocial behaviour.

In summary, according to learning theory, antisocial behaviour and the attitudes and beliefs supporting antisocial behaviour are most likely to develop when a child is surrounded by 'models' (in real life and in the media) who engage in antisocial behaviour, when antisocial cues (unlearned cues such as guns; or learned cues such as oppressive authority) are common in the child's environment, and when the child receives reinforcements for behaving antisocially (such as obtaining tangible goods).

Principles of operant conditioning and punishment

Given this background, let us now turn back to a more detailed discussion of the theory of punishment. As we said above, punishment is viewed as the presentation to a person of something aversive or the removal of something pleasant. The principles of operant conditioning explain the relation between a person's behaviour and the antecedent and consequent events like punishment. Consider the following scenario:

> A 10-year-old boy walks into a shop and sees his favourite candy bar on display. He grabs it, runs out of the shop, and starts to eat it. It tastes really good. But a policeman has seen him run out of the shop and grabs him and takes him to the police station.

The learning theorist would interpret this scenario as follows. The antecedent event is 'the boy seeing the candy bar on display'. The behaviour is 'shoplifting the candy bar'. The first consequent event is 'getting to eat the candy bar'. The second consequent event is 'being detained by the police'. Getting to eat the candy bar is a favourable consequence; being detained by the police is an unfavourable consequence.

Now the fundamental principle of operant conditioning is that *emitted behaviours increase in frequency if the behaviours are followed by favourable consequences and decrease in frequency if they are followed by unfavourable consequences.* Favourable consequences occur either when a rewarding stimulus happens, e.g. eating the candy bar *(positive reinforcement),* or an aversive event is ended or avoided *(negative reinforcement).* Both of these outcomes increase the likelihood of the behaviour recurring. Unfavourable consequences happen either when an aversive event occurs, e.g. the policeman apprehending the boy, or a rewarding event is stopped or prevented. Both of these later cases are called *punishment,* and both should reduce the likelihood of the behaviour recurring.

In the above example, the favourable consequence of getting to eat the candy bar has two favourable parts. First, the boy is rewarded by the good taste of the candy bar he eats. This is positive reinforcement. The boy may also have his hunger reduced by eating the candy bar. This is negative reinforcement – the termination of aversive stimulation, i.e. hunger. Both increase the probability that the child will shoplift candy bars again. However, then the policeman catches the boy running away and detains him. This is punishment by presenting an aversive event, and it should decrease the probability of the behaviour recurring. The policeman could also simply refuse to let the child eat the rest of the candy bar. That would be punishment by preventing a rewarding event.

For consequences to influence the behaviour, they must be *contingent* on the behaviour, and the person must detect the contingency (though not necessarily consciously). In the above example, detaining the boy might not have much effect on his behaviour if he did not connect being detained with shoplifting, i.e. if the police regularly detained him for little reason.

In some cases, a particular consequence is dependent on a certain antecedent. For example, if the policeman is not in sight, the child does not need to worry as much about a policeman detaining him. Antecedent events that signal whether or not a reward or punishment will be delivered are called *discriminative stimuli.* Research has shown that increases or decreases in behaviour due to reinforcement and punishment are most likely when the discriminative stimuli that were present during the initial reinforcement or punishment recur.

It is also true that behaviours generalise to similar situations in proportion to how similar the situation is to the discriminative stimulus. This is known as *stimulus generalisation.* For example, if a boy has successfully shoplifted in one shop, he is more likely to try it in another shop that is similar to the first one. Operant conditioning also produces *response generalisation* – that is, the frequency of behaviours similar to the reinforced or punished behaviour also changes. In the above example, the shoplifting boy who is reinforced will become more likely to shoplift other items besides candy bars.

One might conclude from the above discussion that punishment is the only way one can reduce the frequency of a behaviour according to the laws of operant conditioning. Not so. Probably the most important operant learning principle about how to eliminate undesirable behaviours is that a behaviour that is no longer reinforced decreases in frequency. Such a process is called *extinction* by psychologists. The boy will stop shoplifting the candy bars if they don't taste good to him or if he does not get to eat them regardless of whether he is punished or not. Furthermore, if a *competing behaviour* is reinforced, e.g. playing football instead of hanging out at the shop, the extinction will occur more rapidly. This is called *counterconditioning* and is the basis for the most successful and lasting uses of operant conditioning to change behaviour. The best way to eliminate a behaviour permanently is to reinforce an incompatible behaviour until it occurs regularly.

Finally, we must mention the important law of *secondary reinforcement and punishment*. This law says that anything, however neutral in meaning initially, that is repeatedly paired with reinforcement or punishment acquires reinforcing or punishing properties itself. Thus, for the boy who is repeatedly beaten by his father, the mere presence of the father and any gestures the father might make that have been associated with beating the boy become very punishing to the boy in themselves. Similarly, a boy who has been praised many times in school should begin to feel pleasure simply from being in school as the school becomes a secondary positive reinforcer.

Problems with using punishment to modify behaviour

While this explanation of operant conditioning and punishment seems fairly straightforward, there are numerous complexities that cloud the picture when one tries to apply these principles to change children's, adolescent's or adult's behaviour. It is not that the laws are wrong; the laws of operant and classical conditioning are as immutable as anything we know about human neurophysiology and psychology. Rather it is that humans are complex information processors whose behaviours at any time depend on perceptions, memories, cognitions, motivations and thoughts of which the rest of us are unaware. This leads to a variety of problems.

Identifying what is rewarding and aversive

First, it is often difficult to identify what are all the relevant rewarding events and aversive events that may be affecting the person whose behaviour we would like to change. For example, consider a boy who is acting out in class. The teacher would like to change his behaviour and decides to punish the boy by speaking to him sharply. But it may be that the boy really craves attention from the teacher, and the attention that the teacher gives him when she chastises him is more of a reinforcement (i. e. the presentation of a reward) than the chastisement is a punishment. Then chastising the boy only increases the frequency of his acting out.

Importance of cognitive interpretations

Second, as described above, and as shown in a variety of studies, aggression and other social behaviours are controlled by a complex series of perceptions, beliefs and cognitions, and learned contingencies (not necessarily conscious). Every social situation triggers memories of other situations, ideas about what to do, and thoughts about what is good or bad. A useful concept posed in psychology is that of information processing (terminology borrowed from computer science in order to explain what occurs cognitively as a person perceives and responds to his/her environment). Another useful term is that of 'cognitive schemata', which refers to the beliefs and ideas activated by a situation (using a computer analogy, it is as if a specific floppy disk were inserted and a data file of information relevant to the situation was brought onto the screen). Although technical terms, these concepts are useful in understanding how cognitions and cognitive interpretations of events impact on behaviour.

The process of interpreting a situation – a person's processing and interpretation of antecedent and consequent events – goes far beyond simply noting if events are favourable or unfavourable. As a result, the rewarding and punishing effects of contingent consequent events may be very small or even opposite to what was intended. When punished, people ask themselves why they were punished or rewarded. They make attributions about the intentions of whoever is doing it. They attend selectively to cues in the environment that are consistent with their beliefs, cognitions and scripts. In the example about the chastised school boy who craves attention, even if he recognises the teacher's displeasure, he might attribute it to simple dislike unrelated to his behaviour. Should this be so, the chastisement will not change the frequency of the behaviour. Similarly, school may not become a secondary positive reinforcer for the boy who does very well in school if being in school cues high anxiety over fear of failure.

Alienation and negative self-schemas/self-concepts

The ways in which one perceives and conceptualises oneself is called a self-schema or self-concept (that is, one's sense of self in terms of attitudes, beliefs, expectations, etc.). An individual's self-schema or self-concept is an important kind of cognition for regulating social behaviour and is closely related to normative beliefs about what is appropriate. An adolescent boy who believes he is 'bad' and feels disconnected from society is likely to behave aggressively. Unfortunately, being habitually punished, regardless of how it changes behaviour, is likely to make you start to believe that you really are bad and an outcast from society. As D.J. Bem's self-perception research has shown (1967), people make attributions about the kind of person they are from what they observe happening to them. These attributions then become beliefs that influence future behaviour: regularly punishing a boy because you believe he is bad can make that belief a self-fulfilling prophecy.

Multiple secondary reinforcers and punishers

The laws of secondary reinforcement and secondary punishment mean that by the time a child is just 7 or 8 years old, a large number of originally neutral stimuli may have acquired reinforcing or punishing properties of which most others are unaware. Just the sight of some people or things may be punishing or reinforcing. School may have become punishing for some kids. Aggressive peers may have become reinforcing for other kids. Being in control, being out of control, being controlled by others, being touched, not being touched, being stared at, not being stared at, men, women, older children – any of these things may have acquired reinforcing or punishing properties of their own, and it is virtually impossible for an observer to understand these complexities. As a result, situations intended to be reinforcing may turn out to be punishing and vice versa.

Suppression versus extinction

Punishment *suppresses* behaviour, but it does not extinguish it. In accord with the laws of operant conditioning, even effective punishment that suppresses an undesirable behaviour may only suppress it when a discriminative stimulus – an antecedent associated with a particular consequence – is present, signalling that punishment is likely. The hungry adolescent who wants to steal a candy bar from a shop may not steal when a cop is in the store because he has previously been caught and punished by the cop, but, as soon as the cop leaves, he may well steal again. If punishment for a behaviour is only likely to be delivered when certain detectable cues are present, and if reinforcements for that behaviour are always delivered, a person will learn to suppress the behaviour only in the presence of the cues. Suppression of a behaviour is not the same as extinction of a behaviour. Lack of reinforcement extinguishes a behaviour, particularly if it is coupled with reinforcement of a competing incompatible behaviour. If the little girl climbing on the kitchen counter to get a biscuit no longer finds any biscuits there and at the same time is given a biscuit after playing on the floor without climbing, the response of climbing will extinguish.

Stimulated aggression and escape

Punishments that involve the presentation of aversive events (e.g. beating, spanking, confinement) may stimulate or teach other undesirable behaviours even while the original undesired behaviour is suppressed. If a man is beating or spanking you, running away from him or aggressing against him can stop the punishment. Furthermore, if the escape succeeds or fighting back stops the punishment, then escape and fighting are reinforced and become more likely in the future.

Emotional reactions, and conditioned hostility and fear

Harsh punishment of a child frequently produces strong emotional reactions in that child even while the undesired behaviour is being suppressed. Hostility, fear, screaming and crying are not unusual responses to harsh punishments. One problem is that these emotional reactions may interfere with the learning of competing behaviours and the extinction of the undesirable behaviour. We know that the highly aroused, emotionally upset child cannot learn new complex scripts for social behaviour very easily. Another problem is that we can expect the hostility and fear that one experiences while being punished to become classically conditioned responses to all sorts of characteristics associated with the punishment – the person, the setting, the institution. This may make future positive reinforcements very difficult to deliver.

Punishments compatible with undesirable behaviour

The wrong choice of punishment may not even suppress the undesirable behaviour because that behaviour is completely compatible with the unconditioned response to the punishment. For example, spanking a child more often than not probably causes the child to cry. Therefore, spanking is unlikely to be an effective punishment for suppressing crying. Yet, many parents still try to suppress a child's crying by spanking or otherwise harshly punishing the child. Similarly, a policeman's beating of an adolescent because he ran away from the policeman is unlikely to suppress running away because the punishment of beating stimulates escape, which is compatible with running away.

Reactance and counter-control

Unlike many animals, humans often recognise when another person is trying to manipulate their behaviour with operant conditioning, i.e. by providing reinforcements or punishments. The source of reinforcement and punishment is usually very clear whether it is a parent, a peer, a spouse or authorities. If a parent offers to give his teenage son the use of the family car for the weekend if the son cleans his room, the son will be aware that his behaviour is being manipulated. If a parent says he will deny his daughter her inheritance if she marries a particular man, the daughter will be aware that her behaviour is being manipulated. The problem is that most humans have a strong aversion to being controlled. This motivation sometimes leads them to react against control and resist the direction in which their behaviour is being pushed, even if it would be in their best interests to go along. Who has not experienced a strong urge not to buy something, e.g. a car, that they really liked, after someone else (the salesman) told them they really should buy it. This is *reactance*. It is particularly a problem when someone tries to use punishment to suppress aggressive or antisocial behaviour. It may well be in the best interest of a person being controlled to stop the behaviour, but his/her resistance to being controlled may lead them even to increase their aggressive or antisocial behaviour causing a *boomerang* effect.

One of the reasons why reactance may be a common phenomenon is that it frequently causes the manipulating person to stop trying to control the other person's behaviour. Suppose a father shouts at his teenage son when he comes home once late for dinner. The son, who is usually pleasant and gregarious during dinner, reacts by being sullen during dinner and leaves right after dinner. This is repeated several nights with the son coming home late each night. Finally, the father gives up and says nothing. Now, suddenly the son is pleasant during dinner and comes home on time the next night. After that the son sometimes comes home late and sometimes on time, but the father never complains. What has happened here? The son in displaying reactance has managed to condition his father not to punish him or try to control when he comes home for dinner. The son has punished the father for shouting at him by being sullen and has suppressed that behaviour in his father. Then the son reinforced his father for saying nothing by being pleasant and coming home on time. This is a good example of what is called *counter-control*. Generally, one can expect attempts at counter-control whenever one tries to use either punishments or reinforcements to overtly manipulate someone's behaviour. Of course, our societies and cultures are conditioning all of us all the time in subtle ways that escape our notice and therefore do not stimulate reactance or attempts at counter-control.

Observational learning of aggression

Finally, one must consider the problem that many punishments are themselves examples of aggressive behaviour and therefore can be expected to teach aggressive behaviour to the person being punished through observational learning. As noted above, observational learning is an extremely powerful process that shapes perceptions about others, scripts for social behaviour, and normative beliefs about how it is appropriate to behave. When a father beats his son to get him to stop doing something, the son may indeed stop doing it (suppression), but the boy is also encoding a script that says that a good way to get someone to do what you want them to do is to beat them. Such scripts readily generalise to other people and other situations. Boys who are beaten by their father because they disrespected their father could soon be expected to be beating peers who disrespect them. Observational learning occurs for the boy regardless of whether the target of the punishment is the boy or someone else around him. The husband who punishes his wife for disobedience by beating her is teaching his son that beating women is a way to make them obey.

The extent to which the child identifies with the person punishing him/her plays a complex role in this observational learning process. Certainly, the more a boy respects and identifies with the person punishing him, the more he is likely to encode the script for it. Also, the more the boy identifies with his punisher, the more he is also likely to interpret the punishment as a sign that he really had done something bad, and the more he is likely to suppress his behaviour. The bottom line is that for children who identify strongly with their parents, harsh parental punishment of aggressive behaviour is more likely to suppress aggressive behaviour, but is also more likely to teach children that harsh punishment is OK, at least 'when a child has been very bad'.

Generalised effects of punishment

So far we have discussed the effects that punishment has on someone who behaves in an undesirable way, but we have not attended much to the effects that punishment might have on the punisher or on other people who observe or are aware of the punishment. Yet these are important considerations for understanding the overall effect of punishment.

The first thing to realise is that the laws of conditioning and observational learning apply to the person or groups doing the punishing just as much as they apply to the person receiving the punishment. If, through punishing them, you get someone to do something rewarding for you or to stop doing something aversive to you, your punishing behaviour is reinforced. Therefore, one can expect you to punish more frequently. In other words, punishment that suppresses behaviour perpetuates punishment because it reinforces it. Unfortunately, this may happen even when the punishment is not really changing the behaviour but only suppressing it temporarily. Reinforcements that occur immediately after a behaviour are much more powerful than reinforcements that are delivered much later.

Harsh punishment may also serve the punisher because it is a socially acceptable way to act against the target of the punishment. A parent or teacher who has been frustrated and irritated by the behaviour of an antisocial person may feel a great aggressive drive towards that person. Punishing the child serves as an opportunity to realise that aggression in ways that are consistent with the parent's or teacher's normative beliefs about what behaviours are appropriate. The same analysis can apply to policeman or jailers who beat prisoners when they are particularly irritated. Their desire to take action against an irritating person may be as important a consideration in beating the prisoner as any desire to get them to change their behaviour. The problem is that using aggression to reduce frustration or irritation often works in such situations; so it is reinforced, and it perpetuates itself even if it does not change the behaviour of the child or prisoner. Aside from providing an opportunity to reduce frustration through aggression, punishment may also increase the punisher's sense of control or power. Just as being controlled by others is aversive and can stimulate reactance, feelings of being able to control others are reinforcing. Thus, getting someone to comply with your wishes through either punishment or reinforcement can be very satisfying and lead to the perpetuation of the techniques you used to gain compliance.

Let us turn now to a discussion of the effects of punishment on observers or third persons. As argued above, observational learning is an even more powerful force in shaping social behaviour than conditioning. Consequently, the observer is likely to learn both from what is happening to the punished person and from what the punisher is doing. Psychological theory is clear that the observer will learn more from the person with whom the observer identifies best. So, to the extent the observer identifies with the perpetrator who is being physically punished, the observer may learn to suppress the undesirable behaviour for which the perpetrator is being punished. On the other hand, to the extent the observer identifies with the punisher, the observer may learn how to suppress other people's undesirable behaviours with physical punishment, how to use punishment to gain power and control over other people, and how to reduce one's own frustration by acting aggressively towards others.

Harsh punishment often produces pain and emotional reactions by the punished child or person that make anyone watching, including the punisher, feel uncomfortable. An inevitable consequence of widespread exposure to painful punishment by the punisher, the punished person or an observer is a lessening of such emotional reactions. We say that the person has been *desensitised*. The emotional reaction one initially experiences deadens over time; in a sense, one becomes 'used to' the punishment in such a way that the punishment no longer evokes an emotional reaction. One simply does not feel the unpleasantness that one first did when confronted with such punishment. Consequently, the more a punishment is used, the more it tends to become acceptable. At the extreme this is the psychological process that allowed concentration camp guards eventually to feel little emotion while watching the inhumane tortures inflicted upon inmates.

One last effect on third persons that must be mentioned concerns *retribution*. In many cultures and societies the aggressive acts of antisocial individuals are seen as requiring retribution. The aggressive feelings stimulated in all of us by the frustrating and irritating behaviours of an antisocial person and our normative belief of 'an eye for an eye' combine to justify punishment. The normative belief of retribution may be invoked equally to justify spanking a child and executing a murderer. The point we want to make here concerns the consequences of not punishing someone when such a strong belief is widely held. Within a family, failure to punish may stimulate disharmony between the parents. Within a society with a strong retribution belief, however, failure to punish may leave a strong residual drive for revenge unfulfilled. The coupling of this drive for revenge and the normative belief that retribution is required is a recipe for vigilantism in society. When a society dispenses with punishment but does not change the belief that 'retribution is required', people are likely to take punishment into their own hands.

Psychodynamic approach to punishment

Psychodynamic theory[1] also offers a mixed view of punishment – a source of both positive and negative effects. The positive and negative effects are different from those hypothesised by learning theorists, however, and are assumed to be innate and less dependent on variations in environment. Psychodynamic writers assert that punishment is not strictly negative. Indeed, according to one theory proposed by Freud, the superego – a part of oneself which attempts to modulate one's impulses in order to coincide with societal and parental restrictions – is formed in part due to the child's internalised parental prohibitions. In this way, the psychodynamic view of punishment is more optimistic than the social learning perspective where punishment is seen as mostly a means through which undesirable behaviours are temporarily suppressed. Indeed, according to psychodynamic theory, castration anxiety (the fear of punishment through castration) leads to repression of oedipal wishes (the wish for intimacy with one's opposite-sex parent to the extent that the child has an unconscious emotional fantasy that the other parent be eliminated as a source of competition), and the subsequent structuring of the superego. A recent study group – the Kris Study Group of the New York Psychoanalytic Institute – reported agreement that such fear of punishment contributes to the formation of the conscience. Although psychodynamic theorists are still debating the mechanisms through which this occurs, it appears that, according to psychodynamic theory, punishment may be an important factor in the development of conscience. For instance, D. Milrod (1994) posits that the source of the punishment (internal vs. external) rather than the distinction between fear of punishment and guilt distinguish between children in different stages of conscience formation.

Psychodynamic theory does, however, postulate negative effects of punishment. For example, a 'superego pathology' is seen to account for conduct disorders. This form of superego pathology results from negative childhood experiences (which may included harsh punishment and abuse). The child internalises the negative qualities of the 'cruel, neglectful, and unloving' caretakers, viewing oneself as 'evil and meriting only punishment and reproof'.

Empirical studies investigating the role of punishment in child development

Given this theoretical background it is easy to see why two questions have dominated the past 25 years of child development research on children's punishment and antisocial development:

1 Is or can punishment be an effective tool in modifying children's behaviour and in reducing the frequency of aggressive behaviours so that the likelihood of adolescent and adult antisocial behaviour is reduced?
2 Does punishment produce deleterious consequences for the punisher, observers and the punished child, including, in particular, increasing the chances of habitual aggressive and antisocial behaviour developing in adolescence and young adulthood?

During the last 30 years over 250 studies have been conducted in order to investigate the relation between children's punishment and aggressive and antisocial behaviour. These studies have included the investigation of parenting style and self-esteem, spanking and aggressiveness towards peers, and parental discipline. The studies have investigated parenting of non-compliant children of various ages including young toddlers and older children, and have also examined short-term effects of various punishment procedures as well as long-term or longitudinal effects. While many of the studies have investigated parental punishment and aggressive behaviour directly, some of them have focused on correlates of antisocial and aggressive behaviour such as identification with the punisher and development of guilt and conscience.

Taken as a whole, these studies have suggested that punishment can be used successfully to manage children's behaviour, but that it may also have deleterious short-term and long-term effects on behaviour. Three important types of studies provide this evidence: true experimental studies; cross-sectional correlational studies; and longitudinal studies. True experimental studies manipulate conditions between an experimental and control group so that the only difference between groups is the kind of punishment, thus allowing cause easily to be discriminated from effect. Cross-sectional studies examine whether certain characteristics, e.g. being punished severely and behaving aggressively, tend to occur together more than one would expect due to chance. Longitudinal studies also examine natural factors; however, rather than looking at immediate relations, longitudinal studies examine relations over time.

Probably the best summary of this empirical research was published very recently by Elizabeth Gershoff (2002). She used a technique called meta-analysis to combine the sizes of the effects found in 88 of the most relevant empirical studies over the past 60 years. She concluded that, while corporal punishment of children by parents did produce immediate compliance by the child, it also had many significant negative consequences associated with it. These included increased aggression, decreased moral internalisation of social standards, decreased quality of relationship with the parents, decrements in mental health and increased risk for later antisocial and criminal behaviour, later poor mental health and later abuse of their own children. However, a number of distinguished researchers in the area, including Diana Baumrind, Robert Larzelere and Phil Cowen (2002) have replied that one must consider studies separately because many mix together different kinds of punishment ranging in severity. Therefore, let us examine some of the specific empirical studies on punishment.

Managing behaviour problems

Many Americans use punishment in order to instruct their children and correct problem behaviours. In a 1979 study by J.S. Solheim, it was reported that 81 per cent of American parents used corporal punishment as a method of disciplining their children. Also, according to a 1995 Gallup Poll, many parents report using corporal punishment with children under 5 years of age. Use of corporal punishment is also generally supported by medical professionals. A report by D.A. Trumbull presented to the American Academy of Pediatrics in 1995 concluded that discipline is an important part of a child's development and that proper use of spanking has positive short-term and long-term outcomes. In a 1992 survey of 800 family doctors and 400 paediatricians, K.F. McCormick found that 70 per cent of family doctors and 90 per cent of paediatricians supported the use of corporal punishment. In general, corporal punishment is viewed as an effective and sometimes necessary means of discipline. However, research supporting the effectiveness of corporal punishment in changing children's antisocial behaviour is not as strong as this consensus might suggest.

It is certainly clear from well-controlled, randomised experiments that spanking and similar punishments will suppress the behaviours that they are intended to suppress when everything else is controlled. Experimental studies with clinic-referred children have shown successful short-term effects of punishment. A number of studies have shown that 'timeout' punishment reduces immediate oppositional behaviour in children. 'Timeout' involves removing the child from his/ her current activity and forcing the child to sit quietly in isolation. Timeout combined with spanking has also been shown to be effective in increasing compliance in young non-compliant children. These studies suggest that punishment can reduce problem behaviours in children in the short term. However, they also indicate that timeout is about as effective as spanking with young children. Most studies indicate that corporal punishment is most effective when used in a very defined manner. In treating children who have clinically diagnosed behavioural disorders, very specific strategies that use punishment have been successfully employed by psychologists to modify their disruptive behaviour. A variety of detailed guides have been developed by psychologists about how to optimise the chances that punishment will actually suppress the behaviour it is intended to suppress. The problem is that in the real-world applications by parents and teachers (as opposed to the therapeutic applications by professionals), punishment is seldom applied in such a considered manner and does not always suppress the undesirable behaviour. For example, C. Madsen and colleagues (1970) tell the story of a teacher who shouted 'sit down' at children who got out of their seats in such a way that the children she shouted at got out of their seats more.

In understanding the likely effectiveness of using corporal punishment, the entire parenting style needs to be taken into consideration. In experimental studies, the use of corporal punishment can be defined and administered according to experimenters' guidelines; however, in understanding actual use of corporal punishment outside of a laboratory environment, other parenting characteristics are also important. For instance, in a study of parenting styles, Diana Baumrind (1971) found that both parents who are authoritarian and parents who are authoritative use corporal punishment but use it differently and with different effects. A parent with a so-called authoritarian style uses withdrawal of love, and stimulation of fear in conjunction with corporal punishment; whereas a parent with a so-called authoritative style uses reason and reinforcement in conjunction with corporal punishment. Corporal punishment was found to be the preferred method of punishment for both kinds of parents but was only effective in changing children's behaviours for the authoritative parents. It is clear that overall parenting style is an important moderator of the effectiveness of punishment on children.

The bottom line is that, despite the clear short-term utility of punishment in suppressing behaviour, whether or not the undesirable behaviour finally extinguishes and is replaced by a more desirable behaviour depends on many other factors affecting the child's learning. Most parents, teachers and even juvenile authorities are not equipped to disentangle these factors. As a result, the long-term application of punishment may, in fact, make the acquisition of better behaviours less likely. For example, at least two studies (one by L. S. Benjamin and colleagues in 1971 and one by R. J. Butler and colleagues in 1988) have shown that harsh parental punishment of children who wet their beds lengthens the time it takes the children to learn control rather than shortening it.

Investigating the role of punishment in the development of aggression

While the above studies indicate that punishment can be an effective short-term behaviour-management tool, they also indicate that punishment can interfere with the learning of a new behaviour (for example, see bed-wetting examples). It appears that punishment is most effective as a way to interrupt and prevent a certain behaviour rather than as an effective method of teaching a new behaviour. Further, a large body of literature has now accumulated which shows that harsh physical punishment is associated with immediate or later antisocial behaviour in the child and adolescent. Of course, when one finds that punishment is related to aggressive behaviour, it is difficult to determine whether this relation is due to the fact that antisocial, aggressive children are punished more frequently or that the punishment increases the likelihood of aggressive, antisocial behaviour on the part of the child. In reviewing the studies, this point must be kept in mind.

Most of the evidence that suggests that punishment is related to aggressive behaviour comes from two sources: cross-sectional and longitudinal studies of parenting style and studies on the relation between physical abuse and antisocial behaviour. Two relatively short-term studies have examined the relation. In a study of 273 kindergarten children which investigated short-term effects, Z. Strassberg and colleagues (1994) found that physical punishment was related to a child's aggression toward peers. In a much larger national interview study with 3,780 mothers which investigated long-term effects, Murray Strauss and colleagues (Sugarman *et al.*, 1994) found that children whose parents used corporal punishment had worse behaviour two years later, even when controlling for initial antisocial behaviour. These studies confirm the findings of a variety of older and longer-term studies. Leonard Eron, Rowell Huesmann and associates, in a 1960 cross-sectional study of 800 third-graders, reported that children who were punished more harshly by their parents were more likely to be nominated by their peers as aggressive, except for the children who strongly identified with their parents. Among the children who strongly identified with their parents as being aggressive, greater punishment by the parents was negatively correlated with aggression. When this sample was followed up ten years later at the end of high school, little relation was found between the youths' early punishment and their current peer-nominated aggression, but, when the sample was followed up again at age 30, a strong relation was found. Harsh parental punishment at age 8 was positively correlated with a male's self-reported serious aggression, his score on a personality test of aggressive tendencies, his number of arrests and convictions, his seriousness of arrests and convictions, his tendency to beat his spouse, and how harshly he punished his own children. However, when the influence of early aggression was removed statistically, this long-term relation disappeared, making it difficult to tell the extent to which the young boy's aggression or the harsh punishment he received started the cycle. Using data from a longitudinal study of 411 London boys in 1991, David Farrington was also able to show that harsh punishment at age 8 or 9 was one of the best predictors of early delinquency. Similarly, also in 1991, Joan McCord, in reviewing the records of 130 families in the Cambridge-Somerville Youth Study, discovered that a father's use of physical punishment was a very significant predictor of his son's criminality years later, even when many other variables were controlled. As with the Eron study, neither of these studies unambiguously suggested the direction of the effect between harsh punishment by parents and aggressive and antisocial behaviour. Even when early punishment precedes much later aggression, it is possible that early aggression could have caused both the early punishment and the later aggression.

A few longitudinal studies have provided some data on the causal question. P. Cohen and J. S. Brook (1995) conducted an investigation of about 1,000 children whom they interviewed first between age 1 and 10 and then when they were between age 10 and 20. The authors did not use the most sophisticated analyses to pick apart the effects, but the analyses they did seemed to suggest effects in both directions – that is, that early antisocial behaviour was causing increased parental punishment and that early punishment was causing increased antisocial behaviour. In an analysis of data from a three-year longitudinal study of 6-year-olds and 8-year-olds in the US, Finland, Poland and Australia, Rowell Huesmann and Leonard Eron found that early harsh punishment and rejection of children as reported by the parents was correlated with later aggression as reported by their peers. Structural modelling analysis – which allows the examination of which factor leads to the other – again suggested that the relation between harsh punishment and aggression is as much due to the aggressive behaviour stimulating harsher punishments as it is to the harsher punishments stimulating aggression.

The studies on abusive parenting reinforce the conclusion that harsh treatment of children and their later aggressive and antisocial behaviour are related. There can be little doubt that abused children grow up to be more likely to commit antisocial and aggressive acts. For example, in a study of a community pre-school sample by B. Weiss and colleagues (1992), children who had been hit by an adult hard enough to require medical attention as pre-schoolers were more likely to be aggressive years later, even controlling for child temperament, socio-economic status, and marital violence. Interestingly, in this study it was found that these abused children were also more likely to perceive other people's innocent actions as hostile (*hostile attributional bias*), and had memorised a greater number of plans for aggressive actions (*aggressive scripts*). This result is particularly interesting because it is consistent with the predictions of the information-processing model of aggression about what cognitions would be affected by harsh punishment. Nevertheless, on the basis of the studies existing to date, it is very difficult to conclude with certainty that the abusive parenting or harsh punishment are causing the antisocial behaviour.

Another important point to remember is that harsh punishment may have different effects depending on the cultural norms about appropriate punishment. In societies or subcultures where harsher punishment is the norm, the effects of harsh punishment on future behaviour may be quite different than if harsh punishment were abnormal. For example, a recent study by Gunnoe reported that spanking stimulated aggression in 4- to 7-year-old white American children but deterred aggression in 4- to 7-year-old black American children. While the results of studies like these may be open to alternative interpretations, they at least suggest that culture should be considered in drawing general conclusions.

The most plausible conclusion may be that parental discipline style has a major effect on the development or non-development of aggressive and antisocial behaviour, but that the use or non-use of punishment is just one element of that style. When used properly, within an appropriate overall child-rearing style, punishment may suppress antisocial behaviour. When used improperly, within the wrong style, it may stimulate antisocial behaviour. What is a 'wrong' style? 'Power-assertive' disciplinary techniques have been targeted as being associated with higher levels of aggression in children. Other parenting behaviours that have been found to be correlates of aggressive behaviour include parental non-acceptance and parental permissiveness and parental inconsistency. As the Eron study mentioned earlier suggested, the child's perception of the parental message and acceptance or rejection of it have been found to be important factors that affect whether or not the child internalises the values which the parent is teaching through punishment. Finally, it has been found that early corporal punishment is not related to adolescent delinquency when controlling for parental involvement.

In 1973 Diane Baumrind suggested that some use of punishment combined with reasoning with children would effectively discipline them without adverse consequences, whereas harsh punishment combined with inconsistent and unreasoned discipline would stimulate aggression. More recently, Gerald Patterson has made a compelling case that lack of effective monitoring and disciplining of children's behaviour is more important in the development of aggressive and antisocial behaviour than punishment *per se*. The argument here is that children become antisocial and aggressive, not because they are punished, but because their parents do not attend to their behaviours, do not differentially reinforce pro-social and punish antisocial behaviours, are inconsistent and unpredictable in how they treat their children, and tend to engage in coercive interactions with their children in which antisocial behaviour is rewarded. Patterson argues that a microanalysis of family interaction patterns generally reveals that the parents have in fact conditioned their children to be aggressive through the misapplication of punishment and reinforcement.

What about empirical evidence supporting the psychodynamic view of punishment? Although few empirical articles on punishment from a psychodynamic perspective have been published, it appears that psychodynamic theory and corresponding clinical observations coincide with the above research which shows that punishment can both lead to and inhibit aggressive behaviour. Key factors appear to be: identification with the aggressor, source of punishment, timing in terms of the age of the child at time of the punishment, and intensity – although this appears to be confounded with abusive and neglectful parenting. In general, very young children who identify less with parents and who are punished more harshly seem more likely to respond aggressively and to internalise a poor self-concept than to internalise parental proscriptions against antisocial behaviour.

Implications for punishment of adult criminals

As is clear from the above review, most of the psychological research on punishment has been conducted with children or youth. Yet the laws of learning and behaviour modification that apply to children generally apply to adults as well. However, the likelihood of a successful application of punishment to *change* the behaviour of an adult is even more problematic for several reasons. Once scripts, beliefs, and attitudes are crystallised, they become much more difficult to change. Punishing an adult for a particular behaviour will probably suppress the behaviour temporarily, but changing the scripts, beliefs, and attitudes that support that behaviour while it is suppressed is much more difficult. As a result, once the punishment is removed, the behaviour is likely to return. In addition, adults are much more prone than children to react to punishment with alienation, aggression, reactance and counter-control. An offender who already feels alienated from society is only likely to feel more alienated from punishment and to have a more negative self-schema, making future antisocial behaviour more acceptable. If offenders can rationalise their behaviour as not completely their fault (e.g. a consequence of an impoverished childhood), their self-schema may not become so negative, but they are likely to feel manipulated by the punishment and to resist changing their behaviour (reactance). Finally, adults may find it more difficult to accept the power differentials that punishment entails (between the punisher and punishee) and therefore are even more likely to respond to punishment with anger and aggression.

Using punishment wisely

The conclusion would seem to be, then, that punishment may have some appropriate role in behaviour management, but it must be applied wisely. What exactly does that mean?

First of all, almost all theorists agree that punishment increases compliance and suppresses antisocial behaviour only for a short time after the punishment. For real behaviour change to occur or real extinction to occur, the reinforcements that had been provided for the antisocial behaviour must be identified and removed, and competing behaviours must be reinforced. This process is known as counter-conditioning. If it is to last, the behaviour change must be supported by changes in beliefs and attitudes that support the behaviour. People must 'internalise' mechanisms that regulate behaviour so that in the absence of the threat of punishment, they will choose not to act aggressively – not because of threat of punishment, but because they agree with the behaviour which has been taught. For example, if the child sees a biscuit on the counter but does not reach for it even when his/her parent is absent (hence, in the absence of threat of punishment), this suggests that the child has 'internalised' the prohibition.

Second, the *contingency* of the punishment must be clear to the punished person and the punishment must be immediate in order to be effective. People must understand the connection between the behaviour and the consequential punishment. Unlike animals, whose behaviour will decrease following any punishment, people must perceive the contingency between the behaviour and the punishment. Furthermore, if the punishment is delayed, its effectiveness will be greatly diminished. Delayed punishments may well affect the frequency of other than the intended behaviour. Similarly, if punishment is to deter a person's behaviour before it happens, the person must be fairly certain punishment is going to happen, i.e. certain of being 'caught'. This requires monitoring and consistency that is hard to achieve either for a parent with a child or for the criminal-justice establishment with adults.

Third, if we don't want the punished person to become more aggressive as a result of being punished, at a minimum the person must understand the reasons behind the punishment – how it is contingent on an inappropriate script for behaviour that the person followed, how it is consistent with the normative belief that antisocial behaviour is wrong, and how it is not motivated by any particular hostility towards the person. Aggressive and antisocial behaviour emerge out of a complex interaction of environmental forces with the person's cognitions and information processing. One needs to focus as much on these cognitions and on what the person is observing as on the person's behaviours.

As Leonard Berkowitz, one of the pioneers in the study of aggression and violence, has said (1993, p. 314):

Punishment works best ... when it is: [1] severe; [2] delivered quickly, before the (persons) whose behavior needs to be controlled can enjoy the pleasures that they might gain from the disapproved behaviour; [3] administered consistently and with certainty, so that there is little doubt that the disapproved action will have at least some negative consequences; [4] (when) attractive alternatives to the disapproved behaviour are available; and [5] (when) the (persons) who are punished have a clear understanding or the reasons for the discipline.

One cannot be sure that, even under these conditions, observational learning, desensitisation, reactance, stimulated aggression and other processes will not make antisocial and aggressive behaviour more likely after punishment: they may. All we can be sure of is that, if we use punishment, these rules seem to be the best for successfully modifying behaviour while minimising the chances of teaching someone to be more aggressive.

In conclusion, careful application of punishment may assist in changing children's antisocial behaviours, but there are serious possibilities that it may increase antisocial behaviours instead. With adults the likelihood that punishment will assist in changing behaviours is much more problematic. There are certainly other reasons for society delivering punishment to adults besides attempting to change their behaviour or to deter repetition of their antisocial behaviour. As discussed in this chapter, punishment may serve valuable purposes for the psyche of victims and in preventing antisocial behaviour by other persons who are not punished but learn from 'observing' the punishment. Punishment is an important means of preventing private action, which could be unlawful and destructive of law and order. Punishment by confinement also incapacitates offenders from committing harmful antisocial acts. However, from a psychological standpoint, there is little reason to believe that any kind of punishment by itself has much of a chance to change an offender's behaviour or to deter future offences unless it is viewed by the offender as an almost certain consequence of the behaviour.

Bibliographic review

A substantial body of published literature on the psychological theory behind punishment and the psychological effects of punishment has accumulated over the past century. In this chapter we have provided precise bibliographical citations for most of our assertions; so the reader can track down the original empirical study or theoretical argument on which our assertion is based. However, for the benefit of the reader interested in pursuing the general topic in more detail, we also offer here a guide to some of the most important sources concerning the major topics we have covered. Detailed citations for all of these sources are provided in the references at the end of this review.

Psychological theory and aggressive and antisocial behaviour

Perhaps the best starting point for the reader interested in the modern psychological theory of aggressive and antisocial behaviour (and punishment) is Berkowitz's 1993 textbook entitled *Aggression: Its Causes, Consequences, and Control*. Another fairly comprehensive treatment that is a little more technical is provided by Coie and Dodge in their 1997 paper in the *Handbook of Child Psychology*.

Learning theory, social learning and social cognition as applied to antisocial and aggressive behaviour

The foundations of modern learning theory are quite old, beginning with Thorndike's (1911) experiments on conditioning animals to behave in desired ways. However, it was not until the early 1960s that Eron and his colleagues (see Eron, Walder and Lefkowitz, 1971) and Berkowitz and his colleagues (see descriptions in Berkowitz, 1993) provided some of the first empirical evidence of the importance of learning in the development of aggressive and antisocial behaviour. It was also in the early 1960s that Albert Bandura first suggested that imitation may be as important as Pavlovian or operant conditioning in shaping social behaviour. His 1977 book, *Social Learning Theory*, and his 1986 book, *Social Foundations of Thought and Action*, summarise the thinking that led psychologists to revise their views of how social behaviour is learned. Then in the 1980s and 1990s psychologists combined these concepts into so-called social/cognitive models that viewed the human mind as an information processor that learned by constructing new 'software' based on observation and conditioning. Two good papers presenting this perspective are Huesmann's 1998 chapter in Geen and Donnerstein's *Human Aggression* book and Crick and Dodge's 1994 *Psychological Bulletin* article.

Psychological theory concerning the effects of punishment in child development

In addition to the books on learning theory mentioned above, Baumrind's 1971 paper in *Developmental Psychology* provides a popular perspective on how different styles of parenting interact with punishment to change its effects. It is well worth reading. Baumrind and Patterson (see Patterson's 1995 paper on punishment and coercion) both write eloquently about why harsh punishment and inconsistent discipline increase antisocial behaviour in adolescents. More generally, Kazdin's 1989 book, *Behavior Modification in Applied Settings*, provides an excellent review of the current theory of punishment's effects in modifying behaviour and how one can go wrong in using punishment.

Empirical studies of childhood punishment and adult antisocial behaviour

A large number of studies have documented the fact that harsh punishment and inconsistent discipline in childhood are often associated with antisocial behaviour later in life. The recent meta-analysis by Gershoff (2002) in *Psychological Bulletin* is a must-read review of the empirical work, as are the comment articles in the same issue. Anyone interested in this topic should also read Widom's 1989 *Psychological Bulletin* paper on how abusive punishment seems to be transmitted across generations. However, the detailed reports on longitudinal studies showing that harsh punishment is associated with increases in adult aggression may be more important. We would recommend the papers by Eron, Huesmann and Zelli (1991), by Farrington (1982), and by McCord (1991). Joan McCord's 1995 book, *Coercion and Punishment in Long Term Perspective*, provides a good summary of many studies. Finally, the papers by Murray Straus and his colleagues provide perhaps the strongest arguments about the negative effects of corporal punishment on children.

Note

1 Psychodynamic theory stems from a theory of psychology in which instincts and drives are viewed as innate forces which compete against societal norms in order to find expression. Two key drives – sex and aggression – are viewed as predominant forces influencing development. When a great deal of conflict exists and drives are inexpressible, emotional and behavioural problems may result. While these drives impact development, so also do significant early relationships. In essence, the emotion-laden interactions with parents and care-takers shape not only the child's behaviours but also his/her emotions and ways of relating. The term 'dynamic' indicates the importance of these early relationships and the ways in which individuals interact together in 'dynamic' relationship. Learning theorists view behaviour as determined environmentally through the various types of learning (enactive and observational learning). Although some theorists attempt to integrate these perspectives, they are generally viewed as being in opposition to each other.

References

Abelson, R.P. (1976) 'Script Processing in Attitude Formation and Decision Making', in J.S. Carroll and J.W. Payne (eds) *Cognition and Social Behaviour*, pp. 33–46. Hillsdale, NJ: Erlbaum.

Arles, H.R. and Garske, J.P. (1982) *Psychological Theories of Motivation*. Monterey, CA: Brooks/Cole.

Axelrod, S. and Apsche, J. (1983) *The Effects of Punishment on Human Behaviour*. New York: Academic Press.

Bandura, A. (1973) *Aggression: A social learning analysis*. Englewood Cliffs, NJ: Prentice-Hall.

Bandura, A. (1974) *Behaviour Therapy and the Models of Man*. New York: Holt, Reinhart & Winston.

Bandura, A. (1977) *Social Learning Theory*. Englewood Cliffs, NJ: Prentice-Hall.

Bandura, A. (1986) *Social Foundations of Thought and Action: A Social-cognitive Theory*. Englewood Cliffs, NJ: Prentice-Hall.

Bandura, A. and Walters, R.H. (1959) *Adolescent Aggression*. New York: The Ronald Press Company.

Baumrind, D. (1967) 'Child Care Practices Anteceding Three Patterns of Preschool Behaviour', *Genetic Psychology Monographs*, 75, 43–88.

Baumrind, D. (1971) 'Current Patterns of Parental Authority', *Developmental Psychology Monographs*, 4(1, pt. 2), 1–103.

Baumrind, D. (1973) 'The Development of Instrumental Competence Through Socialization', in A.D. Pick (ed.) *Minnesota Symposia on Child Psychology*, Vol. 7, pp. 3–46. Minneapolis: University of Minnesota Press.

Baumrind, D., Larzelere, R.E. and Cowen, P.A. (2002) 'Ordinary Physical Punishment: Is it Harmful? Comment on Gershoff (2002)', *Psychological Bulletin*, 128, 580–589.

Bean, A.W. and Roberts, M.W. (1981) 'The Effect of Time-out Release Contingencies on Changes in Child Noncompliance', *Journal of Abnormal Psychology*, 9(1), 95–105.

Bem, D.J. (1967) 'Self-perception: An Alternative Interpretation of Cognitive Dissonance Phenomena', *Psychological Review*, 74, 183–200.

Benjamin, L.S., Serdahely, W. and Geppert, T.V. (1971) 'Night Training Through Parents' Implicit Use of Operant Conditioning,' *Child Development*, 42(3), 963–966.

Berkowitz, L. (1974) 'Some Determinants of Impulsive Aggression: The Role of Mediated Associations with Reinforcements for Aggression', *Psychological Review*, 81, 165–176.

Berkowitz, L. (1993) *Aggression: Its Causes, Consequences, and Control*. New York: McGraw-Hill.

Bernal, M.E., Duryee, J.S., Pruett, H.L. and Burns, B.J. (1968) 'Behaviour Modification and the Brat Syndrome', *Journal of Consulting and Clinical Psychology*, 32(4), 447–455.

Brehm, J.W. (1966) *A Theory of Psychological Reactance*. New York: Academic Press.

Butler, R.J., Brewin, C.R. and Forsythe, W.I. (1988). 'A Comparison of Two Approaches to the Treatment of Nocturnal Enuresis and the Prediction of Effectiveness Using Pretreatment Variables', *Journal of Child Psychology and Psychiatry and Allied Disciplines*, 29(4), 501–509.

Cloninger, C.R. and Gottesman, A. (1987) 'Genetic and Environmental Factors in Antisocial Behaviour Disorders', in S.A. Mednick, T.E. Moffitt and S.A. Stack, (eds) The Causes of Crime: New Biological Approaches, pp. 92–109. New York: Cambridge University Press.

Cohen, P. and Brook, J.S. (1995) 'The Reciprocal Influence of Punishment and Child Behaviour Disorder', in J. McCord (ed.) Coercion and Punishment in Long-term Perspectives. Cambridge: Cambridge University Press.

Coie, J.D. and Dodge, K.A. (1998) 'Aggression and Antisocial Behaviour', in W. Damon and N. Eisenberg (eds) Handbook of Child Psychology. New York: John Wiley & Sons.

Crick, N.R. and Dodge, K.A. (1994) 'A Review and Reformulation of Social Information Processing Mechanisms in Children's Adjustment', Psychological Bulletin, 115, 74–101.

Day, D.E. and Roberts, M.W. (1983) 'An Analysis of the Physical Punishment Component of a Parent Training Program', Journal of Abnormal Child Psychology, 11(1), 141–152.

Dodge, K.A. (1986) 'A Social Information Processing Model of Social Competence in Children', in M. Perlmutter (ed.) The Minnesota Synmposium on Child Psychology, Vol. 18, pp. 77–125. Hillsdale, NJ: Erlbaum.

Eron, L.D. (1987) 'The Development of Aggressive Behaviour from the Perspective of a Developing Behaviourism,' American Psychologist, 42, 435–442.

Eron, L.D. and Huesmann, L.R. (1984). 'The Relation of Prosocial Behaviour to the Development of Aggression and Psychopathology' Aggressive Behaviour, 10, 201–211.

Eron, L.D., Huesmann, L.R. and Zelli, A. (1991) 'The Role of Parental Variables in the Learning of Aggression', in D. Pepler and K. Rubin (eds) The Development and Treatment of Childhood Aggression, (pp. 169–188). Hillsdale, NJ: Lawrence Erlbaum Associates.

Eron, L.D., Walder, L.O. and Lefkowitz, M.M. (1971) The Learning of Aggression in Children. Boston: Little, Brown & Co.

Farber, I.E. (1963) 'The Things People Say to Themselves', American Psychologist, 18, 185–197.

Farrington, D.P. (1978). 'The Family Backgrounds of Aggressive Youths', in L. Hersov, M. Berger and D. Shaffer (eds) Aggression and Anti-social Behaviour in Childhood and Adolescence, pp. 73–93. Oxford: Pergamon.

Farrington, D.P. (1982) 'Longitudinal Analyses of Criminal Violence', in M.E. Wolfgang and N.A. Weiner (eds) Criminal Violence, pp. 171–200. Beverly Hills, CA: Sage.

Farrington, D.P. and Hawkins, J.D. (1991) 'Predicting Participation, Early Onset and Later Persistence in Officially Recorded Offending', Criminal Behaviour and Mental Health, 1(1), 1–33.

Feshbach, S. (1970) 'Aggression' in P.H. Mussen (ed) Carmichael's Manual of Child Psychology, Vol. 2, pp. 159–259. New York: Wiley.

Fisher, W.W., Piazza, C., Cataldo, M., Harrell, R., Jefferson, G. and Conner, R.

(1993) 'Functioning Communication Training With and Without Extinction and Punishment', *Journal of Applied Behaviour Analysis*, 26, 23–36.

Gallup Organization (1995) *Disciplining Children in America: A Gallup Poll Report.* Princeton, NJ: Gallup Organization.

Gershoff, E.T. (2002) 'Corporal Punishment by Parents and Associated Child Behaviours and Experiences: A Meta-analytic and Theoretical Review', *Psychological Bulletin*, 128, 539–579.

Grusec, J.E. and Goodnow, J.J. (1994) 'Impact of Parental Discipline Methods on the Child's Internalization of Values: A Reconceptualization of Current Points of View', *Developmental Psychology*, 30(1), 4–19.

Guerra, N.G., Eron, L.D., Huesmann, L.R., Tolan, P. and VanAcker, R. (1997) 'A Cognitive/Ecological Approach to the Prevention and Mitigation of Violence', in K. Bjorkqvist and D. Fry (eds) *Styles of Conflict Resolution: Models and Applications from Around the World*, pp. 199–214. New York: Academic Press.

Guerra, N.G., Huesmann, L.R., Tolan, P.H., VanAcker, R. and Eron, L.D. (1995) 'Stressful Events and Individual Beliefs as Correlates of Economic Disadvantage and Aggression Among Urban Children', *Journal of Consulting and Clinical Psychology*, 63(4), 518–528.

Gunnoe, M.L. and Mariner, C.L. (1997) 'Toward a Developmental-Contextual Model of the Effects of Parental Spanking on Children's Aggression', *Archives of Pediatric Adolescence Medicine*, 151, 768–775.

Hetherington, E.M., Stouwie, R.J. and Ridberg, E.H. (1971) 'Patterns of Family Interaction and Child-rearing Attitudes Related to Three Dimensions of Juvenile Delinquency', *Journal of Abnormal Psychology*, 78(2), 160–176.

Hoffman, M.L. (1994) 'Superego Analysis Report of the Kris Study Group: Response to David Milrod, M.D., *Journal of Clinical Psychoanalysis*, 3(2), 228-230.

Hoffman, M.L. (1960) 'Power Assertion by the Parent and its Impact on the Child', *Child Development*, 34, 129–143.

Huesmann, L.R. (1982) 'Television Violence and Aggressive Behaviour', in D. Pearl, L. Bouthilet and J. Lazar (eds), *Television and Behaviour: Ten Years of Scientific Programs and Implications for the 80's*, Vol. 2, pp. 126–137. Washington, D.C.: US Government Printing Office.

Huesmann, L.R. (1988) 'An Information Processing Model for the Development of Aggression', *Aggressive Behaviour*, 14, 13–24.

Huesmann, L.R. (1998) 'The Role of Social Information Processing and Cognitive Schema in the Acquisition and Maintenance of Habitual Aggressive Behaviour', in R.G. Geen and E. Donnerstein (eds.) *Human Aggression: Theories, Research, and Implications for Policy*, pp. 73–109. New York: Academic Press.

Huesmann, L.R. and Eron, L.D. (eds) (1986) *Television and the Aggressive Child: A Cross-National Comparison.* Hillsdale, NJ: Erlbaum.

Huesmann, L.R. and Eron, L.D. (1991) 'Modeles structurels du development de l'agressivite' [Structural Models for the Development of Aggression], in

R.E. Tremblay (ed.) *Les Comportements Agressifs*, pp. 181–214. Montreal: University of Montreal Press.

Huesmann, L.R., Eron, L.D., Lefkowitz, M.M. and Walder, L.O. (1984) 'The Stability of Aggression Over Time and Generations', *Developmental Psychology*, 20(6), 1120–1134.

Huesmann, L.R. and Miller, L.S. (1994) 'Long-term Effects of Repeated Exposure to Media Violence in Childhood', in L.R. Huesmann (ed.) *Aggressive Behaviour: Current Perspectives*, pp. 153–186. New York: Plenum.

Huesmann, L.R., Moise, J. and Podolski, C.P. (1997) 'The Effects of Media Violence on the Development of Antisocial Behaviour', in D. Stoff, J. Breiling, and J. Masser (eds) *Handbook of Antisocial Behaviour*, pp. 181–193. New York: Wiley.

Kagan, J. (1988) 'Temperamental Contributions to Social Behaviour', *American Psychologist*, 44, 668–674.

Kanfer, F.H. and Hagerman, S.M. (1985) 'Behaviour Therapy and the Information-processing Paradigm', in S. Reiss and R.R. Bootzin (eds) *Theoretical Issues in Behaviour Therapy*, pp. 3–33. New York: Academic Press.

Kazdin, A.E. (1982) 'Symptom Substitution, Generalization, and Response Covariation: Implications for Psychotherapy Outcome', *Psychological Bulletin*, 92, 349–365.

Kazdin, A.E. (1987) 'Treatment of Antisocial Behaviour in Children: Current Status and Future Directions', *Psychological Bulletin*, 102, 187–203.

Kazdin, A.E. (1989) *Behaviour Modification in Applied Settings* (4th edn). Pacific Grove, CA: Brooks/Cole Publishing Co.

Kuczynski, L., Kochanska, G., Radke-Yarrow, M. and Girnius-Brown, O. (1987) 'A Developmental Interpretation of Young Children's Noncompliance', *Developmental Psychology*, 23(6), 799–806.

Lagerspetz, K. and Lagerspetz, K.M.J. (1971) 'Changes in Aggressiveness of Mice Resulting from Selective Breeding, Learning and Social Isolation', *Scandinavian Journal of Psychology*, 12, 241–278.

Lax, R.F. (1992) 'A Variation on Freud's Theme in "A Child is Being Beaten" – Mother's Role: Some Implications for Superego Development in Women', *Journal of the American Psychoanalytic Association*, 40, 455–473.

Lefkowitz, M.M., Walder, L.O. and Eron, L.D. (1963) 'Punishment, Identification and Aggression', *Merrill-Palmer Quarterly*, 9, 1060–1074.

Lefkowitz, M.M., Eron, L.D., Walder, L.O. and Huesmann, L.R. (1977) *Growing Up to be Violent: A Longitudinal Study of the Development of Aggression'*, New York: Pergamon Press.

Luntz, B.K. and Widon, C.S. (1994) 'Antisocial Personality Disorders in Abused and Neglected Children Grown Up', *American Journal of Psychiatry*, 151(5), 670–674.

Madsen, C.H., Becker, W.C., Thomas, D.R., Koser, L. and Plager, E. (1970) 'An Analysis of the Reinforcing Function of "Sit Down" Commands', in R.K. Parker (ed.) *Readings in Educational Psychology*, pp. 265–278. Boston, MA: Allyn & Bacon.

Martin, B. (1975) Parent-Child Relations', in F.D. Horowitz (ed.) *Review of Child Development Research*, Vol. 4, pp. 463–540. Chicago: University of Chicago Press.

Matson, J.L and Kazdin, A.E. (1981) 'Punishment in Behaviour Modification: Pragmatic, Ethical and Legal Issues', *Clinical Psychology Review*, 1(2), 197–210.

McCord, J. (1983) 'A Forty-year Perspective on Effects of Child Abuse and Neglect', *Child Abuse and Neglect*, 7(3), 265–270.

McCord, J. (1988). 'Parental Behaviour in the Cycle of Aggression', *Psychiatry*, 51(1), 14–23.

McCord, J. (1991) 'Questioning the Value of Punishment,' *Social Problems*, 38(2), 167–179.

McCord, J. (ed.) (1995) *Coercion and Punishment in Long Term Perspective.* New York: Cambridge University Press.

McCord, W., McCord, J. and Howard, A. (1961) 'Familial Correlates of Aggression in Nondelinquent Male Children. *Journal of Abnormal and Social Psychology*, 62(1), 79–93.

McCormick, K.F. (1992) 'Attitudes of Primary Care Physicians Toward Corporal Punishment', *Journal of the American Medical Association*, 267(23), 3171–3165.

Mednick, S.A., Gabrielli, W.F. and Hutchings, B. (1984) 'Genetic Influences in Criminal Convictions: Evidence From an Adoption Court', *Science*, 224, 891–894.

Meltzoff, A.N. and Moore, K.M. (1977) 'Imitation of Facial and Manual Gestures by Human Neonates', *Science*, 109, 77–78.

Milrod, D. (1994) 'Superego Analysis Report of the Kris Study Group: Discussion,' *Journal of Clinical Psychoanalysis*, 3(2), 221–227.

Noshpitz, J.D. (1993) 'Superego Pathology in Conduct Disorders', *Israel Journal of Psychiatry and Related Sciences*, 30(1), 3–14.

Noshpitz, J.D. (1994) 'Self-destructiveness in Adolescence', *American Journal of Psychotherapy*, 48(3), 330–346.

Olweus, D. (1979) 'The Stability of Aggressive Reaction Patterns in Males: A review', *Psychological Bulletin*, 86, 852–875.

Olweus, D., Mattsson, A., Schalling, D. and Low, H. (1988) 'Circulating Testosterone Levels and Aggression in Adolescent Males: A Causal Analysis', *Psychosomatic Medicine*, 50, 261–272.

Paik, H. and Comstock, G.A. (1994) 'The Effects of Television Violence on Antisocial Behaviour: A Meta-analysis', *Communication Research*, 21, 516–546.

Parke, R.D. and Slaby, R. (1983) 'The Development of Aggression', in P.H. Mussen (ed.) *Handbook of Child Psychology*, Vol. 4, pp. 547–642. New York: John Wiley & Sons.

Patterson, G.R. (1986) 'Performance Models for Antisocial Boys', *American Psychologist*, 41(4), 432–444.

Patterson, G.R. (1995) 'Coercion – A Basis for Early Age of Onset for Arrest', in J.McCord (ed.) *Coercion and Punishment in Long-term Perspective*, pp. 139–168. New York: Cambridge University Press.

Patterson, G.R., Capaldi, D.M. and Bank, L. (1991) 'An Early Starter Model for Predicting Delinquency', in D.J. Pepler and K.H. Rubin (eds) *Systems and Development: Symposia on Child Psychology*, pp. 139–168. Hillsdale, NJ: Lawrence Erlbaum.

Pulkkinen, L. (1993) 'Continuities in Aggressive Behaviour from Childhood to Adulthood'. *Aggressive Behaviour*, 19(4), 249–263.

Raine, A. and Jones, F. (1987) 'Attention, Autonomic Arousal, and Personality in Behaviourally Disordered Children', *Journal of Abnormal Child Psychology*, 15, 583–599.

Rizzolatti, G., Fadiga, L., Gallese, V. and Fogassi, L. (1996) 'Premotor Cortex and the Recognition of Motor Actions', *Cognitive Brain Research, 3,* 131–141.

Roberts, M.W. and Powers, S.W. (1990) 'Adjusting Chair Timeout Enforcement Procedures for Oppositional Children', *Behaviour Therapy*, 21, 257–271.

Scarboro, M.E. and Forehand, R. (1975) 'Effects of Two Types of Response-contingent Time-out on Compliance and Oppositional Behaviour of Children', *Journal of Experimental and Child Psychology*, 19, 252–264.

Sears, R.R., Maccoby, E.E. and Levin, H. (1957) *Patterns of Child Rearing*. Evanston, IL: Row, Peterson and Company.

Simons, R.L., Johnson, C. and Conger, R.D. (1994) 'Harsh Corporal Punishment versus Quality of Parental Involvement as an Explanation of Adolescent Maladjustment', *Journal of Marriage and the Family*, 56, 591–607.

Solheim, J.S. (1982) 'A Cross-cultural Examination of use of Corporal Punishment on Children: A Focus on Sweden and the United States', *Child Abuse and Neglect*, 6(2), 147–154.

Staub, E. (1996) 'Cultural-societal Roots of Violence: The Examples of Genocidal Violence and of Contemporary Youth Violence in the United States', *American Psychologist*, 51(2), 117–132.

Strassberg, Z., Dodge, K.A., Pettit, G.S. and Bates, J.E. (1994) 'Spanking in the Home and Children's Subsequent Aggression Toward Kindergarten Peers. *Development and Psychopathology*, 6(3), 445–461.

Straus, M.A. and Kanton, G.K. (1994) 'Corporal Punishment of Adolescents by Parents: A Risk Factor in the Epidemiology of Depression, Suicide, Alcohol Abuse, Child Abuse, and Wife Beating', *Adolescence*, 29, 543–561.

Sugarman, D.B., Straus, M.A. and Giles-Sims, J. (1994) 'Corporal Punishment by Parents and Subsequent Anti-social Behaviour of Children'. Presented at conference on Research on Discipline: The State of the Art, Deficits, and Implications. University of North Carolina Medical School.

Thorndike, E.L. (1911) *Animal Intelligence: Experimental Studies.* New York: Macmillan.

Trumbull, D.A. (1995) 'Disciplinary Spanking by Parents', AAP District IV Meeting, November.

Weiss, B., Dodge, K.A., Bates, J.E. and Pettit, G.S. (1992) 'Some Consequences of Early Harsh Discipline: Child Aggression and a Maladaptive Social Information Processing Style', *Child Development*, 63(6), 1321–1335.

Westen, D. (1986) 'The Superego: A Revised Developmental Model', *Journal of American Academy of Psychoanalysis*, 14(2), 181–202.

Wicklund, R.A. (1970) 'Prechoice Preference Reversal as a Result of Threat to Decision Freedom', *Journal of Personality and Social Psychology*, 14(1), 8–17.

Widom, C.S. (1989) 'Does Violence Beget Violence? A Critical Examination of the Literature. *Psychological Bulletin*, 106(1), 3–28.

Chapter 3

Lost youth and the futility of deterrence

Mark Fleisher

America has a gang problem. The 2000 National Youth Gang Survey collected gang-related police data in a sample of rural, suburban and urban communities across the United States. An analysis of these data estimates that there are some 24,500 gangs and 772,500 gang members in 3,300 police jurisdictions. This chapter sets out the findings of an ethnographic study of the Fremont Hustlers, a violent youth gang in Kansas City, Missouri. This research shows the Fremont Hustlers to be similar in group structure and dynamics to youth drug gangs in cities, such as St Louis (Missouri), Seattle (Washington), Milwaukee (Wisconsin) and Columbus (Ohio). It also shows that the personal lives of the adolescent males and females who comprise the Fremont Hustlers are similar to teenagers in youth gangs in other cities.

The research results should be helpful to gang intervention and prevention initiatives. I discuss the following topics: a summary of daily life among the Fremont Hustlers; an examination of Fremont kids as victims of family violence; a synopsis of their of early family life; a discussion of punishment as a balance of 'costs' versus 'benefits'; a critical review of deterrence-based crime policy; an abstract of Fremont kids' opinions on punishment; and a number of proposals for non-punishment-based youth gang intervention.

The Fremont Hustlers call themselves simply 'Fremont'. This youth gang is comprised of adolescents who are black, white and Mexican, males and females. I refer to them intentionally with the words 'kids', 'boys', and 'girls'. In 1994 when I met Wendy and Janet, two of Fremont's founding members, they were 17 and among Fremont's elders. Age notwithstanding, the Kansas City police consider the Fremont Hustlers to be one of the city's most active gangs. These kids are involved in drug trafficking and a number of them have been arrested for or convicted of shootings, robberies and assaults, and murder. One adolescent was twice on Kansas City's Most Wanted list, each time linked to a killing. But when legislators intend to modify the behaviour of kids like the Fremont Hustlers with punishment-based interventions, it is important to remember that the 'targets' of such state and federal punishment are children.

Fremont Hustlers research was conducted for three reasons. First, more than 70 years of youth gang literature includes few long-term ethnographic, or first-hand, studies of youth gangs, and even less systematic research focusing on female gang members within a dual-sex youth gang, such as the Fremont Hustlers. This research captures in detail daily life inside a mixed racial, dual-sex youth gang over a period of nearly two years. Second, Fremont Hustlers research emphasised the social processes of gang members' family lives and how these family processes influenced young gang members' life courses. Ethnographic data include: interviews with Fremont members and their parents; participation in daily Fremont gang life, including interactions between Fremont and other Kansas City youth gangs and non-gang-affiliated adolescents and adults; and observations of interactions between Fremont kids and police and probation officers. Third, an extended first-hand study of a mixed racial, dual-sex youth gang could make significant contributions to the national debate on how best to prevent the formation of youth gangs, to intervene in the lives of gang-affiliated adolescents, or to suppress further crime related to youth gang activity by imprisoning young offenders.

An inside look at a youth gang

Fremont Avenue, a narrow north–south road in an out-of-the-way, low-income, high-crime neighbourhood, is the home territory of the Fremont Hustlers. The Fremont neighbourhood is located in East Blue Valley on Kansas City's northeast side. Census data gathered in 1990 is revealing and instructive. In this area, 85 per cent of the 2,387 residents were white, 9 per cent black. The average annual income in East Blue Valley was $9,238: 18.8 per cent earn less than $9,999 per year; 26.6 per cent between $10,000 and $19,999; and 11.2 per cent over $40,000. East Blue Valley has 617 dwellings: 74.7 per cent are valued at less than $29,999; 1.6 per cent are valued over $60,000. There are 1,531 residents over age 15: 42.8 per cent have less than a high-school diploma. In the late 1960s, East Blue

Valley's major employers, a steel mill and a commercial warehouse, closed. Census data show that 68.7 per cent of East Blue Valley residents moved into this area after 1970.

Fremont members say they 'own' the intersection of Fremont and 13th Street and the 10 to 20 blocks around it. Ownership means they have the right to sell drugs in that area and that they will defend that right with violence. Fremont members spray-painted the letters FH and dollar signs ($) on the sides of houses and on local businesses. Green is Fremont's colour: it represents money and marijuana, one of the gang's chief commodities. Fremont teenagers grew up on or near Fremont Avenue, and have known one another since they were pre-teenagers. Many members are siblings, step-siblings and cousins.

There were some 70 Fremont members in June 1995; among them, 20 girls aged 14 to 17 hung out regularly on Fremont and were gang members. Like other youth gangs, Fremont membership is fluid, which means that the membership list is not hard-and-fast. Fremont has a 'hardcore' group comprised of some 25 to 30 boys and girls who devote themselves to gang activities. These 15-, 16-, and 17-year-olds are chronic truants with multi-year criminal histories. Most of them ran the streets unsupervised and committed their first crimes before the age of 12.

This youth gang, unlike some reported in the gang literature, does not have an initiation ritual, which purportedly tests a prospective member's mettle. This means that prospective members are never ordered to shoot a stranger, or to shoot at or fight a member of a competing gang, or asked to defend themselves in a fight against Fremont members. Gang research reports that in some dual-sex youth gangs boys require prospective female members to have sexual intercourse with all of the gang's males, or at least those who wish to participate. A Fremont girl said that she and other girls would not stand for that 'nonsense'. Girls said they would kill any boy who tried to rape them or they would simply walk away and join another gang. In any case, Fremont's male and female members agree that violence attracts the police to the neighbourhood, and with the police parked at Fremont and 13th Street, drug sales would suffer and they would likely to go jail.

Fremont is egalitarian. Members do not differentiate themselves by a group-defined status system. There is no talk of differential status or prestige assigned by gender to Fremont members. Wendy calls herself a 'straight G', or a gang member willing to do whatever boys do, and they know it. Boys do not try to exclude girls from any activities, including incidents of physical violence or the use of firearms. If girls wish to join in, they do; if they do not, they were not chided or criticised by boys or girls who chose to participate. In Fremont's most profitable activity, drug selling, I anticipated chinks in the gang's egalitarian nature as more aggressive boys pushed less aggressive girls aside and took their drug customers. This did not happen. Drug selling was a co-operative activity. In fact, Wendy was one of Fremont's main drug sellers.

Fremont Hustlers have no formal political statuses, no positions carrying a name, such as 'shot-caller', 'secretary', or 'sergeant-at-arms'. There is no appointed or self-proclaimed gang leader; no one has power over members by virtue of holding a particular status in the gang social system. A member's ability to coerce or leverage assistance or property from other members is a matter of interpersonal skill. Fremont kids, especially hardcore members, are aggressive, irascible, and shun adolescent or adult authority figures and, when necessary, have fought to retain their freedom from authoritarian control. These kids do not tolerate anyone telling them what to do nor would they allow anyone to garner their cash as a so-called tribute, or payment, to self-proclaimed gang leaders. Rather than differentiating themselves within the group by leadership, they distinguished themselves by their preferences for criminal activities, drug sellers versus car-jackers, and by excellence at crime ventures, such as drug selling.

Fremont members aver racial equality. They openly discuss the group's racial admixture and overlook differences in skin colour. Race and ethnicity do not interfere with the gang's social and economic activity. Kids hang out with or set up drug-selling partnerships with whomever they wish, independent of race, ethnicity and gender. Dating relationships are not controlled by race or ethnicity, either. In fact, in the summer of 1995, there were only two same-race relationships, and in one of these cases, the young lovers were step-siblings.

While the Fremont Hustlers do not have a formal system of statuses, they do differentiate themselves into informal categories defined by the amount of time a kid spends at Fremont and 13th Street and by denoting who is 'tight' with whom. Kids who are tight hang out together, share drugs for use or sale, and in the cases of the tightest kids, once shared membership in another Kansas City youth gang prior to joining. Fremont. Kids use the following expressions to denote degrees of participation; the numbers in parentheses indicate the number of days spent on Fremont to be considered in one category or another: 'here all the time' (six to seven), 'here a lot' (three to five), 'comes around' (one to two) and 'will be here if we need [him/her]' (several times a month). The first category is the 'everyday', or regular, group. These are kids 'who's in the shit everyday', said Cara, one of Fremont's hardcore members. These labels are merely descriptive; kids who participate more than others are not granted special status or privileges.

Fremont kids recognise gang-related and personal crime. A gang-related crime is facilitated by the gang. Fremont operates a drug house on Fremont Avenue, which Wendy initiated in 1994. She was responsible for ensuring its constant supply of drugs, until the police closed it in the autumn of 1996. In its heyday, individuals or partnerships of two or three kids bought drugs at discount from Wendy and then resold those drugs at a profit to their own network of customers. Some portion of the profit earned in this network of Fremont drug sellers was voluntarily re-invested to purchase larger quantities of drugs.

The Fremont drug house had a stream of customers, especially on weekends and at night. But drug customers attracted the attention of competing gangs who wanted to sell to Fremont's customers. Competition did on occasion lead to violence, such as a drive-by shooting, committed by a competing gang trying to discourage Fremont's customers. Kids call this type of violence 'cutting off [someone's] money'. Fremont protected the drug house and retaliated. Such behaviour is gang-related violence, because it is an outcome of the social group's self-interest in economic activity. By contrast, Fremont had several subgroups who specialised in non-drug crime. One group burgled residences, another car-jacked. Although these kids were Fremont Hustlers their crimes were committed outside the Fremont neighbourhood, were not facilitated by the gang itself, and the proceeds of those crimes were not shared by other Fremont Hustlers or voluntarily invested in any communal Fremont activities.

Common threads informally bond these kids, at least temporarily. They were reared in poor families on or near Fremont or in other neighbourhoods on Kansas City's northeast side; over many years they have shared companions and lovers; and they have had similarly bad experiences with schools and law enforcement. More immediately important to Fremont kids is a common need to survive, and every Fremont kid knows that he or she cannot survive alone on the street.

Life on the street is tough, and these kids have experienced violence and loneliness. Fremont teenagers must provide for themselves the basics of daily life. No one prepares meals for them, no one buys them clothing, provides them shelter or gives them an allowance. They must co-operate with one another and, to their credit, have worked out a survival mechanism that has not allowed divisive factors, such as race and gender, to interfere with social and economic survival activities. A youth gang lifestyle is not ideal, but it is the only lifestyle available to the Fremont Hustlers.

Children: victims of family violence

Fremont research findings on issues such as gang initiation, political dynamics, crime-related economics and causes of inter-gang violence are corroborated by ethnographic and survey research on youth gangs in many American cities. However, Fremont research was more than a gang study. This ethnography explored the relationships Fremont kids had with their parents, and then watched as Fremont kids became parents. While parenting style has not been a pre-eminent topic in gang research, decades of criminological research have linked the quality of a child's early family life to the emergence of deviant behaviour in adolescence and adulthood.

Research has shown that juvenile offenders whose deviant behaviour began by early adolescence, 10 to 12 years old, are likely to remain involved in criminal activity into adulthood. Such an early onset to crime has been linked to family life abuse and neglect. Abuse means, among other things, beatings and verbal haranguing; neglect means a prolonged lack of attention to children's physical, medical and educational well-being. Gang research has shown that as delinquency proceeds to gang involvement, and then to gang membership, some delinquents may increase the frequency and/or the severity of illegal activities. Once they leave the gang, most commit many fewer and less serious crimes. Fremont research confirms these findings.

Generally speaking, interviews with Fremont adolescents reveal common themes in their pre-adolescent family lives and in their adolescent lives as delinquents and gang members. Those who are teenage parents also share similar patterns of parenting behaviour.

Many Fremont kids' parents, often the hardcore members' mothers and fathers, were violent and substance abusers (marijuana, heroin, cocaine). Wendy said her best marijuana and rock cocaine customers were the parents of her gang companions. Many kids' fathers were criminals, often active or convicted drug dealers; some were convicted killers and armed robbers serving long prison terms. Kids' mothers, aunts and grandmothers were also directly involved in the criminal activities of their husbands and brothers, or of their sons and daughters, nephews and nieces – the Fremont Hustlers. Sometimes these women were passive observers, but they were always active consumers of the money and goods that were the proceeds of crime. Fremont kids' parents assaulted each other and whipped with belts and punched and slapped their children, too.

When they reached late pre-adolescence or early adolescence, Fremont kids fled the violence at home and went to the street searching for peace and companionship. At first they stayed away for a few days or a week at a time, but as they adjusted to street life and became part of its action, these stints grew longer until they rarely, if ever, returned home. They hung out on Kansas City streets in loosely knit social groups and committed crimes, such as robbery, burglary and car theft. Such a group is a youth gang. Kids who founded the Fremont Hustlers pronounced themselves to be an 'official' youth gang in the summer of 1992, and then began using gang symbols. Prior to that, Fremont kids hung out with one another on Fremont or in other northeast Kansas City neighbour-hoods; many were also in other neighbourhood gangs.

While gang membership affords a modicum of safety and protection, it exposes youngsters to drugs and violence and severs social relationships with school peers and teachers and other community members who might be able to help them. By junior high school, nearly all Fremont kids were chronic truants and indulged freely in marijuana, alcohol and 'dank', a concoction of formaldehyde or liquid PCP diluted with brake fluid, nail polish or other solvents. A cigarette dipped into dank is called a 'dank stick'. Depending on the length of the cigarette dipped into dank, a dank stick sells for five, ten, or twenty dollars.

Fremont Hustlers as young as nine practised street trades, including burglary, car theft, drug selling, car-jacking and assault and robbery. More than a dozen earned income exclusively by selling marijuana, rock cocaine and dank. Others sold drugs part-time and also did burglaries and sold stolen property, including rifles, shotguns and handguns. Whenever a kid needed a few dollars, drug selling was a quick, easy and reliable income source.

Fremont kids do not work too hard at crime. It takes little effort to earn enough cash to support a meagre youth gang lifestyle. Fremont kids are not the flashy drug sellers seen in movies. They earn enough money to buy fast-food, or a few CDs or a new shirt now and then, but little else. A few drug entrepreneurs earned more cash than others. They bought older used cars and rented apartments; some bought gold jewellery, stereos and televisions. This property was owned temporarily, however, and served as a 'street' bank account.

Drug sellers were eventually arrested and jailed for selling drugs or some other crime. When that happened, an imprisoned drug seller relied on his or her tightest companions to sell or pawn the accumulated property to get cash for a bail bond. Sometimes that happened; usually it did not. As often occurs on the street, once a kid is out of sight, even his or her tightest companions look out for themselves first. It was not uncommon to find an imprisoned kid's apartment door kicked in and his or her property stolen by Fremont companions or acquaintances from other neighbourhoods. In these cases, there is no retaliation against his or her companions, once the kid gets back to the street. Such behaviour would alienate him or her from the companions he or she needs to survive. Kids say that if drug money bought goods once, it will again. 'Easy come, easy go' is the ethic.

Fremont kids became parents. When they did, they behaved toward their children as their parents did towards them. It was customary for 16- and 17-year-old mothers to neglect their children's emotional and medical needs and ignore their children's need for physical safety. Gang boys hit, slapped and beat pre-school age children as punishment for trivial acts, such as spilling soda onto a filthy threadbare carpet in a gang-operated drug house. Young mothers did not demonstrate by example that alcohol and drugs are dangerous nor did young parents encourage education: no one bought school-age children school supplies; no one encouraged children to read and write; no one read to children.

Pregnancy and parenthood always worsen the already bleak life of a Fremont girl. A newly pregnant teenager talked brightly about a future with her boyfriend. However, the reality of pregnancy and parenthood drove off a teenage father-to-be, who showed equal disregard for his future child and his lover by abandoning both long before childbirth. A young father-to-be almost always found another girl and the pattern of attachment–sex–pregnancy–abandonment recurred. In such cases, a boy's newest girlfriend always knew of her boyfriend's former girlfriends and his children, and always the new lover swore to her companions that he would be different with her.

Young parents-to-be were not married, nor were child support or visiting rights legally arranged. These kids avoid voluntary contacts with the court. They do not have the resources to hire a lawyer nor do they even discuss such an option. When a child is born, a teenage father neglects financial responsibilities to his child and to his child's mother, having left her months earlier to fend for herself and find social support and money. To do that, she first seeks support from her fellow gang girls. If that proves fruitless, she turns to her mother, aunts or grandmother. A maternal kin tie does not entitle a teenage mother to social or financial assistance from relatives. These families are the working poor and, even with good intentions, a limited income must be used first on the immediate costs of daily life, including rent, food, car insurance and repairs, and utility and medical bills. There is never extra income. Pregnancy and motherhood strain low incomes, and poverty worsens weak emotional and social attachments between a pregnant teenager or youth mother and her kinswomen. An estranged mother–daughter relationship is not patched by pregnancy or motherhood.

In the eyes of adult women, pregnant teenagers and teenage motherhood do not require their assistance. Privately, adult women criticise a girl for getting herself into trouble, and announce that a girl who is old enough to have sex should be able to care for herself. Despite such rhetoric, the aid that older women may give a pregnant girl or teenage mother is limited less by estrangement than poverty. Adult women most often live without gainfully employed husbands or boyfriends; women share overcrowded small houses or apartments with other women, some of whom have children; always these household units subsist on persistently low incomes.

To new teenage mothers, the novelty of motherhood is soon lost and replaced by a need to party. It was common to find that a 16- or 17-year-old mother begins the slow process of abandoning her child within a month or two of the child's birth as she lets whomever is nearby worry about feeding and caring for the baby. Motherhood, said new mothers, is boring. These young mothers are teenage girls, too, and they want to hang out and resume the gang lifestyle. And most did just that. Generally speaking, at this point the formerly reluctant-to-help mother of a teenage mother sometimes relents and cares for her grandchild, sharing child-rearing responsibilities with her sisters and mother, the baby's aunts and grandmother. When a teenage mother's maternal relatives did not relent, a responsible neighbour would care for the baby full-time. On Fremont Avenue, there was a woman who cared for her own children as well as the abandoned children of Fremont's mothers. In fact, the Fremont kids call her a 'Fremont mom', because she cared for many of them when they were early teenagers and had run away from their parents' homes.

The social and financial pressure of pregnancy and parenthood frequently leads to violence. A young father-to-be or father quickly grew tired of hearing via mutual companions that his former girlfriend was 'badmouthing' him about being a 'bad' father. Fremont research shows that Fremont boys' most common act of violence was committed against former or current lovers, or both.

Fremont kids recall family life

Criminologists have long argued that social and economic settings influence where crime occurs and who commits it. Fremont gang members did not emerge from every household in East Blue Valley. Directly across the street from the Fremont drug house resided two Latino families. The children in those households and the Fremont

Hustlers have no interaction with one another. Why did delinquents emerge from some households but not others? Fremont household ethnography suggests a partial answer to this question.

The majority of Fremont's members have not been involved in serious crime. Most sold drugs but not in quantities sufficient to attract police attention, nor were they involved in serious incidents of violence, such as drive-by shootings. In fact, most Fremont kids shy away from face-to-face physical confrontations. But the hardcore group was different. These kids were the most active drug sellers and the most violent adolescents. Their families, compared with those of the other kids, were characterised by extreme disorganisation and conflict, including child abuse and neglect and spouse abuse, exacerbated by parents' drug use and criminal behaviour. The hardcore group included siblings (Angie and her brother; Cheri and her sister and brother), cousins (Cheri and her siblings are cousins to Afro, one of Fremont's most violent boys, and his siblings), step- and half-siblings (Cara and her three sisters have three fathers).

In their early lives, Fremont's hardcore kids were victims of parental abuse and neglect. To these youngsters, family life was so painful that a gang lifestyle and subsequent periods of juvenile detention and prison were a relief. 'My mom was 19 when I was born, and my dad was 15,' said Cara, a 17-year-old who has been pregnant three times. She was shot with an AK-47 in a gang shooting in the summer of 1994. 'Dad went to prison for murder after I was born. Dad was bad off into drugs. He was deranged too.' Cara's mother divorced her father when Cara was two and married a man who reared Cara from age three to nine. 'He was a real bad alcoholic. He used to beat us real bad. He put knives at mom's throat, threw things at us kids [Cara has one younger and two older siblings], hit us in the face. Mom put locks all around my bedroom door but he kicked down the door. He was always drunk, all the time. He was just mean.' At the age of ten, Cara began a series of placements in residential treatment programmes, hospitals and juvenile detention facilities. She was told that she had 'an anger problem and a chemical imbalance'. Between the ages of 10 and 17, she was hospitalised or imprisoned seven times. The longest time was for nearly a year in a state hospital at age 13. During her last hospital commitment, Cara met Wendy.

Wendy's natural father and mother were married in a county jail, just before her father was transferred to a state penitentiary to serve a sentence for murder. He was a violent alcoholic, she said, and so was her step-father, who married her mother when Wendy was nine. At age eight, Wendy smoked her first joint. By age 12, she drank and smoked 'bud' (marijuana) every day, gambled, enjoyed an occasional street fight, and stole cars. Then, after a car theft, Wendy was recommended by a juvenile court to serve a 30-day psychiatric evaluation. But she rebelled, and 30 days turned into four years. 'I hated the matrons,' she said with a scowl across her face. 'I fought them, jumped 'em, beat 'em whenever I could, and I ran away. But they kept bringing me back.' Wendy adjusted slowly and learned to live with counselling, planned recreation, good food and a clean bed.

Fremont kids have spent most of their teenage years living in juvenile treatment and detention facilities. Rosa, Taz, Wayne, TJ, Angie and her brother Roger, Christina and Harold, among others, were inmates in the same residential adolescent treatment facility. They all escaped at different times, according to Angie, who was locked up almost continuously from the age of 12 until she was 17. Angie's father was an armed robber who went to prison for seven years when she was five. Memories of family life before her teenage years are fuzzy, but she recalls clearly her first arrest for car theft and possession of a weapon at age 12. 'From then on out, I never went to school, I never went home.' Her mother divorced her father after he was imprisoned and, according to Angie, had a series of boyfriends. The man she remembers best is the one who beat her mother and put a knife to her throat and threatened to kill her. 'He was always mean. He kicked our dog's teeth out. He was a hateful person.'

At about the time Angie's mother was suffering at the hands of her boyfriend, Angie's father was released from prison and was committed to an 'honor center' (a minimum-security half-way house). He escaped, returned to his former wife's house, found her boyfriend, and stabbed him. He was returned to prison.

'When I was twelve, I used coke [cocaine] but I didn't make a habit of it. I almost ODed [overdosed]. But I started smoking weed and drinking and getting high every day.' And at about the same time, her brother Roger, who is a year younger than Angie, 'started getting in trouble robbing houses'. His first arrest was for the possession of a gun. 'I was in and out of group homes for four years, finally they committed me to state, DYS [Department of Youth Services] custody. I just got released from that May 17, 1994.' Between the ages of 12 and 17, Angie said she was arrested at least 50 times and was confined for periods of weeks up to months. 'I spent every holiday in custody.'

Like Cara, Wendy and Angie, Cheri's father is a penitentiary inmate. He has been serving a sentence for murder in Angola Penitentiary since Cheri was an infant. She says she gets a letter from him every day. But she doesn't. 'It's not his fault that he's locked up. He did what he had to.'

So does Cheri. Her outbursts of anger scare even her Fremont companions. 'When she gets pissed and heads for the kitchen to get a knife,' says Wendy, 'we all leave.' Cheri has thought about her anger and says that she has two personalities: Cheri and Penelope. Cheri said:

> Cheri loves to have fun, talk about people's problems, help people with their problems, she like to do [things] for people. Know what I'm sayin'. When I get older I want to help kids, tell them what I been through in my childhood that I don't want them to go through, and I also want to be a doctor. Penelope comes when I'm real stressed out. She will never hurt my mother, but she does not like my sister at all. She hates my sister. She'll throw something at her like a knife or something. She loves my brother, though. She's cool with him. She won't never do nothing to him. You'll know when Penelope's comin'. I'll sit there. My eyes'll get real big, and I'll black out for a minute, and when I look up, I'm not Cheri. I have more control over Penelope [now] than when I was little. When I was little, she had control over me.

Now 15, Cheri has been pregnant several times, has not attended school in a year, was stabbed three times in fights at school, and smokes weed every day and dank sticks whenever she can get them. Her 19-year-old brother is also a member of Fremont and serving time in a Missouri state prison for a probation violation (drug offence). Cheri's sister, age 17, also a member of Fremont, has a two-year-old son who hangs out on Fremont and is exposed to violence, guns and drug use. 'If it weren't for my homeys', said Cheri, 'I'd have nothing. At Fremont, I can do whatever I want.'

Punishment: a balance of 'cost' versus 'benefits'

Fremont research suggests that current juvenile justice practices, such as imprisonment and probation, do not meet the social, economic and emotional problems of youth-gang members; they possess neither sufficient resources nor are they suitably proactive. The juvenile justice system reacts to offenders with a series of incrementally more severe punishments. Generally speaking, the US criminal justice system operates on the behaviour-modification strategy known as deterrence. This assumes that offenders' illegal behaviour may be modified towards lawful behaviour by increasing the 'cost' of rule-breaking behaviour, while simultaneously decreasing its 'benefits'. The latter may include the thrill of participating in high-risk, high-income street occupations, such as selling illegal drugs. Cost refers to one or another type of punishment, including community custody (probation), institutional custody (prison), financial penalties, or a combination of these costs. In principle at least, as the cost of crime increases, the benefits decrease.

Within the context of the criminal justice system, a deterrence strategy assumes that offenders are rational thinkers who calculate the costs and benefits of their behaviour. As such, a person faced with the choice between criminal and lawful behaviour would choose lawful behaviour, with its high benefits and relatively low costs, over an illegal lifestyle, with its high costs and relatively low benefits. The criminal justice system tries to be fair in meting out the level of cost by adjusting it to such things as the frequency and severity of crime and the age and gender of the offender. A first-time 13-year-old offender arrested selling marijuana would be treated more leniently than a 17-year-old repeat offender who committed the same offence.

At first glance, deterrence seems to be a rational approach as it delivers punishment in measured amounts, as parents might to children who continuously break or bend family rules. However, Fremont research shows that the deterrence model, at least in this case, is too simplistic or even unrealistic if the concepts of cost and benefit are interpreted within the actual context of Fremont members' early lives and a gang lifestyle. Two problematic issues emerge when trying to predict the influence that a deterrence strategy might have on Fremont kids' behaviour. First, there is the assumption that young offenders share with the mainstream community the notion of what is and is not punishment. In fact, Cara's response, and her family's, to her being jailed repeatedly is similar to the response of other Fremont members and their families who have experienced imprisonment.

Fremont teenagers are simply apathetic about being jailed. This is not to say they are thrilled with it, but they say it 'comes with the territory'. Fremont kids' parents feel a sense of relief, not devastation or loss, when their kids are jailed. These parents say the children are physically safer inside a correctional or treatment centre than they are hanging out on the street and that inside, their kids 'get help'. Off the record, parents say that their households are quieter and more stable than when their sons and daughters and their kids' gang companions hang around.

The local jail and juvenile detention centre are only a few miles from the homes of Fremont kids and still, during 21 months of Fremont research, no parent ever visited a jailed child. Fremont kids do not feel that imprisonment pulls them away from friends and constructive school activities. Fremont's most active members had not attended school for many years. Cara stopped attending school at age 14 and Angie had not attended school regularly after age ten. When a Fremont kid is detained, he or she reunites inside with other Fremont kids or companions from other neighbourhoods. In the end, the cost of criminal behaviour is low and the benefits of a gang lifestyle are relatively high, even if that lifestyle leads to imprisonment.

Imprisonment has influenced the life course of Cara and other Fremont members. Fremont's most criminally active members have been arrested, sentenced to juvenile treatment centres and then placed on years of probation; in some cases, Fremont's most violent young offenders were sentenced to prison. One of them began a term in an adult state prison at age 15. In this case, a prison sentence was supposed to punish a young offender as well as offer him opportunities to gain an education, vocational training and drug treatment or psychological counselling. Generally speaking, Fremont ethnography shows that imprisonment has the opposite effect: it pushes adolescents farther from mainstream life, isolates them with other young offenders, and stigmatises them as the community's criminal gang members.

Fremont research shows that imprisonment gets kids off the street; however, imprisonment has long-term negative effects on the life course of gang members which, in turn, adds to a community's long-term crime-control burden. Fremont, as well as other research, has shown that the stigma of imprisonment lasts longer than gang affiliation and a prison term. The stigma alone blocks post-imprisonment job opportunities and prevents young, once-imprisoned gang members from renting apartments outside of high-crime neighbourhoods.

The transition from adolescence to adulthood is difficult at best, even for well-educated young adults without criminal histories. Fremont research shows that juvenile and adult imprisonment worsens gang members' opportunities to enter the mainstream community and has pushed them farther away from legitimate employment. This problem is worse for a teenage or young adult mother who receives no economic support from her relatives or her baby's father. Such an economic dilemma forces even well-intentioned young adults back to profitable criminal street trades.

From the perspective of young adult gang members, life has a tragic irony: the most direct means of getting social and education services or job training is to go to prison, but the stigma of a criminal history prevents good employment. Fremont research shows that stopping gang participation and street crime is as difficult as preventing it. By the time adolescents are fully enmeshed in gang life, they are alienated from the community. Even if they want to leave gang life behind, they have no social bridge leading them to positive relationships with school teachers, family members and non-gang-affiliated or non-delinquent adolescents.

Gang members like Cara are socially and economically stuck: if she walks away from Fremont, she has nowhere to go. Such a conflict points out the core weakness of the deterrence strategy and points to the double-bind it causes: law-breaking gang members are punished, but then, when they try to go 'straight,' they are stigmatised, alienated and helpless. Teenagers cannot resolve such problems on their own and communities fail to assist them.

Failure of deterrence-based crime policy

Fremont research does not support the notion that the imprisonment of juvenile offenders is a punishment that has a deterrent and a rehabilitative effect. Life inside a juvenile institution, the Kansas City jail or an adult prison is more predictable and safer than a gang lifestyle. When Fremont kids were locked up in the county jail, they complained about not hanging out on the street with companions and not being allowed to smoke cigarettes or marijuana, but they were physically safer, lived a more stable lifestyle and had access to programmes such as Alcoholics Anonymous, Narcotics Anonymous and basic education programmes.

No Fremont member reported being seriously injured in a fight inside the Kansas City jail or juvenile detention centre, nor did Fremont members report incidents in which Fremont members they knew were seriously injured inside a local jail or a state prison. On the street, they were continuously at risk. Many Fremont girls were victims of their boyfriends' violence. Some Fremont boys and girls were injured critically, some fatally, in gang-related violent incidents, such as drug-related inter-gang shootings. Some instances of inter-gang violence were motivated by boys' jealousy over the attention of a girl who once dated a Fremont boy and then gave him up to date a boy in another gang. In a few cases, a Fremont boy accidently killed another one while handling a handgun.

While juvenile detention has advantages, it strains youths' tenuous links to school and tosses them in the mix with kids who are not gang members. Meeting one another in detention forges social ties which serve gang and non-gang members well inside and may also lead to connections on the street. Wendy and Cara met inside an institution and their relationship has been sustained into young adulthood. Except for those kids who face serious felony charges, Fremont kids are released, often on probation.

Probation fails to alter Fremont kids' lives in positive ways. Despite probation requirements intended to promote personal responsibility, Fremont kids miss court dates, ignore community service requirements and curfews, and leave fines and court costs unpaid. Kids on home confinement use and sell drugs, hang out inside their residences with gang companions, and stay in touch with one another with pagers and telephones. Wendy was convicted of selling marijuana and assigned to a year-long probation programme designed to supervise adolescents who are 'one short step' from prison. During her probation she did not satisfy a single requirement, failing to do even one of her 100 required hours of community service, and yet no one intervened. If juvenile probation's goal, in the case of Fremont kids, was the readjustment of their life course, it failed.

Generally speaking, correctional institutions intend to redirect the social and economic paths of inmates, moving them from crime to mainstream life. For my informants this has not happened. What did happen, however, was that former inmates in their late teens and older had job skills and earning power equivalent to those of adolescents who earn minimum wages while attending high school or college. In other words, social adolescence is matched by a period of economic adolescence. But college students graduate and have the skills to move into economic adulthood. Former inmates like my informants, armed with a high-school equivalency diploma and basic vocational skills, rarely emerge from economic adolescence. They are socially and economically alienated. Even citizens without a criminal record cannot support themselves, let alone a family, on minimum wages.

Realistically, former inmates with good intentions but with little else to offer the job market are predisposed to economic failure. That failure is reinforced by a highly competitive and increasingly specialised job market. With many high school, junior college and college graduates competing for entry-level jobs, 'ex-cons' pose a risk that employers would rather avoid. Now former inmates are either unemployed or join the ranks of the working poor. And there is nothing a former inmate can do about the socio-economic nature of American life and the demanding prerequisites for good jobs. At this point many informants said life in prison seemed tolerable, if not preferable to unemployment and temporary residence in missions, shelters or rundown houses like the Fremont drug house.

Fremont youngsters know they are inadequately educated, do not fit into the scheme of economic life in free society, and are ostracised from the mainstream community. These facts (poor education, economic alienation, social marginalisation) are to some extent effects of imprisonment. If these facts about my informants also characterise the hundreds of thousands, if not millions of offenders in America, then it is fair to say that the overuse of prisons has created more social and economic problems than it has resolved.

Fremont kids' talk about punishment

Fremont kids have definite opinions on the value and fairness of punishments, such as imprisonment and probation, and the consequences of these measures on their lives. Cara says:

> Punishment is a reaction to an action. It's a consequence you receive when you do something you know is not right. If you don't know it's not right you shouldn't be punished. Everything starts in the home and no one realizes that. That's where it starts at. When I think of punishment, it's hitting. I used to get my ass beat, and when I asked my mamma why she smacked me across my face she's say 'cause I'm your mamma'. That ain't good enough. You can't punish someone for something you do. I see women beat the shit out of their kids for touching shit and those kids will never know why. Then they grow up and smack somebody, hit they own kids, and they get punished. It ain't right.

Carmen, 15, reported a life-long pattern of ingesting lithium to control seizures and anger. 'I been in and out of jail since I was twelve for assault with a deadly weapon, fighting, stealing cars, and running away.' In September 1995, she was released from a juvenile hall in St Louis, Missouri, after 18 months of a sentence of one to six years.

> I liked it in there and didn't want to go home. I set fires, set off fire extinguishers, started fights with group members, hit staff, took their keys. I told them I'd get in trouble if they let me go, but they threw me out. I didn't want to go back to my mother. She used to punch me in the head, throw [water] glasses at me, and choke me.

Carmen returned to her mother's house for two weeks and was kicked out and came to Kansas City. She said she can't trust anybody on the street, not even her sisters. Carmen met and is staying with Cara. 'She is my mother for now.' I asked if she'll return to her mother's house. 'I'd rather go to jail than go back to her.'

Fremont youngsters are not angry about getting arrested and sentenced to juvenile hall and expelled from school. Carmen expressed what angers them:

I don't see why I have to get punished for some stupid stunt my mother does. 'She threw me out of the house, then calls the police to report I'm a runaway. I get arrested. That just ain't fair. If I'm going to get punished the parents should get punished too. It ain't all the kid's fault. Look at my mamma. Half her kids do drugs, half gangbang. Why would all her kids just walk off and do all that stuff. It has to be something wrong at home, but, nope, nobody even looks at that. They just look at the kids all the time. If parents ain't getting punished, I ain't getting punished.

Intervention without punishment

To be sure, violent street crime and the distribution of illegal drugs are community safety issues of utmost importance. But looking beyond crime, Fremont ethnography offers insights into three intervention dilemmas. The single most important one for interventionists is teenage pregnancy and child care for the children of gang-affiliated teenage parents. Adolescents who are the most active in crime and sexually most active are Fremont's hardcore group, the same kids who were victims of serious parental abuse and prolonged neglect.

The link between teenage pregnancy, parenthood, low-income employment, child care, gang boys' victimisation of gang girls, and the eventual neglect and abuse of children with adolescent gang parents is the single most intractable problem facing interventionists. Between July 1994 and August 1996, one girl was pregnant three times, another twice; each pregnancy ended with a spontaneous miscarriage. By December 1996, the girl who had been pregnant twice was pregnant a third time, and three other Fremont girls had given birth.

In June 1995 a 17-year-old was the mother of an infant whose father was serving a prison term for murder. By September 1995, this young mother was pregnant again, this time with a child fathered by a teenager who was imprisoned in August 1995 on a parole violation and new conviction for drug distribution. By late 1996, this young mother of two was pregnant again with a child fathered by the cousin of her second child's father. She is now 19, unemployed, sells and uses drugs, and shares daily child supervision responsibilities with whomever is nearby.

The account of three sisters shows the integration of gang crime, drug use and child-rearing; the two youngest sisters were core members, the eldest was peripheral to gang crime but deeply involved in gang social life. The youngest sister is a 16-year-old prostitute and stripper and active in Fremont crime; in the fall of 1996 she was pregnant with a Fremont drug seller's baby. The middle sister is a 24-year-old heroin and rock cocaine addict who had participated in Fremont crime for a number of years; in the fall of 1996 she was pregnant. The eldest is a 28-year-old mother of three children: an 11-year-old-boy and two pre-school daughters, one five, the other two. The boy stays with his aunt, the pregnant heroin and cocaine addict, in her apartment in another neighbourhood but returns to Fremont at night and on weekends to hang out. He has begun to fight, use drugs, skip school and engage in property crime.

Two houses away from the Fremont drug house, the other two children reside with their mother in a rented, ramshackle two-bedroom house. One bedroom was rented to one of Fremont's rock cocaine sellers and his 16-year-old pregnant Fremont girlfriend. In this house, the pre-schoolers breathe second-hand cigarette and marijuana smoke and in the absence of a television, these pre-schoolers watch real-life gang members selling cocaine. One of the pre-schoolers, a five-year-old girl, often shows black-on-blue marks on her buttocks and face, bruises inflicted by gang boys who cannot control their anger. She cannot read the simplest words or write her name. In the winter of 1996 this girl's mother was pregnant with her fourth child. The 18-year-old father of this child is an active drug seller, car thief and burglar and the son of a rock cocaine addict.

Fremont's gang lifestyle is antagonistic to the physical, emotional and medical demands of pregnancy and the financial and personal responsibilities of parenthood. Pregnant girls receive virtually no pre-natal care; most do not think they need it or say they do not have the money to ride the bus to go downtown to the hospital where they can receive cost-free medical care. Most girls do not stop smoking cigarettes, and many continue to use illegal drugs and consume alcohol.

In America, nearly 35 per cent of births are to unwed mothers; on Fremont, that number is 100 per cent. There are no court-ordered child-support arrangements, no child-support payments, no stable house-holds, no stable sources of non-government income.

Education-based institution intervention programmes had little effect on altering Fremont kids' behaviour outside prison. Once these programmes ended, young former inmates return to street companions and a neighbourhood where there is no available employment for youngsters with few job skills. To find employment outside the Fremont area, somewhere else in Kansas City, these kids would need job-hunting and interviewing skills and sufficient income to support the infrastructure (a stable household, work clothes, reliable transportation) of full-time employment. What's more, full-time work means Fremont adolescents would be on their own, without the support of companions, parents and professionals to guide them through the maze of work life. To Fremont Hustlers, work life is scarier than gang life and jail.

Finally, some Fremont Hustlers are violent and threaten community safety. For their own protection and the community's, these youngsters need the treatment that is available to them in well-managed institutions. The majority of Fremont kids are not dangerous criminals but are imprisoned anyway, largely for non-violent offences. Serving time in juvenile detention centres has not taught them how to get and keep a job, nor has time behind steel doors allowed them to participate in the customary adolescent activities necessary to move into a lawful lifestyle. Prisons do not teach young or adult inmates to be lawful, economically productive citizens.

These dilemmas point to intervention opportunities. Delinquency policy and, more specifically, youth gang policy should mandate comprehensive early intervention programmes. The most active Fremont Hustlers used drugs and committed crime sometime between the ages of 10 and 14. Such high-risk kids must be found as early as possible. Waiting until they are arrested means we have waited too long. Adolescents are high risk if they say they are members of or have some affiliation with a gang; are identified as a member of gang by other kids, police, teachers, neighbourhood residents and former gang members; hang out regularly with gang members; act on behalf of a gang by using gang signs, painting gang graffiti, wearing gang colours; have siblings, parents, cousins, step-siblings or other relatives involved in a youth or an adult gang. High-risk kids engage in delinquent behaviours, fail at school or are chronically truant, use drugs and alcohol, and are sexually promiscuous. In the families of high-risk adolescents, research shows spouse abuse, abuse and neglect of children, alcohol and drug abuse, and adults engaged in street crime.

Juvenile justice policy prescribing an incapacitation–rehabilitation approach is short-sighted and sets the stage for failure. A more effective approach would be to implement comprehensive intervention and prevention programmes in high gang-crime neighbourhoods with a focus on high-risk adolescents and their families. Once interventionists select a 'target' site, they should set up on-site professional offices. From these offices, professionals can become part of the community and offer services to neighbourhood clients. On-site offices will instill a sense of commitment to neighbourhood activities and, with time, should effect a sense of rapport and confidence from neighbourhood citizens, and may even quell the signs of social disorder (open drug selling, homelessness) common in such neighbourhoods.

The arrest and imprisonment of violent gang members maintain community order. In well-managed juvenile or adult correctional facilities, troubled adolescents receive the treatment they would miss on the street; however, as noted above, imprisoning adolescents in order to treat them has its costs. Fortunately, most gang members are not egregiously violent and should not have to be imprisoned. To be effective over the long term, gang intervention must do more than suppress crime.

Long-term delinquency and gang intervention must be able to develop and implement realistic, community-based solutions to social and economic problems. Fremont research has identified core problems in adolescents' lives. The most serious problems include: family abuse and neglect; homelessness; chronic truancy; adolescent pregnancy; teenage parenthood; drug and alcohol addiction; and the victimisation of adolescent women and their children. Arrest and imprisonment of adolescent gang members will not stop family abuse and neglect or adolescent drug abuse.

High-risk adolescents are created by the neglect of community leaders who ignore serious community social problems. Threats and punishment mean nothing to adolescents who were beaten and whipped before they ran away from home and ended up on Kansas City's streets. Preaching abstinence to youth like the Fremont Hustlers will not end teenage pregnancy. Advertisement campaigns like 'Just Say No' will not stop youth like Cara, Wendy, Angie and Cheri from using drugs and alcohol. Surely, the arrest and imprisonment of an increasing number of high-risk adolescents will never resolve the complex set of problems that created the Fremont Hustlers.

We do know, however, that the best chance of intervening in and/or preventing youth violence will only come when community leaders stop blaming adolescents for problems they did not cause and take responsibility for improving the social and economic conditions in the poorest neighbourhoods. Entrenched social and economic problems will never end if imprisonment is the only crime-intervention strategy. If the money spent on imprisonment were invested in school treatment and enrichment programmes and community-based intervention and prevention programmes, the outcome would be a socially and mentally healthy generation of youth.

Voters and elected officials may feel good as they bluster about increasing the rates of imprisonment and lengthening prison terms. Threats of more and greater punishment have no necessary connection to the real outcome of filling our prisons with offenders who do not belong in prisons.

The criminal justice system that brought Fremont Hustlers to prison is extremely expensive and our short- and long-term return (crime deterrence) on investment is very low. The Fremont Hustlers' core members have been to juvenile detention and adult jails; most have been to state prison. Some youth left prison and returned to Fremont and within hours resumed drug use and selling.

Imprisoned adolescents return to drug-filled neighbourhoods, abusive homes, unemployment, no job training, no treatment for substance abuse and/or mental health problems, and no assistance from anyone in the dominant community who may be able to provide much-needed services. Young people are trapped in a social world created by racial, economic and political forces they do not understand and cannot control. This is a dramatically bad situation and imprisonment worsens it by further isolating marginal youth. Ill thought-out, politically popular policies like imposing more punishment, building more prisons and increasing the number of prisoners exacerbates today's problems and ensures that the social and economic problems caused by imprisonment will continue to recur.

There is a solution, but it is not quick and easy. Crime prevention and intervention take planning and money; however, well-designed intervention programmes can slow the rising tide of crime and decrease the number of emotionally damaged youth who join gangs like the Fremont Hustlers. Putting an end to gangs and crime means access to, among other things, easily available drug and alcohol treatment, more available training to better than minimum-wage job markets, and readily available, no-cost medical and psychological care located in poor neighbourhoods.

In neighbourhoods like Fremont no one wants to be poor. No one wants to be a drug addict or a victim of crime. The bravado of gang youth street talk is deceptive and masks the painful reality they know all too well. Cara and Carmen and the others are children trapped in and by poverty and find themselves in a depressing and hopeless scene. Our anger at gang youth cannot solve their problems nor will it resolve the community problems they cause. They need our help.

If we refuse to act on behalf of adolescents like the Fremont Hustlers, we will continue to be victimised by the enormous economic drain of failed punishment and crime deterrence policies. Our wrong-headed policy decisions such as issuing long prison sentences to non-violent offenders have cost society billions of dollars and have not improved the quality of life of people at most risk of committing crime. Spending billions on failed crime control means weakening societal infrastructure by reducing revenue available to, for instance, public schools and local-level economic development programmes.

Crime control research has shown what works well and what fails. Given that, we have to make a serious choice: either we continue to build and fill prisons, which leads only to expanding the number of prisoners who will eventually have virtually no chance of legitimate and gainful employment; or we invest in a higher quality of life for everyone by ensuring that comprehensive treatment programmes reach pre-adolescent victimised children before they too stand on a corner like Fremont and 13th Street.

Bibliographical review

Gangs have been a topic of intense research focus in America for more than 100 years. They are a complex research phenomenon for two reasons. First, they are the outcome of the interaction of cultural, political, social and economic forces. Second, they are the initiator of community problems such as violence, property and drug crime. Jeffrey Fagan's 1990 study of high-school students and school dropouts showed that gangs have significant influences on violence and on communities. Field studies of gangs have yielded a close look at gang social and economic dynamics. Studies such as Joan W. Moore's 1978 field research in Mexican-American neighbourhoods of East Los Angeles is a first-hand illustration of how the social and economic isolation of a community can result in the emergence of gangs (*Homeboys: Gangs, Drugs, and Prison in the Barrios of Los Angeles*. Philadelphia: Temple University Press). Moore's 1991 study (*Going Down to the Barrio: Homeboys and Homegirls in Change*. Philadelphia: Temple University Press) returned to the study area of her 1978 research. She showed that further erosion in employment, education and demographic changes effected an entrenchment of gangs in their neighbourhoods and an increase in criminal behaviour.

Field studies also include Ruth Horowitz's 1983 *Honor and the American Dream* (New Brunswick, NJ: Rutgers University Press), Diego Vigil's 1988's *Barrio Gangs* (Austin: University of Texas Press), and Felix Padilla's 1992 *The Gang as an American Enterprise* (New Brunswick, NJ: Rutgers University Press). Recent gang field studies include Mark S.

Fleisher's *Dead End Kids: Gang Girls and the Boys They Know* (1998, Madison: University of Wisconsin Press) and Jody Miller's 2001 *One of the Guys: Girls, Gangs, and Gender* (2001, New York: Oxford University Press). Fleisher's and Miller's studies examine the role of girls in gangs. Miller found that girls in gangs are victimised and witness violence more than non-gang peers and that in a seemingly contradictory way, girls know that gang participation increases the likelihood of victimisation but also offers them the protection they need while on the street. Fleisher's 1995 *Beggars and Thieves: Lives of Urban Street Criminals* (Madison: University of Wisconsin Press) shows that gang members were reared in neglectful and abusive early-life homes and that gang membership is an integral process in the maturation of street criminals.

Fleisher's 2002 field study of female gang participants (*Women and Gangs: A Field Research Study*, Grant Number: 2000-JR-VX-0006, Washington, D.C.: US Department of Justice, Office of Juvenile Justice and Delinquency Prevention) is a multi-year comprehensive study of the lives of adolescent and young-adult female gang members who reside in a poor African-American community. This study collected three types of data. Sociological data examine employment and education history, among other topics. Public health data explore their knowledge of birth control and describe sexual behaviour, among other topics. Social network data carefully describe the nature of social interaction among gang girls in the community's principal gangs. These are known as Vice Lords, Gangster Disciples and Black P-Stones. An analysis of gang girls' friendship networks, such as social support and mutual child care, shows that girls in each gang have friends in other gangs, and that strong friendships exceed social boundaries imposed by one or another gang affiliation. Fleisher argues, as did James F. Short (1997, *Poverty, Ethnicity, and Violent Crime*. Boulder, CO: Westview, p. 81), that gangs are not necessarily committed to a 'criminal orientation', as argued by Malcolm Klein in *The American Street Gang: Its Nature, Prevalence, and Control* (1995, New York: Oxford University Press).

Another comprehensive study of gangs is Scott H. Decker and Barrik Van Winkle's *Life in the Gang: Family, Friends, and Violence* (1996, New York: Cambridge University Press). This study is based on field interviews with St. Louis gang members and systematically reviews gang membership, gang structure and gang-member relationships, gang-member activities, gang crime and related issues. This research also explores the often-neglected relationship between gang members and their families.

What to do about gangs has occupied a good deal of scholars' efforts. In *Dead End Kids*, Fleisher argues that gang-involved girls and young adult women should be physically removed from the gang area, which in turn socially removes them from the influences of the gang group. Given the frequency of violence directed at gang girls, physical removal alone should provide some social and emotional relief. Fleisher's 2002 analysis of gang girls' friendship networks strongly suggests that friendships precede other types of relations and provide a long-term mechanism of social and economic survival in a poor community. These conclusions suggest that gang prevention and intervention programmes must begin as early as possible in the lives of high-risk girls. Intervention and prevention should include remedies for a wide range of health issues, such as mental health and substance abuse, rather than an exclusively suppressive approach. Fleisher's 2001 essay, 'Doing Field Research on Diverse Gangs: Interpreting Youth Gangs as Social Networks' (in C. Ronald Huff [Ed.] *Gangs in America III*. Thousand Oaks, CA: Sage) compares a risk-factor and a social network approach of gang data. He argues that the interpretive model of gang data is critical, because the model will determine the nature of prevention and intervention initiatives.

Studies on gang violence commonly report that gang members witness violence. If these gang members are parents, their children are likely to witness a continuous barrage of violent behaviour at home and/or in their neighbourhood and at school. In a recent important study of children's exposure to violence, Mark Singer and Daniel Flannery found that exposure to violence has damaging effects on the development of youth. Their research also finds that exposure to violence commonly precedes violent behaviour, substance abuse and mental illness ('The Relationship Between Children's Threats of Violence and Violent Behavior', *Archives of Pediatrics and Adolescent Medicine*, 154, 785–790, 2002; Singer, M., Miller, D., Guo, S., Flannery, D., Frierson, T. and Slovak, K. 'Contributors to Violent Behavior Among Elementary and Middle School Children', *Pediatrics*, 104(4), 878–884, 1999). The link between gang violence and its psychological and emotional effects on children may be a strong contributing force that perpetuates youth gang violence, drug abuse and mental illness.

The newest compilation of gang research essays, including chapters on gang intervention, is *Gangs in America III* (edited by C. Ronald Huff. Thousand Oaks, CA: Sage, 2002). Huff's book is a good place to begin reading about American gangs and it includes a comprehensive list of references to gang literature.

Gangs are not, however, found exclusively in America. Poverty, migration and the socio-economic dynamics in complex multi-cultural urban settings have led to the increase in youth gangs in European urban centres. American and European gang researchers, sociologists and criminologists and policy-makers have created a systematic approach to study of street crime and teamed up to create the first edited book on European gangs and problematic youth groups (Malcolm W. Klein, Hans-Jurgen Kerner, Cheryl L. Maxson and Elmar G.M.Weitekamp (eds) *The Eurogang Paradox: Street Gangs and Youth Groups in the U.S. and Europe.* Dordrecht: Kluwer Academic Publishers, 2000).

There is ample literature for anyone interested in youth gangs and gang intervention and prevention. Gang intervention and prevention initiatives and policy recommendations appear in many gang studies, but the most comprehensive study on the topic is Irving A. Spergel's *The Youth Gang Problem: A Community Approach* (1995, New York: Oxford University Press). Current research findings and publications are also available at http://ojjdp.ncjrs.org.

Suggested reading

Ball, Richard A. and G. David Curry (1995) 'The Logic of Definition in Criminology: Purposes and Methods for Defining "Gangs"', *Criminology,* 33(2), 225–245.

Bourgois, Philippe (1995) *In Search of Respect.* New York: Cambridge University Press.

Campbell, Anne (1984) *The Girls in the Gang.* New York: Basil Blackwell.

Curry, G. David (1998). 'Female Gang Involvement', *Journal of Research in Crime and Delinquency,* 35, 100–118.

Decker, Scott H. and Barrik Van Winkle (1996) *Life in the Gang.* New York: Cambridge University Press.

Esbensen, Finn-Aage and David Huizinga (1993) 'Gangs, Drugs, and Delinquency in a Survey of Urban Youth', *Criminology,* 31, 565–589.

Esbensen, Finn-Aage and Elizabeth Piper Deschenes (1998) 'A Multi-Site Examination of Gang Membership: Does Gender Matter?', *Criminology,* 36, 799–828.

Fleisher, Mark S. (1995) *Beggars and Thieves: Live of Urban Street Criminals.* Madison: University of Wisconsin Press.

Fleisher, Mark S. (1998) *Dead End Kids: Gang Girls and the Boys they Know.* Madison: University of Wisconsin Press.

Fleisher, Mark S. (2001) 'Doing Field Research on Diverse Gangs: Interpreting Youth Gangs as Social Networks' in C. Ronald Huff (ed.) *Gangs in America II.* Thousand Oaks, CA: Sage Publications, pp. 199–217.

Fleisher, Mark S. (2002) *Women and Gangs: A Field Research Study,* Grant Number: 2000-JR-VX-0006. Washington, D.C.: US Department of Justice, Office of Juvenile Justice and Delinquency Prevention.

Howell, James C. (1998) *Youth Gangs: An Overview. Juvenile Justice Bulletin*, August. Washington, D.C.: US Department of Justice, Office of Juvenile Justice and Delinquency Prevention.

Howell, James. C. and Scott H. Decker (1999) *The Youth Gangs, Drugs, and Violence Connection.* (Juvenile Justice Bulletin, Youth Gang Series, NCJ No. 171152.) Washington, D.C.: US Department of Justice, Office of Juvenile Justice and Delinquency Prevention.

Huff, Ronald C. (2001) *Gangs in America III.* Thousand Oaks, CA: Sage Publications.

Klein, Malcolm W. (1995) *The American Street Gang.* New York: Oxford University Press.

Krienert, Jessie and Mark S. Fleisher (2003) *Crime and Employment: Issues in Crime Reduction for Corrections.* Walnut Creek, CA: AltaMira Press.

Miller, Jody (2001) *One of the Boys: Girls, Gangs, and Gender.* New York: Oxford University Press.

Moore, Joan (1991) *Going Down to the Barrio: Homeboys and Homegirls in Change.* Philadelphia: Temple University Press.

Short, J.F., Jr. (1968) *Gang Delinquency And Delinquent Subcultures.* New York: Harper & Row.

Short, J.F., Jr. (1997) *Poverty, Ethnicity, And Violent Crime.* Boulder, CO: Westview.

Short, J.R., Jr., and Strondtbeck, F.L. (1965) *Group Process And Gang Delinquency.* Chicago: University of Chicago Press.

Spergel, Irvin (1995) *The Youth Gang Problem.* New York: Oxford University Press.

Taylor, Carl (1993) *Girls, Gangs, Women, Drugs.* East Lansing: Michigan State University Press.

Thornberry, Terence P., Marvin D. Krohn, Alan J. Lizotte and Deborah Chard-Wierschem (1993) 'The Role of Juvenile Gangs in Facilitating Delinquent Behavior', *Journal of Research in Crime and Delinquency,* 30, 55–87.

Chapter 4

Punishment, markets and the American model: an essay on a new American dilemma

Marcellus Andrews[1]

Theory and punishment

The American model as a promise, and a warning

This chapter uses economics, tentatively and in a modest way, to explore the long-term economic consequences of punishment policy in America. Specifically, I use economics to explore the economic dimensions of the problem of punishment, and especially the use of prisons to control crime in a racially divided society with vast and growing economic inequality.

My focus on the United States is not due to narrow nationalism or laziness. In many ways, the United States has pursued the logic of free markets and individualism with a peculiar mixture of zeal and dread. The miracle of the market as an engine of growth and the wellspring of liberty is an article of faith among Americans. Yet, Americans are also obsessive worriers who know, but can't quite acknowledge, that crime may well be the price we pay for the mixed blessings of an economy and society that honours so many of the unlimited desires of the self. Legal historian Lawrence Friedman has noted, in his magisterial *Crime and Punishment in American History*, that the culture of liberty and of self-determination at the heart of American being casts a sinister shadow – crime – over social life:

> The shadow of crime haunts 'respectable' society ... There is no free lunch. American liberty comes at a price. Total societies, traditional societies, disciplined societies, sometimes keep crime

under firm control. After the Soviet Empire collapsed, we are told, street crime increased, along with general disorder. A well run prison may have iron discipline and perfect order. Not many of us would prefer a well-run prison to the way we live. Yet, this must be said: a rich culture of liberty has evolved in the United States, but it casts a dark and dangerous shadow. The culture of mobility and the culture of the self are not costless. They have brought with them, like pests imported on exotic cargo, side effects of crime and social disorganization, and society, so far, has been unable to eradicate these pests, or bring them under control.[2]

The idea that crime is the mirror image of liberty, that choice necessarily means that careless, desperate, angry or heedless people will make bad or evil choices that require society to punish them is hard for Americans to accept. To an economist, though, the idea that self-interest and free choice are the source of social problems as well as social wealth is simply part of the order of things. Punishment, from an economic point of view, is one set of devices for controlling the inevitable damage that accompanies free markets and bad choices. Despite our best efforts as parents, teachers, preachers, neighbours, pundits and presidents, the wounds of childhood and young adulthood will lead some people into self-destructive and socially destructive ways of life. Even worse, the normal rhythms of economic life in American capitalism create an economic underclass that supplies forbidden goods and pleasures to the well-off classes, whose piety and sobriety are never so complete that they forswear their keen appetites for narcotics or young flesh. Accordingly, economics helps us map out the ways that punishment regulates both the nasty side of commerce and the social damage that comes from the inevitable failure of families, churches and schools to disarm the savage side of the human spirit.

Punishment as an economic problem: a brief primer

The traditional division of economics into two broad categories, microeconomics and macroeconomics, will be quite useful in organising our thoughts about punishment. Microeconomics is the study of individual choices as well as the social consequences of the unco-ordinated choices of actors (persons, businesses and governments) under a variety of circumstances. In contrast, macroeconomics is the study of whole economies, especially the evolution of employment, wages, prices, living standards and the distribution of wealth, income and well-being in a nation or aggregate population. Our brief exploration of the economics of punishment pays close attention to the impact of punishment on behaviour. One of the fundamental assumptions of economics – that people and enterprises make choices so as to maximise their well-being – will shape our discussion of punishment. First, we use the idea of incentives to explore the extent to which different forms of punishment are effective in shaping individual criminal behaviour. Second, our analysis uses economic criteria, particularly the idea that governments should design policy in order to maximise the difference between the social benefits of policies and their associated social costs, to consider the logic or folly of different punishment schemes.

Macroeconomics enters into our analysis of punishment policy as well. Punishment is an institution that tries to shape people's choices (a subject considered in more detail below). However, the economic environment, including the extent of unemployment, the distribution of income and wealth, the nature and extent of technological change, real wages and living standards across class and colour divides, and government policy shape the choices that men and women make. Changes in the economic environment have important effects on employment, wages and income distribution, which in turn affect the social consequences of punishment policy. Further, punishment policies are likely to have significant effects on the economic well-being of large segments of the population, particularly on the poor, unskilled workers and racial outcasts. This makes punishment policy an important part of overall economic policy precisely because decisions about punishment necessarily affect the choices that poor men and women make in their struggle to survive. In turn, governments make critical economic and social policy mistakes when they treat punishment policy as wholly separate from other aspects of economic and social policy, not least because the link between poverty, social distress and crime connects inequality to social welfare and criminal justice questions.

Choice, deterrence and punishment

To begin with, Friedman's observation cited above makes the claim that crime is a problem because some people make bad choices that threaten or take the property, security or lives of others, thereby undermining the capacities of each of us to pursue our own interests and enjoy our freedom to the maximum extent possible. In turn, punishment is an economic issue for two reasons. First, one economic purpose of punishment is to impose a cost on various kinds of criminal activity in the hope of deterring crime.[3] Punishment policy helps to deter crime by raising the penalties associated with law-breaking. The public invests in police, courts and prisons in the hope that increases in the certainty (and with longer prison terms, the severity) of punishment will reduce the potential gain from crime and thereby deter criminal activity. Longer prison sentences also deter crime, according to theory, by increasing the costs of incarceration in terms of the income, opportunities and pleasures that a criminal loses by being incarcerated.

The deterrence function of punishment is not unlike the impact of pollution taxes and charges that a government will impose on activities that foul the environment. The primary purpose of pollution taxes is to force both the buyers and sellers of noxious products to bear the full cost of their activity in the hope that they will either find a better way to make and sell goods or simply reduce the scale of the polluting activity. Similarly, a positive function of punishment is credibly to threaten offenders with loss so that there is no profit in criminal activity.[4] While some people can be dissuaded from breaking the law by the threat of sanctions, others will need to feel the sting of sanctions – including arrest, trial, fines, or, at the extreme, prison – before they change their behaviour.

The economist's tendency to reduce human action to the calculus of rational choice is deeply flawed in at least one important way when it ignores the possibility that people may act without giving much thought to the consequences of their behaviour. The economist, like most well-behaved, educated and well-socialised achievers in modern society, has a deep commitment to the idea that human beings conduct their affairs on the basis of coherent, integrated life plans that reasonably link their objectives and activities in both the short and long term. But the economist's presumption is simple prejudice to the degree that it blinds us to the possibility that many actions may be undertaken with little thought as to their long-run costs and benefits. Compulsion is just as important a force in life as reason, though the typical economic model rarely admits that men and women may be motivated by desires or hatreds that are simply outside the realm of rational thought. There are whole categories of actions and, in our case, criminal offences, particularly those related to consumption of addictive substances or the commission of sexual offences, that do not fit easily into the framework of rational decision-making that guides economic thinking.

Compulsions have murky origins, at least from the perspective of economists. More importantly, criminal activities that are driven by compulsions, or at any rate by non-rational sources of motivation, are simply beyond the reach of deterrence. One cannot deter someone from action if they pay no attention to the balance between the costs and benefits of their actions. Punishment can only be a deterrent if one can threaten a potential offender with loss and if this person includes the economic value of punishments into their calculations. There is a great deal of evidence (much of it summarised in other chapters in this volume) that suggests that a huge volume of crime is committed by people for reasons that cannot be reduced to narrow economic logic. But this leads us back to the age-old question of the causes of crime. The public, aroused by reports of ever-worsening violent crime (despite ample evidence of falling violent crime rates in major American cities over the past decade), is understandably impatient with the notion that coherent crime policy requires that social scientists answer this seemingly impossible question. Nonetheless, unless we face the fact that crime may not be driven solely, or even primarily, by rational choice, societies that adopt a rational-choice view of crime may well commit themselves to policies that do far more harm than good, as we will see below.

Punishment, particularly imprisonment, is a social device for removing criminals from society and in that way reducing the incidence of crime. Prisons, from an economic point of view, are warehouses that quarantine or incapacitate those men and women who either cannot be deterred by the threat of sanctions or whose actions are so harmful to society that they are best kept away from the rest of us. In either case, prisons are forms of public capital that insure society against the failure of education, social customs, laws and intermediate sanctions to deter criminal behaviour.

The resources used to operate and maintain prison facilities are funded by taxes, or in the case of governments plagued by budget deficits, borrowing, thereby requiring any rational government to think about its punishment policies in relation to all of its other economic and social policies. Public-sector budgets are tight in the modern world, in part because citizens in all countries chafe at the price tag of the public services they demand, and because taxation and public spending priorities have very important effects on the economic well-being of nations. Governments faced with insistent demands for extensive and high-quality public services and limitations on their taxing and borrowing powers must carefully weigh the costs and benefits of spending extra money on everything, including police and prisons. For example, a government is on solid economic ground in building another prison rather than more schools if the economic benefits from housing more felons exceeds the economic gain from providing high-quality schooling to the community's children. Conversely, a society that goes on a prison-building binge without carefully considering whether limited funds are better spent on other things, like schools, is being foolish, at best.

A narrow economic perspective on the punishment process shows that a government has to weigh a number of items as it tries to deal with crime. We have already seen that punishment can only deter crime if the threat of arrest, trial and the imposition of sanctions is credible, which requires significant investments in police and in the court system. In addition, the system of sanctions must be carefully constructed to both deter crime and, where necessary, handle felons in a cost-effective manner. An economically rational punishment policy will match the sanction to the crime in ways that lead to the greatest possible social benefit. This means that there should be a link between the severity of the sanction, in terms of the type of sanction imposed and, in the case of imprisonment, length of sentence, and the social cost of the criminal act *on economic grounds*. Policies that sentence petty drug dealers to long mandatory prison terms ignore the economic logic of using scarce prison resources to maximise safety and social welfare. The cold logic of economics tells us that a greater share of resources should be devoted to offenders who do great social harm, like those who repeatedly commit murder, rape and other forms of violent crime, with less severe sanctions being meted out to felons whose crimes inflict smaller social costs.

The distinction between the deterrent and incapacitation effects of punishment requires governments to consider the proper balance between deterring crime and warehousing felons when making decisions about punishment policy. As always, the proper balance between deterrence and incapacitation is at that point where the extra social benefits from spending another dollar on deterrence – which may increase the certainty of punishment – is just equal to the additional social benefits from putting an extra dollar toward incapacitation. If societies can reduce crime more by increasing the likelihood of punishment (by spending on police and courts) than by increasing the length of incarceration, then the proper allocation of public resources will shift funds and people towards policing and away from prisons. Similarly, if crime can be prevented by increased long-term investments in education, health care, job training and the development of effective policies to increase the rewards for work among the unskilled, then egalitarian social policy can be said to have a deterrent effect. Simple economics tells us that if we want to maximise social welfare we must choose the right combination of punishment – both deterrence and incapacitation – along with employment, welfare, education and macroeconomic policies in order to realise our goals.

The lay reader will no doubt object to all of this since it says that punishment policy must be developed in light of all other policy. Since everything in life is related to everything else, the lay reader will throw up his or her hands in disgust and say that we are proposing an unreasonable standard that requires governments to consider the indirect consequences of their punishment policies on employment, income distribution and other seemingly separate economic policy matters. It is certainly true that the economic perspective advocated here, a general equilibrium perspective that insists that the full direct and indirect effect of policies be assessed when making critical public choices, is asking a lot. Still, the only way to make sure that punishment policy is not making matters worse is to be sure that it makes sense in light of the other things that society is trying to do.

Public investment in prisons imposes three different direct economic costs on society. Each of these costs is associated with special economic and political problems that need to be considered carefully in the analysis of rational punishment policy.

1 First, the cost of constructing a prison must be financed either by current taxes or future taxes (through borrowing) or by cuts in other areas of government spending. Any decision to pay for new prisons on the basis of current taxes is necessarily a decision to reduce current private-sector consumption or investment activity in the interest of increasing society's capacity to warehouse criminals, presumably because the net social benefits of deterring and incapacitating offenders exceeds the value of forgone consumption and investment opportunities. By contrast, decisions to build prisons on the basis of future taxes – since borrowing funds to finance current public spending is a decision to rely on future resources – substitutes future consumption and investment activity for the benefits of more prison space. Finally, decisions to cut other government programmes in order to construct prisons is a sensible policy if the social benefits of prison building exceed the net benefits of reductions in other government activities as noted above.

2 A decision to raise current taxes in order to build prisons is the most transparent way to force the public to consider the economic cost of punishment policy. Yet, the transparency of this policy approach makes it appear to be the most costly in the eyes of a public that resents taxation. Similarly, policies that would finance punishment schemes by reducing other categories of spending are likely to be resisted by the taxpaying public unless prison construction is paid for by reductions in spending directed at politically powerless or unpopular groups like the poor or racial outcasts. Still, there are limits to the extent to which governments can shift spending away from poor relief and social welfare spending to punishment policy,

not the least of these being that the expansion of punishment brings with it a long-term commitment to expenditure that may prove to be economically risky for reasons explained below. The least politically difficult method for financing a punishment regime is by public-sector borrowing since the full costs of the punishment regime are put off into the future. However, the general limits on public-sector borrowing impinge on prison construction by forcing governments to choose between using debt to finance tax reductions or investments in other areas and building prisons.

3 A decision to build a new prison requires the government not only to pay for prison construction but also to pay yearly operation and maintenance costs associated with monitoring and caring for inmate populations. These expenditure commitments must be met on the basis of tax revenues that fluctuate with changes in economic conditions as well as changing fiscal policy priorities. For example, conservative governments committed to reducing tax rates and the cost of government face a potentially severe fiscal problem if they also insist on building prisons in order to manage crime. The tight connection between crime, poverty and unemployment means that rising crimes rates are one social cost of any obsessive programme of tax cuts. Yet, a law-and-order conservative will be hard pressed to support low tax rates, lower levels of public spending and increased reliance on longer prison terms as well as larger police forces. A harsh punishment policy that requires larger police forces and more prisons can only be consistent with lower taxes and lower level of poor support or anti-poverty spending if the overall economy is growing fast enough to offset the negative effects of lower tax rates on government revenues. In the event of recession due to a decline in aggregate economic activity or due to negative economic events like the terrorist attacks on New York City in 2001, falling tax receipts will raise the fiscal burden of punishment policies to governments, thereby requiring tough choices between the punishment regime, other priorities, borrowing more heavily or raising taxes. Since even conservative governments spend more on poor support in times of recession or economic downturn, prior commitments to harsh punishment policy may lead to later situations where conservatives must partially rescind their harsh stance in the interest of fiscal stability, as has happened recently in a number of US states where inmates have been released in order to reduce budget deficits. These considerations suggest that there is a fundamental fiscal contra-diction at the heart of modern, small-government conservatism – one cannot have a commitment to a large prison system, low taxes and

low levels of poor support at the same time without making unrealistic assumptions about the sustainability of high rates of economic growth. It seems that a commitment to harsh punishment policy, like a commitment to equality, requires high tax rates.

The social costs and benefits of punishment

The foregoing survey has been a bit abstract. We need to know how to apply economic criteria to the real world, which requires that we attach money values to the costs and benefits of punishment. In particular, how should we judge the effectiveness of punishment policies? How should we go about comparing the impact of punishment policy on social welfare as against other policies, particularly in situations where tight public-sector budgets force governments to choose between increased spending on criminal justice at the cost of reduced spending in other areas?

Evaluation of the effect of punishment on social welfare has two components. First, how large is the deterrent effect of various punishments on offending behaviour and, second, how large are the net social benefits of incapacitation? If offending behaviour is very sensitive to the probability of arrest and conviction, even if punishments are only moderately severe, then policies that tilt towards policing and away from incarceration are called for. However, if variations in the prospects of arrest and conviction have little effect on offending behaviour then governments should put resources into incarceration and increase the length of prison terms.

The balance between deterrence and incapacitation hinges on the relative strengths of these two effects. A survey of the economics literature on crime and punishment by Erlich (1996) presents mixed findings about the relative importance of the deterrent and incapacitation effects of punishment. Statistical studies by a number of authors imply that, in the US, an increase in the certainty of punishment (that is, in the probability of arrest and conviction) has a greater effect on offending behaviour than does an increase in the severity of punishment (as measured by the length of prison sentences). Unfortunately, an extensive survey of the economics literature on deterrence by Cameron (1988) reports that most statistical studies fail to establish a significant relationship between the size of a police force and the probability of arrest. A review article by Anderson (1997) on the recent decline in rates of violent crime points to the effect of an increased emphasis on new forms of policing (including the well-documented trend towards 'community policing' in major metropolitan areas in the US) and increased police visibility in the enforcement of both major and minor violations of law in deterring crime.[5] For example, an increased police presence on the street in New York has been matched by investments in the capacity of lower courts and probation authorities to process and supervise felons, thereby both increasing the chances of arrest and conviction for criminal offences and enabling the State to supervise felons outside prison walls.[6] This particular case suggests that changes in the organisation of policing activity, combined with adequate court and supervisory facilities for the management of offenders, may have potentially powerful deterrent effects.[7]

Taken as a whole, the literature on deterrence offers the hope that a high likelihood of arrest will reduce crime rates and thereby improve social welfare. In contrast, one certain benefit from incarceration is the reduction in crime associated with a larger prison population. Levitt (1996) has estimated that the average crime costs society US$3,332 (in 2000 dollars) while the average offender commits 15 crimes per year.[8] If we use Levitt's estimates for the sake of argument, then each imprisoned felon increases social welfare by $49,980 per year (again in 2000 dollars): the detention of one more average offender will mean $49,980 less harm due to criminal activity. Of course the gain from punishment, whether through deterrence or through incapacitation, must be set against the cost of deterring crime or incarcerating offenders before we can know the net direct effect of punishment on social welfare. If we once again rely on Levitt's estimates, the operating cost of incarceration is approximately $33,321 per year per inmate in 2000 dollars (including the cost of maintaining prison facilities), with the consequence that placing one more convicted offender in prison increases social welfare by approximately $16,659 per year.

But there are still more economic benefits from a reduction in crime. Millions of men and women make decisions about where to live, work and play on the basis of their perceptions of personal safety. Free markets respond to consumer demands for safety by supplying home security devices, anti-theft devices for cars, handguns and handgun training, attack dogs, private security guards for apartment buildings, and private police forces for wealthy residential communities and prosperous urban districts. Businesses pay out enormous sums of money for bank security, retail shop security (against theft by employees, shoplifting and robbery), security forces in large shopping areas (especially shopping malls) and other protective measures.[9]

The money value of private security services and products is both a measure of the public's demand for protection against crime and, in its own way, a type of 'tax' that crime imposes on the citizenry. This 'crime tax' is the market response to the perceptions of the risk of injury, assault and theft that individuals and corporations believe they face. In turn, private spending on security is ultimately reflected in the prices of most goods and services produced in the United States, thereby shifting a significant portion of the cost of private efforts at crime prevention onto buyers of goods and services.

Prison maths

Punishment, particularly imprisonment, may have beneficial effects by reducing the threat of harm. A high incarceration rate and long prison terms for a wide range of crimes is, from the perspective of an economist, a signal that government sends to both criminals and an anxious public that it is serious about reducing crime. If the public believes the government, and thereby reduces its demand for security devices in favour of other goods and services, then the economic costs of crime are shifted from the private to the public sector (and hopefully reduced if public authorities can handle crime more efficiently than private-sector enterprises). Even small declines in the fear of crime may lead to millions or even billions of dollars in savings on private crime control. The costs of providing goods and services may fall a bit; fewer men and women will be employed as security personnel; the demand for home and business security systems may fall, with the savings realised from a lower level of anxiety about crime being channelled into other areas.

The arithmetic of an even greater investment in prisons, for the purposes of both warehousing criminals and deterring crime, is truly daunting. Assume that Levitt is right, so that putting a 'average' felon in prison increases social welfare by $16,659 per year. According to the Bureau of Justice Statistics, the average time served for a violent crime in a state prison in 1999 was 51 months of an average sentence of 87 months; felons served just over 55 per cent of their sentence.[10] One clear way to reduce crime rates is to keep criminals under lock and key longer, since so many studies suggest that most prisoners released on probation or parole (two-thirds of the population under supervision by the criminal justice system) will commit crimes within a year of their release. The average turnover rate for violent offenders is 23.53 per cent per year, with an average of 51 months served in prison, i.e. 23.53 per cent of all prisoners are released from prison each year.[11] Simple arithmetic shows that if the average amount of actual time served in prison is increased by one year (from 51 to 63 months) then only 19.04 per cent of prisoners will be released each year. It is important to note that a rise of one year in the time served by the average felon will mean that the prison population rises by 19.04 per cent (assuming that there is no increase in the number of admissions into the system).[12]

The 2001 edition of the *Sourcebook of Criminal Justice Statistics* reports that 1,962,220 people were incarcerated (in prison or jail) in the United States in 2001. If the average prison term rose by one year, the number of prisoners released in 2001 would have fallen from 461,710 to 374,391 so that the incarcerated population would increase by 87,319 people. If the prison system is already working at capacity when the decision to lengthen prison sentences is made, then the state must make capital investments in prison facilities and in training the required correctional personnel. The most common estimate of the cost of a new prison cell is $50,000. Since Levitt's calculations indicate that incarcerating the average offender yields $16,659 per year in increased social well-being net of the operating costs of incarceration, the social rate of return on investment in a prison cell is approximately 199 per cent, assuming that each cell houses two felons.[13] This means that the authorities would be able to build jails and thereby improve social welfare (in the narrow economic sense) so long as the cost of borrowed funds, in this case the interest rate on bonds issued by the authorities in order to finance new prison construction, is less than 199 per cent. Since interest rates rarely rise beyond 25 per cent (given the remarkable financial stability of the American economy and the aims of American economic policy), prison building is certainly a 'viable' economic undertaking.[14]

Of course, this illustrative calculation is certainly not the most accurate assessment of the economic gain from longer prison terms. A lower estimate on the social costs per crime will certainly lower the rate of return from lengthening prison terms, as would a higher estimate of the cost of a new prison cell. Public-sector cost–benefit analysis is notorious for its inaccuracy; it is very hard to assign the proper monetary value to the many costs and benefits associated with a public-sector capital project that is being provided in a non-competitive setting by a producer that has little incentive to provide goods or services efficiently (a point we return to below). Further, if advances in technology or, as we will see later, the privatisation of prisons actually reduce the operating costs of incarceration, then the rate of return from lengthening prison sentences must increase.

The foregoing calculation, though sobering and more than a bit frightening, is biased to the extent that it is based on an estimate of the social damage done by the 'average criminal'. Different types of violent and non-violent crime impose different costs on society, thereby requiring governments to choose those offences that warrant prison and those that are better addressed through other forms of punishment.

Crimes like murder, manslaughter and rape are, from an economic perspective, very 'expensive' offences whose prevention through incarceration can be expected to yield great social returns. However, other offences, such as non-violent drug offences and petty property crimes, impose much lower social costs and yield correspondingly lower rates of return from imprisonment. John DiIulio and Anne Piehl in 'Does Prison Pay, Revisited?' argue that the high costs of violent crime call for long mandatory prison sentences for violent criminals but that economic considerations argue against subjecting non-violent offenders to long spells of imprisonment.

We should mention one other set of costs that need to be included in any prison calculus before leaving the narrow economics of incarceration. Punishment is, by its very nature, the deliberate use of public power to inflict pain on offenders. Proponents of deterrence hope that inflicting pain on inmates will alter the calculations of other offenders and thereby reduce their incentives to commit crimes. For others, especially proponents of incapacitation, the pain that inmates suffer as a result of incarceration is an inevitable by-product of the reduction of crime that comes from warehousing repeat offenders.

The economic analysis of incarceration requires that the pain associated with punishment be applied up to the point where the social benefits of the additional harm are just equal to the additional costs of administering pain. Any comprehensive economic analysis of punishment must include the costs of incarceration to inmates and their communities into the balance of costs and benefits. There is clear evidence that incarceration imposes severe mental, emotional, physical and economic costs on inmates and those who watch them – including everything from violence between inmates, conflict between inmates and prison authorities, and rape. Badly run prisons wound people in permanent ways that inevitably affect the lives of men and women outside prison walls, since most prisoners are released from confinement.[15]

There are further hidden costs that, though almost impossible to calculate, must nonetheless be included in the balance in some way. While society has an image of the felon as disconnected social trash, the reality of the lives of men and women who become inmates is so much more complex, in part precisely because these people are so ordinary. Most inmates come from impoverished families and communities where they play a variety of social roles. Imprisonment deprives families of husbands and wives, sons and daughters, fathers and mothers, breadwinners and caregivers (of both genders). The disruptions of inmates' mini-communities of families, neighbourhoods and larger social units by virtue of incarceration (especially when punishment is meted out on a mass scale, as with the current American experiment with imprisonment) surely destroys a portion of the social capital that is one of the bulwarks against social disorganisation. Though it is fashionable for economists to talk about social capital in matters of economic growth and business organisation, middle-class prejudice (at least among the literate and chattering classes) should not blind us to the fact that incarceration disrupts important patterns of care and association in inmates' communities of origin, thereby undermining these communities' ability to survive and thrive.

The political economy of bad choices

Our meditation on punishment has only considered criteria for the efficient mixture of incarceration and deterrence policies. Yet punishment policy must be considered in the broader context of overall social policy that seeks to contribute to the citizenry's well-being in a variety of ways. The reduction of the considerable social costs associated with crime, as well as the reduction of the 'crime tax', certainly improves economic efficiency by reallocating resources away from private efforts at crime control toward other areas. Punishment policy is also shaped by larger social and economic forces that can be influenced by governmental activity. As we have already noted, the economic view of crime suggests that criminal offences happen because there are net benefits from breaking the law, after due consideration for the risk of arrest, conviction and punishment. According to this view, punishment deters when the gains from criminal behaviour fall short of the benefits of obeying the law, which include the considerable benefits associated with work, pay, consumption and leisure under conditions of liberty. Effective forms of punishment impose large enough costs on potential offenders to discourage criminal activity, either through stiff fines or through the costs of forgone income and opportunities associated with incarceration.

The economic approach to punishment directs our attention to two aspects of the problem of crime and choice. First, social norms and taboos play a critical role in shaping the range of choices that men and women make, principally by inhibiting certain choices in the light of moral and ethical standards. The absence of these sort of inhibitions among certain social groups, due perhaps to structural conditions like poverty, family breakdown, community disorganisation or racism, will lead to more bad choices regardless of the certainty and severity of punishment. It is important to recall that punishment is, by its very nature, a device that society uses when moral and ethical injunctions fail to restrain antisocial behaviour. Therefore, social conditions that weaken ethics and morality will necessarily weaken the ability of punishment to deter bad behaviour.

Second, the lost income and opportunities that are associated with punishment matter most when potential offenders have incomes and opportunities to lose in the first place. An economic view of punishment clearly suggests that punishments are less effective when criminal activity is more lucrative than work, study and other law-abiding activities. If wages are low, unemployment chronic and long-term income and educational prospects slim compared with the returns from criminal activity, then offenders are rationally choosing to break the law, especially if they come from social circumstances where ethical and moral restraints on bad behaviour are weak.

Governments trying to control crime must consider the effects of the broad range of economic and social policies, including employment, trade, tax, fiscal, monetary and regulatory policies, on the social conditions that contribute to criminal activity. If the social forces that generate violent crime are largely beyond the reach of social policy, then governments are obliged to build as many prisons and hire as many police as are necessary to manage criminals, even if it means that they also reduce investments in education, health and social welfare spending. If, on the other hand, crime is strongly related to economic and social forces that can be influenced by social policy, particularly by education, child care, health care and poor relief policies, then governments may have an option beyond bolstering the punishment capacity of the state. The particular mixture of punishment and social welfare expenditure that society ultimately settles upon will not simply depend on the relative effectiveness of different policies, but also on fundamental values of social justice and fairness. Even if prisons are more cost effective than schools and the dole as devices for managing poverty and structural unemployment (a distinct and depressing possibility that we have noted above), the balance between confinement of the poor and redistribution towards the poor will depend on the willingness of the well-off to share the burdens of the poor. A stingy, angry or racially hostile middle-class majority (particularly in countries, like the United States, where crime has a powerful racial element) may well decide that it will opt for prisons instead of welfare because prisons are cheaper and the poor are thought to be racially inferior.

Broadly speaking, conservative scholars emphasise the role of morals and incentives (or more precisely, the lack thereof) as the fundamental causes of social breakdown and criminal behaviour. Liberals and leftists, by contrast, see structural forces such as poverty, social (including racial) oppression and other 'macro-social' forces as the culprits. This dichotomy, like all extreme divisions, is obviously a bit of a straw man. There is little doubt that morals, character and incentives are influenced by forces that extend far beyond a particular individual's control. Indeed, the recent conservative emphasis on the role of absent fathers, teenage child-bearing and bad child-rearing practices in poor black communities as a primary cause of lawlessness in these communities can be thought of as a structural analysis, of a sort. Similarly, many liberal writers take great pains to note that bad character and predatory behaviour among young poor men from racial pariah groups are due not only to material deprivation and social oppression, but also to retrograde ideas of masculinity and the breakdown of communal morality. Still, the primary difference between liberals and conservatives on the issues of crime and punishment is one of emphasis as well as origin: conservatives assign the blame for growing crime and lawlessness among the poor and the dark-skinned to the decay of social norms and moral rules that are largely separate from economic forces; whereas liberals insist that material forces, including economic conditions, play a large role in shaping the power of social norms and moral rules to control criminal behaviour among the young.

John DiIulio is a well-regarded exponent of the view that crime is, at bottom, the inevitable consequence of the breakdown of the moral norms and social rules of a community. In a long series of books, articles and congressional testimony, DiIulio had made it clear that a rational government, faced with the prospect of managing crime, must be willing to use incarceration to minimise the violence and social destruction caused by badly raised young outcast men who are simply beyond the hope of progressive social reform.[16] DiIulio had once insisted that the large-scale social breakdown that he saw as the cause of the inner-city crime problem must call for government policy aimed at replacing, as much as possible, dysfunctional families, if need be by a system of publicly funded orphanages and group homes that try to instil proper ethical norms into the wounded hearts of poor children. The bleakness of this view, which treats poor black families as unable to mould good character for black children, was matched by his frank prescription to use jails to lock up the children of the black poor. Long prison terms, including mandatory minimum sentences, 'truth-in-sentencing' regulations (which require an inmate to serve at least 85 per cent of the pronounced sentence), restrictions on plea bargaining and on the use of parole, are all ways of keeping violent criminals detained for longer periods, thereby reducing the social costs of crime.

DiIulio has in recent years turned against using punishment – particularly imprisonment – as a primary government response to the problem of urban crime, in favour of a sort of 'social Christian' structuralism that sees crime as the result of a spiritual and religious crisis in poor black communities. While DiIulio's current stance could still be broadly called 'conservative' in the sense that it views crime as a problem that ultimately arises because of the spiritual maladies of specific populations, it is also a structuralist stance that connects the presumed moral crisis of poor black communities to economic and social conditions that both contribute to and reflect the underlying spiritual disjunction. In recent years, DiIulio has spearheaded efforts to use 'faith-based' approaches to public policy to rebuild civil society in crime-ridden parts of urban America, though his well-publicised recent break with the Bush administration has put him at some distance from parts of the American Right.[17] This 'preceptoral' approach to the problem of crime and social disorder is, needless to say quite, controversial.

Suppose that either 'early' or 'late' DiIulio is right. If so, then crime, though associated with poverty and certainly worsened by material deprivation, is ultimately due to bad parenting – specifically child abuse and neglect by teenage parents who are no more than children themselves – or moral decay in communities that have lost their bearings. In such a setting, criminals are simply people who lack any training in civilised modes of being: these are people whose horrific family lives and psychotic subcultures have made them heedless, thoughtless, sullen, angry, violent and deaf to the basic claims of moral life. Hence, they are willing to consider the cost and benefits of crime in many cases (moral people would simply refuse to consider crime as an option), though some, maybe many, of their number may be so wounded by their bad family lives and dysfunctional cultures of origin that they simply career through life like mindless, destructive dervishes, driven by compulsions that are beyond their understanding or control. These people commit crimes – especially violent crimes – on the basis of 'motives' that have no connection to the limited rational calculus of economic theory. The rich stew of obsessions, notions and psychoses that drive ordinary men and women to murder, rape, torture and abuse others cannot be understood through the lens of rational choice, no matter how obsessed economists and other social scientists are with the claims of formal reason.

Class, crime and punishment

DiIulio's view, though traditionally associated with conservative perspectives on crime and society, need not be confined to the right end of the political spectrum. Indeed, it can be readily folded into some (though by no means all) leftist views of the role of social class and economic crisis in creating conditions of social breakdown requiring radical solutions, including a reliance on punishment.

Although DiIulio's claims that moral decay and the breakdown of social norms may undoubtedly play a role in young, poor men's willingness to commit crime, there must still be an economic incentive for young men to risk punishment. Economist Richard Freeman of Harvard has noted that the wages of young American workers with the lowest levels of education have declined between 20 and 30 per cent since 1973. Freeman goes on to show why this decline in the wages and job prospects of young workers, combined with the prospects of higher earnings from criminal activity and the relatively low risk of imprisonment, can plausibly be understood as a cause of growing youth crime, particularly robbery, burglary and other types of property crime.[18]

Of course, the declining economic prospects of unskilled workers has no direct connection with the frightening increase in violent crimes among the young. Yet, Freeman's analysis of the role of low wages, high unemployment and bad long-term economic prospects in generating a rising crime rate among the young is linked to the problems of family breakdown and the instability of poor, urban neighbourhoods explored by William Julius Wilson in his path-breaking analyses of the American underclass, *The Truly Disadvantaged* and *When Work Disappears*. Wilson notes that low wages and poor employment prospects among young, poor men have greatly reduced the pool of 'marriageable' men that is available (as in outside-of-jail) and economically stable (employed and capable of earning above poverty-line wages) in poor neighbourhoods relative to young women. This relative scarcity of potential marriage partners for young women must mean, as a matter of logic and arithmetic, that young women who want to have children must be willing to do so without the help of gainfully employed young men or the economic support of extended families. Indeed, one of the ironies of tough punishment policies is that a prison-building spree will simply make this shortage of marriage partners and potential parental partners much worse. No amount of breast beating about moral decay or terrible black families or any other belief-based or race-based cause of crime can escape the most basic fact of American economic life: the low (and falling) real wages and employment prospects among the young, poor and modestly educated means that, short of an economic miracle, American capitalism has a vast pool of largely marginal or even unemployable people who are having trouble sustaining working marriages or stable parenting partnerships, thereby creating the conditions of limited parental and community control over the behaviour of the young that results in criminal activity.

The only way to deal with this problem, which is basically a problem of a growing population of the economically useless, is to either reduce their numbers (through better and more broadly available education for the children of the poor and working classes, an exceedingly expensive proposition that the American middle class has consistently rejected for a very long time) or increase the demand for the unskilled and modestly educated workers. One way to boost the demand for unskilled labour is through significant increases in public spending for public works projects – largely programmes to rebuild the airports, roads, bridges, schools, parks, dams, sewers and other parts of the nation's physical infrastructure by employing unskilled labour. However, no argument for massive increases in public spending is likely to appeal to an American public that is wary of higher taxes in the face of stagnant real wages. Further, many of these kinds of public works projects require workers with technical, scientific and literacy skills that are well beyond the qualifications of the underclass. Even this kind of programme would not ultimately deal with the central problem: unskilled and low-skilled labour in the United States is simply not able to command a high enough wage because it is cheaper to produce cars, steel, textiles and other mass-market goods abroad. Temporarily boosting the wages and employment prospects of unskilled workers through public works programmes is certainly helpful, but it doesn't address the basic problem.

The question of how to raise the real wages of the modestly educated without creating welfare traps or increasing structural unemployment is receiving increasing attention among economists and policy-makers. Edmund Phelps of Columbia University, a distinguished economic theorist, has proposed that the United States develop a national system of wage subsidies in order to boost the earnings of low-wage workers. Phelps' proposal, presented in great detail in his *Rewarding Work* as well as in a number of technical articles in academic journals, explicitly acknowledges the need for modern societies to develop policies that encourage work effort among members of the underclass while simultaneously boosting the rewards from work. Phelps notes that the decline in real wages among the most poorly educated members of the adult population has created conditions of low labour force participation and increasing crime among the underclass. In order to counter the destructive social consequences that low wages and low degrees of labour force participation have on poor communities, Phelps proposes that the government replace most current income support and poor-relief programmes with a system of wage subsidies where employers receive a subsidy for hiring every employee whose pay is below a level that affords a full-time worker an income above the poverty line (calculated at $7.00 per hour in 1997 dollars). Though Phelps claims that this programme would be self-financing (if it fully replaced existing welfare programmes and if the resulting rise in real earnings among poorly paid workers reduced crime somewhat), his proposal is rather expensive (on the order of $100 billion per year in 1997 dollars or $106 billion in 2002 dollars) and, though fully consistent with the ethos of workfare and mandatory work requirements for the poor, unlikely to pass muster in the current conservative political setting.

If we put all these considerations together, we can see that the nature of modern labour markets, particularly the poor job prospects for so many of the young, are perfectly consistent with the brutal description of social disorganisation and family breakdown provided by DiIulio. Economic marginality and the social disorganisation of poor neighbourhoods are mutually reinforcing states that used to be thought of as the usual and destructive consequences of poverty, at least before it became fashionable to blame the poor for being poor. The poverty, inequality and unemployment that Freeman sees as a major driving force behind youth crime is ultimately linked to the education and preparation of the young to work in a modern, skill-driven world economy. Young workers who have modest levels of academic attainment are simply no longer going to secure industrial and service jobs that will pay adequate real wages. The sad truth is that the blue-collar road to the American middle class has crumbled and no one knows how to rebuild it.[19]

The private provision of punishment

A primary justification for the state's monopoly over the use of legitimate violence is the need to mete out punishment in order to protect citizens from each other. Yet, from an economic perspective, the state's monopoly on the use of approved force does not necessarily mean that it should also be the sole provider of punishment services. Punishment is a complex set of public goods that generate a host of positive and negative social costs, which forces governments to choose whether these goods should be provided through public-sector bureaucracies or through markets. Though most of us tend to see punishment as linked to the state's prerogatives over the use of force, the question of whether punishment should be provided by the government or through the market has a long and brutal history in America. The essential issue is whether private prisons are less costly than public prisons. The answer to this question is complicated.

There has been a significant increase in the proportion of prisons and jails managed privately in the US. For example, the number of states opting to use private firms to manage incarceration facilities grew from 14 in 1991 to 23 in 1994, before rising to 33 in 2001. In addition, 23 of the 33 states utilising private prison facilities in 2001 were in the South and West, accounting for 68 per cent of the 91,828 persons held in detention for profit. Some states rely on private operators to manage a substantial portion of their inmate populations including Montana (32.7 per cent), Washington D.C. (35.9 per cent) and New Mexico (43.8 per cent). The percentage of total capacity managed by private firms grew from 2.61 per cent in 1991 to 6.5 per cent in 2001 over the same period.

The reader will remember the calculations presented earlier that suggested that prison expansion may well be an efficient use of scarce public resources, at least by narrow economic criteria. Evidence of the impact of the privatisation of prisons on the costs of operating corrections facilities is mixed. For example, the state of Texas, the third most populous state in the United States, has aggressively pursued a policy of prison building as part of its anti-crime programme. In July 1991, according to a report in the 16 March, 1994 edition of the *Wall Street Journal*, the Texas Performance Review Board of the Texas Comptroller of Public Accounts (a public agency that monitors the efficiency of public-spending programmes in the state) reported that the per person cost of operating a private prison was $30.62 per day, which is between $6.00 and $6.50 less than state prison operating costs. This fall in prison operating costs of between 16.56 per cent and 17.53 per cent, if applicable to other private prison operations in Texas and throughout the country, would certainly increase the social rate of return from building prisons and incarcerating more criminals. A study of the cost of private as against public prison operations in Louisiana in 1996 showed that two private facilities operated at lower average costs per inmate than a similar public facility, with the additional bonus that the private facilities had fewer disciplinary problems with inmates than the public prison.[20] However, a 1996 report by the General Accounting Office (GAO), an investigative agency of the US Congress, reports that the evidence on cost savings associated with privatisation is quite mixed.[21] While the GAO report confirms the Texas experience, it also notes that studies on the effect of privatisation on correctional costs in California, New Mexico, Tennessee and Washington state show no clear pattern. In these other cases, operating costs were either similar for private and public facilities or (in one case) higher in the private facility. Further, the GAO report noted that there were few significant differences in service quality between private and public facilities.

Market failure and private punishment

The usual problems with unregulated markets, particularly for services involved in supervising society's untouchables, have played a major role in the private provision of prison services.[22] The economic problem with unregulated, market-based punishment systems is relatively straight-forward, if harrowing. Private corrections enterprises, like all private entities, have few incentives to think about the *social* costs and benefits of punishment. At best, a private prison has powerful incentives to pay attention to how it provides a limited range of services for a specific group of inmates on behalf of a particular client in a specific facility over a limited period of time. The problem is that the primary customers for private prison services are governments, which in turn represent communities, not prisoners. Indeed, prisoners are not all that different from slaves in one important sense: though they are human beings, they are the mute objects of commercial transactions. A recent theoretical analysis of the economics of privatisation, with a special emphasis on prisons, has noted that private prisons have powerful incentives to cut the costs of prison services by reducing the quality of these services.[23]

The tunnel vision that the profit motive encourages, and that is vitally important to economic efficiency in the narrow sense, necessarily ignores all aspects of a problem that have no direct bearing on profitability. This is a classic example of a negative social cost where a third party, in this case prisoners, must bear the burden of transactions completed by others. As a practical matter a minimally regulated, competitive private punishment industry might provide cheap services, narrowly defined, though society must bear the brunt of problems that private jailers are allowed to ignore. However, if government forces private enterprises to incorporate the full cost of punishment into their profit calculations, there is no guarantee that even the most socially efficient prisons can be cheap prisons. For example, most prison inmates are poorly educated, with relatively few marketable skills in a skill- and technology-driven economy. Many are drug addicts, emotionally disturbed or mentally unbalanced, in part because of terrible personal histories of family abuse, sexual abuse, or the dysfunctional families and communities that DiIulio writes about. If governments demand that private prisons not only incarcerate these people, but also provide the therapy, counselling, education and training that they did not get from their families, schools, churches or communities, then they are asking prisons to perform important and costly social services. Indeed, the GAO study noted above suggests that private and public imprisonment may be equally expensive.

To the extent that a 'free' market in prisons can reduce the costs of prison services, local and state governments have compelling reasons for privatising punishment. An article in *The Wall Street Journal* on 12 July 1994 contains the following summary of the state of play in the market for private punishment:

> Americans' fear of crime is creating a new version of the old military-industrial complex, an infrastructure born amid political rhetoric and a shower of federal, state, and local dollars. As they did in the Eisenhower era, politicians are trying to outdo each other in standing up to the common enemy (crime); communities pin their economic hopes on jobs related to the [prison] buildup; and large and small businesses scramble for a slice of the bounty. These mutually reinforcing interests are forging a formidable new 'iron triangle' that arms makers, military services, and lawmakers formed three decades ago.

The article goes on to mention a number of cases where poor, rural communities are scrambling to be sites for the construction of new prisons.[24] Prisons have virtues that recommend them as prime vehicles for community economic development in a conservative, free-market age: they are labour-intensive, recession-proof enterprises that offer substantial job opportunities to unskilled and semi-skilled workers as prison guards and administrative personnel.[25]

Conclusion

Our brief survey of the economics of punishment in the US is inconclusive, which is neither a surprise nor a disappointment given the complexity of the subject. The deterrent effect of punishment is mixed. Increases in the certainty of punishment and the evolution of policing – particularly in the form of 'community policing' – are associated with reductions in crime, while increases in the length of prison terms do not have much of an impact. Of course, longer prison sentences along with more prison cells will certainly improve social welfare by detaining dangerous people. Yet, economic considerations suggest that governments should limit their use of prisons and long prison terms to warehousing violent people. The imprisonment of non-violent offenders, particularly non-violent drug offenders, makes little economic sense in light of the social costs of their crimes relative to the high costs of incarceration.

An economic approach to the problem of crime control requires governments and citizens to weigh the costs and benefits of punishment against those of other social policies. Though most of us tend to think about punishment in terms of justice and retribution, punishment is, to an economist, a device for improving social well-being by penalising those whose criminal behaviour undermines social order. Punishment derives its limited power to shape behaviour by threatening potential offenders with harm, thereby reducing the benefits of deviant behaviour relative to the rewards of obeying the law. It is obvious that no system of policing and punishment can, by itself, compel a population to conform to the social contract embodied in the criminal code. The fundamental institutions of character formation – schools, families, churches and, in modern times, the vast machinery of persuasion and propaganda called 'the media' – mould hearts and minds in ways that create consensus on the essential goodness of existing social arrangements, including the criminal law. Punishment is limited to those people who have not been properly indoctrinated, and who do not find the threat of force credible, or worse, those who simply do not care.

These considerations mean that the power of punishment largely depends on larger social conditions, including the ability of communities to mould their children into conforming citizens, and the material rewards of obeying the law. In recent years, the collapse of real wages for young, unskilled workers has blunted the power of punishment to control behaviour, particularly since the rewards from illegal activity, especially the drug trade, have risen relative to earnings from legal work. Though economically efficient punishment policy will certainly imprison violent people, a society that uses incarceration to lock away young men whose poverty gives them little material incentives to obey the law is pursuing a risky *economic* policy. Our analysis strongly suggests that governments intent on reducing non-violent crime must search for ways to raise the rewards from work, thereby giving young, unskilled men something to lose.

The only economic justification for relying heavily on punishment policy to control crime is that ameliorative social policy is impossible or ineffective, and the institutions of character formation are far too expensive to repair or are simply beyond repair. If the American model of free markets, racial fragmentation and limited social solidarity is in such a sad state that we must rely on threats to maintain social order, then the American model is likely to become an outstanding example of the social failure of market society.

Bibliographical review

There is an enormous technical literature on the economics of crime and punishment that is, unfortunately, almost completely obscure to all but the few who have been trained in 'economese'. Much of this literature uses formal economic analysis, including rather sophisticated mathematics and statistical methods, to explore the nature of crime and punishment from an economic point of view. Gary Becker's classic statement of the economic approach to crime and punishment, 'Crime and Punishment: An Economic Approach' (*Journal of Political Economy*, March/April 1968, pp. 169–217) is an excellent starting point for those who want to explore what traditional economic theory brings to the analysis of crime. James Q. Wilson's *Thinking About Crime* (New York: Basic Books, 1975) presents a more accessible economic analysis of crime and punishment. George Akerlof is a major economic theorist who, like Becker, tries to use formal economic theory to provide insight into pressing social problems. Unlike Becker, however, who uses a rather narrow theory of rational choice to construct an economic theory of crime and punishment, Akerlof integrates insights from sociology, psychology and anthropology into an economic approach to social life, including crime, that is both more useful and less reflexively right-wing than Becker's work. In particular, Akerlof's 'The Economic Consequences of Cognitive Dissonance' (*American Economic Review*, June 1982, pp. 307–19) and 'Gang Behavior, Law Enforcement, and Community Values', in Henry Aaron, Thomas E. Mann and Timothy Taylor (eds) *Values and Public Policy* (Washington D.C.: Brookings Institution, 1994, pp. 173–209) are good examples of a more nuanced approach to crime than Becker's Chicago view. Isaac Erlich provides a fine update and summary of recent, Becker-inspired writing on the economics of crime and punishment in 'Crime, Punishment, and the Market for Offenses' (*Journal of Economic Perspectives*, Winter 1996, pp. 43–68) while John Fender develops a more complete general equilibrium model of crime and punishment along Beckerian lines in 'A General Equilibrium Model of Crime and Punishment' (*Journal of Economic Behavior and Organization*, August 1999, pp. 437–53). Finally, readers can consult a slightly older but nonetheless useful summary of economic thinking on the deterrent effect of sanctions by consulting

Samuel Cameron's 'The Economics of Crime Deterrence: A Survey of Theory and Evidence' (*Kyklos: International Journal of Social Sciences*, September 1988, 41, 301–323).

Richard Freeman of Harvard University has done extensive work on the role of labour markets, and especially the declining wages and employment prospects for young men, in creating conditions for growing crime. Four articles by Freeman are particularly important: 'Crime and the Labor Market', in *Crime and Public Policy*, edited by James Q. Wilson, (San Francisco Institute for Contemporary Studies, 1983). 'The Relation of Criminal Activity to Black Youth Unemployment' (*Review of Black Political Economy*, Summer/Fall 1987, pp. 99–107); 'Crime and the Employment of Disadvantaged Youth', in *Urban Labor Markets and Job Opportunity* (Peterson, George and Wayne Vroman (eds), 1992; Washington D.C.: Urban Institute, pp. 201–237); and 'Why Do So Many Young American Men Commit Crimes?' (*Journal of Economic Perspectives*, Winter 1996, pp. 25–42). These articles explore different aspects of the role of poverty, inequality, unemployment, bad schools and poor neighbourhood conditions in promoting crime among young, poor men over an extended period of time. The relationship between the declining economic prospects of the young, and larger economic trends over the past two decades have been surveyed by Sheldon Danzinger and Peter Gottschalk in *America Unequal* (New York: Russell Sage Foundation and Cambridge, MA: Harvard University Press, 1995). Danziger and Gottschalk's survey provides the background material for both Freeman's more detailed study of the link between youth unemployment, low wages and crime, and William Julius Wilson's investigations of the social consequences of the disappearance of work in *The Truly Disadvantaged* (Chicago: University of Chicago Press, 1987), and *When Work Disappears* (New York: Knopf, 1996). Wilson's analysis of the forces creating and sustaining the urban underclass in the US was partly a response to the popular success of Charles Murray's claim in *Losing Ground* (New York: Basic Books, 1984) that liberal social welfare policy was largely responsible for the growth of a criminal underclass. Robert Moffit's survey article on the findings of empirical economists about the role of welfare policy in promoting family instability, teenage childbearing and welfare dependency, 'The Incentive Effects of the U.S. Welfare System' (*Journal of Economic Literature*, 30, March 1992, pp. 1–61) shows that Murray either badly overstates the effect of welfare on social breakdown or is wrong about every claim he makes. Michael Katz's *The Undeserving Poor: From the War on Poverty to the War on Welfare* (New York: Pantheon Books, 1989) is fine summary of American thinking about poverty and anti-poverty efforts from the 1940s to the 1980s that provides the reader with a better sense of how debates about unemployment, low wages, poverty and crime fit together. Richard Freeman and William Rodgers have done extensive statistical work that illustrates the link between crime, unemployment and low wages among young men in US metropolitan areas during the late and lamented 1990s boom in 'Area Economic Conditions and the Labor Market Outcomes of Young Men in the 1990's Expansion' (Working Paper w7073. National Bureau of Economic Research: Cambridge, MA, 1999).

Steven Levitt's 'The Effect of Prison Population Size on Crime Rates: Evidence From Prison Overcrowding Litigation' (1996) in *The Quarterly Journal of Economics* contains a good, concise summary of the economic costs and benefits of imprisonment. In addition, Anne Piehl and John DiIulio's article on the net social benefits of incarceration, 'Does Prison Pay?, Revisited' (*Brookings Review*, Spring 1995), presents a clear, direct analysis of the issues involved in the questions of optimal incarceration, without any 'economese'. *The Sourcebook of Criminal Justice Statistics* from the Bureau of Justice Statistics of the US Department of Justice is a convenient and complete source of data on incarceration, probation, parole and other aspects of punishment in local, state and federal jurisdictions. The Sentencing Project, a non-profit research group associated with the Landesmith Center, provides information and criticism of American criminal justice policies, especially sentencing policies, from a left-liberal perspective. Finally, *The American Prospect* has presented survey articles on the success and failures of community policing efforts in major American cities. Two particularly illuminating articles are 'Eyes on the Street: Community Policing in Chicago' by Jonathan Eig (November–December 1996) and 'The Mystery of the Falling Crime Rate' by David Anderson (May–June 1997).

David Shicor has recently published an extensive review of the literature on private prisons in *Punishment for Profit: Private Prisons/ Public Concerns* (Thousand Oaks, CA: Sage Publications, 1995). The *Wall Street Journal* is a valuable source of information about private prisons and the whole private punishment industry. Eric Schlosser's three-part series, 'The Prison-Industrial Complex', in the December 1998, January and February 1999 issues of *The Atlantic* is a useful journalistic account of the profound contradictions associated with private punishment. On the other hand, Professor Charles Logan of the University of Connecticut (www.fraserhtml.htm) presents a spirited defence of private prisons on the grounds that the legendary efficiency properties of competition and market incentives is a new method for dealing with the cost and other difficulties of incarceration policies that are not likely to be any worse than publicly run prisons. In fact, Logan makes the interesting point that the major problems with prisons have less to do with whether incarceration is publicly or private managed and more to do with the fact that prisons are problematic institutions.

The American Correctional Association Internet site is a treasure trove of information about private prisons and private punishment more generally. However, the *Journal* is a far better source for specific information about the profitability of private prison operations, though Internet sites for two major private prison operators, the Esmor Corporation and the Wackenhut Group, do from time to time contain interesting facts about actual private prison operations. Finally, Elliot Curie, a well-respected left-liberal sociologist who has written extensively on crime, has recently presented an accessible summary of research evaluating the impact of the American experiment with incarceration in *Crime and Punishment in America* (New York: Metropolitan Books, 1999). This slim volume is an excellent introduction to revised liberal thinking on crime and prisons that makes the left-liberal case against punitive punishment policy while fairly considering the conservative case.

Notes

1 Special thanks go to Lilian Quah for her brilliant and timely research assistance. Lilian collected data, read endless drafts and helped me turn this paper into a decent piece of work.

2 Lawrence Friedman, *Crime and Punishment in American History*, p. 14.

3 The economic logic behind the idea of deterrence, which was first fully developed by Nobel laureate Gary Becker of the University of Chicago, is quite simple. According to the economic theory of crime and deterrence, criminal acts are simply the result of choices made by self-interested people seeking to maximise the gain or satisfaction they derive from their actions. Just as each of us chooses a product, job, or pursues some other course of action when the benefits from that action exceed the associated costs, so too does a criminal choose to break the law in one area as against another, or maybe even to refrain from criminal acts altogether, depending on the balance of costs and benefits. In one sense, the only difference between the criminal and the law-abiding citizen is that criminals are more willing to violate social taboos and laws if the gain from so doing exceeds the costs, perhaps because criminals come from families or communities that do not instil sufficient respect for social norms and the law (as some conservative analysts insist) or for some other reason. Nonetheless, crimes are

committed when the gain from crime exceeds the associated costs of criminal actions and vice versa.

4   A second function of pollution taxes and charges is to encourage polluting firms to search for new, less environmentally damaging ways of producing goods and services. The economic theory behind this approach is perfectly sound: governments want to make polluting technologies more costly, thereby giving firms incentives to switch to alternate technologies that yield lower environmental costs. It is perfectly clear that governments do not want punishment policy to encourage technological innovation in criminal activity though, regrettably, the sad history of anti-narcotics policy in the United States shows that harsh punishments may give drug dealers an incentive to increase the technical sophistication of their operations.

5   Community policing efforts, which try to build strong bonds of trust, respect and mutual support between the police and residents in particular neighbourhoods, are an interesting attempt to build 'social capital' as part of an overall crime control policy. From an economic perspective, community policing attempts to deal with problems of imperfect information, particularly the problems of detecting criminal activity and monitoring the behaviour of potential offenders, especially young men, by enlisting the co-operation of neighbourhood residents in reporting criminal activity and testifying in criminal trials. These efforts lead to an increase in the certainty of punishment by creating networks where trust between the police and neighbours extend the capacities of the community to monitor behaviour. The increased surveillance capacity of the community requires local governments to invest in a number of community services as well as restructure systems for the provision of public services in order to improve a community's incentives to co-operate with the police. Jonathan Eig's report on community policing efforts in Chicago in the December 1996 issue of *The American Prospect* shows the considerable difficulties involved in creating this form of social capital.

6   Nonetheless, Erlich gives good reasons to believe that the claim that the certainty of punishment has a larger effect on crime than the severity of incarceration is problematic, in part because of the complexity of the statistical analyses necessary for disentangling the effects of the likelihood of punishment on the incentives to commit crime from the clear negative effect of incapacitation on crime.

7   One interesting thing to note about the relative effects of deterrence and incapacitation is that policies focusing on particular crimes are less effective than policies that try to reduce crime in general. Economist Steven Levitt (1996) has shown that the attempt to deter particular categories of crime causes offenders to shift their activity into other areas of illegal activity, strongly suggesting that different types of crime are 'substitutes' for each other. Incarceration and general increases in deterrence have greater effects on crime than targeted deterrence; incapacitation removes offenders who commit a wide array of crimes, whereas general deterrence reduces the net benefits from criminal activity across the board. Levitt

(1998) emphasises the way that arrest rates for particular crimes lead offenders to shift from one set of criminal activities to others with lower arrest rates.

8 This estimate of the costs that a typical criminal imposes on the public includes the various medical costs, lost wages, higher insurance costs and greater security expenditures that crime victims must bear as a result of victimisation. These figures have been converted from 1995 dollars to 2000 dollars using the GNP deflator from the 2002 Economic Report of the President of the United States.

9 Total spending by individuals and businesses on security has been estimated to exceed $65 billion in 1994 ($72.2 billion in 2000 dollars). This figure is to be found in *The Real War on Crime: The Report of the National Criminal Justice Commission*, edited by Steven R. Donziger (Harper/Perennial, 1996), p. 54.

10 Table 6.0007 of the 2001 edition of the *Sourcebook of Criminal Justice Statistics* (www.albany.edu/sourcebook/1995/pdf/t60007.pdf).

11 If the average felon serves a sentence of 51 months, or 4.25 years, then this must mean that each year 1/ 4.25 or 23.53 per cent of felons are released each year.

12 Note that if the evolution of the prison population over time is represented by the simple dynamic system $Z_{t+1} = (1 - \delta) Z_t + a_t$, where Z is the size of the prison population, $0 < \delta < 1$ is the exit rate, and $a > 0$ is the number of new inmates admitted to the system, then the 'steady state' or long-term level of the prison population Z^* is $Z^* = \dfrac{a}{\delta}$, which implies that $\dfrac{\Delta Z^*}{Z^*} = -\dfrac{\Delta \delta}{\delta}$ i.e. that the percentage rise in the long-term prison population is minus the percentage decline in the prison exit rate δ (assuming that $a_t = a$, constant for all values of t).

13 The rate of return on investment in this case is simply the internal rate of return for this project. If n_t is the net social benefit at time t from housing an additional felon for the year (after accounting for all direct operating costs and maintenance charges), x is the price of a new prison cell, and T is the expected lifetime of a prison cell, then the internal rate of return λ is the largest positive root of the equation

$$\sum_{t=0}^{T} \frac{2n_t}{(1+\lambda)^t} - x = 0$$

if we assume that there are two felons per cell. Using Levitt's figures, $n_t = \$16,659$ and $x = \$50,000$ for all time t, which lead to a rate of different values of the rate of return (λ) for various values of T. Note that if we assume that a prison cell is used for 50 years then the internal rate of return is $\lambda = 1.997$ or 199.7%.

T	1	3	5	10	20	30	50
λ	0.997	1.917	1.989	1.997	1.997	1.997	1.997

Of course, an increase in the number of prisoners per cell will, all other things equal, increase the rate of return on new prison construction. However, the prospect of lawsuits and regulations against prison overcrowding reduce incentives to increase the average number of occupants in a prison cell.

14 Shicor (1996) notes that the cost of new prisons cells depends on the type of prison facility under consideration. Low-security units cost as little as $40,000 per cell (in 1988 dollars) whereas high-security units could cost in excess of $110,000 per cell. Yet if the average prison cell cost as much as $150,000 and was in use for 30 years, the social rate of return would still be 25 per cent. Since the rate of return on the Dow Jones index of the 30 premier common stocks is a little over 10 per cent historically, our calculations suggest that prison building – even of high-security units – is very lucrative in economic terms.

15 Elliot Curie's excellent summary of crime and punishment in America (in a volume of the same name) points out that incarceration has been shown to raise the recidivism rates of offenders, especially young offenders, thereby greatly reducing the social benefits of punishment. Indeed, Currie notes that the criminogenic effects of incarceration are a well-known criminological fact that seems to escape the notice of politicians and the public. See Currie (1998) for an excellent discussion of all matters related to problem of incarceration in the United States.

16 In testimony before the then newly elected conservative majority in the US House of Representatives on 20 January 1995 (entitled 'Crime in America: Three Ways to Prevent It') Professor DiIulio presented a blunt summary of his views on the origins of crime, which in turn shape his recommendations for the use of jails and prisons to control crime:

> Most predatory street criminals – people who murder, assault, rape, rob, burglarise, and deal deadly drugs – are very bad boys from very bad homes in very poor neighborhoods, that is, places where child abuse and neglect, substance abuse, and crime itself are common. The single most comprehensive and widely cited review of the scientific literatures on criminal behavior concludes that we must 'rivet our attention on the earliest stages of the life cycle' for 'after all is said and done, the most serious offenders are boys who begin their careers at an early age.'

[This latter quote is drawn from Wilson and Herrnstein's *Crime and Human Nature*, where the Herrnstein in question is none other than the co-author, with Charles Murray, of *The Bell Curve*.]

After quoting a National Academy of Sciences report finding that children who come of age in poor, inner-city neighbourhoods are harmed by the lack of good role models and thereby become prone to commit crime themselves, Professor DiIulio remarked:

That is a polite and politic way of stating that many of the young black inner city males who end up committing serious crimes, going to prison, or being buried in the graveyard before their time, start life born out-of-wedlock to single-parent homes where they are severely abused and neglected, and in neighborhoods where many of the adults with whom they have contact are themselves deviant, delinquent, or criminal.

17 A brief yet intriguing statement of these themes can be found in 'Supporting Black Churches: Faith, Outreach and the Inner-City Poor' in *The Brookings Review*, Spring 1999.

18 A few facts about the wages and prospects of young workers in America. Sheldon Danzinger of the University of Wisconsin and Peter Gottschalk of Boston College, in their comprehensive summary of the causes of income inequality in the United States since 1973, *America Unequal*, have shown that the inflation adjusted wages of young high-school graduates in 1992 were 18 per cent lower than they were in 1963. Further, the gap between the wages of college trained workers and those without college degrees has exploded since the mid-1970s. First, the inflation-adjusted wages of male college-trained workers have risen by 8 per cent while those for male high-school graduates (across the age spectrum) have fallen by 40 per cent since 1973. This latter result follows directly from the simple law of supply and demand: the wages of the college-trained rose because the demand for their services exceeded their numbers; just the opposite happened to less well-educated workers. Second, the wage premium associated with a college degree, that is, the percentage difference between the wages of young college-trained workers and young high-school graduates, has risen from 23 per cent in 1979 to 43 per cent in 1989. Finally, surveys of labour force participation by young men have consistently shown that a lower fraction of young men are actually in the labour market now than in the 1960s and 1970s. This is perfectly consistent with what economists know about people's work behaviour: the drastic decline in wages for young workers will lead many of them to seek out alternatives to working in the low-wage sector of the economy, including crime. Freeman and Rodgers (1999) have shown that the boom of the 1990s has been associated with lower crime rates in those parts of the economy that have experienced low rates of youth unemployment and substantial real wage growth. However, those regions that did not benefit from the 1990s boom experienced high crime rates and high incarceration rates.

19 Danzinger and Gottschalk in *America Unequal* show that the United States has a high degree of income mobility relative to other nations; that is, that workers are able to move up the income ladder in the US more quickly than elsewhere. Nonetheless, the vast increase in income inequality with little change in mobility in the past 20 years implies that class mobility is likely to be lower for the foreseeable future. The authors' calculations show that 67

per cent of those who are in the lowest income quintile in any given year are still in the lowest quintile in the next year. If a larger fraction of the population falls into the lowest quintile as a result of unemployment or a drastic decline in the wages of unskilled workers, then a greater fraction of the population will find itself locked into the lower classes even if the probability of any particular person escaping poverty remains unchanged. See Danzinger and Gottschalk (1995), pp. 120–123.

20 *Cost Effectiveness Comparisons of Private vs. Public Prisons in Louisiana: A Comprehensive Analysis of Allen, Avoyelles, and Winn Correctional Centers: PHASE I,* by William G. Archambeault and Donald R. Deis, Jr. of Louisiana State University to the Louisiana Legislature, December 1996.

21 *Private and Public Prisons: Studies Comparing Operational Costs and/or Quality of Service* (Letter Report, 8/16/96 to Representative William McCollum, Chairman Subcommittee on Crime, House Committee on the Judiciary, GAO/GGD-96-158).

22 John DiIulio has recounted the sorry history of private incarceration in the US in his article 'What's Wrong With Private Prisons' in the conservative policy journal *Public Interest.* An extended quote from the article will serve to capture the flavour of his remarks:

> For much of the nineteenth century and as late as the 1960's, prisons and jails in many parts of the United States were privately owned and operated. In the current debate over private-sector involvement in corrections, these precedents have not been duly acknowledged. In Texas, California, Michigan, Louisiana, Oklahoma, and many other states, all or part of the penal system has at one time or another been administered privately. The pre-1980 record of private-sector involvement in corrections in unrelievedly bleak.

23 The theoretical analysis referred to in the text is a brilliant, but rather technical, piece of economic analysis by Oliver Hart, Andrei Shleifer and Robert Vishny, three gifted economic theorists. The paper, 'The Proper Scope of Government: Theory and an Application to Prisons', is in the November 1997 edition of *The Quarterly Journal of Economics.*

24 One especially revealing and poignant set of reports on the contradictions involved in the use of private prisons in New York and California by Eric Schlosser were published in *The Atlantic* in a three-part series in December 1998 and January and February 1999.

25 Schlosser's reports in *The Atlantic* series provide vivid accounts of how depressed regional economies in rural New York and California have come to rely on prisons as engines of economic growth, thereby tying the well-being of an economically marginal white rural underclass to the imprisonment of a largely black and Latino urban underclass. The bitter racial implications of these practices in modern America are rich indeed.

Chapter 5

States of insecurity: punishment, populism and contemporary political culture

Richard Sparks

In many Western societies today, but perhaps most flagrantly in the United States and United Kingdom, questions of crime and punishment are rarely (perhaps never) absent from public discourse. For contemporary politicians, punishment seemingly provides a standing, and often irresistible, temptation – to promise that more will urgently be done, to demonstrate strength of conviction and will, to emote in ways that are presumed to chime with the passions of an angry and anxious electorate.

It is no doubt possible both to overstate and to oversimplify this relation. The place of penal politics in the public life of nation-states varies in intensity and texture from time to time and place to place. It comes in flurries as major stories break and scandals and *causes célèbres* are played out. It responds, as sociologists have long argued, to a range of surrounding conditions from the popularity of incumbent governments, to the condition of the national and international economy, to the distractions of other urgent public issues. One need not argue, therefore, that punishment is a constant, or fixed, or singular thing or theme in order to suggest that it is an aspect of contemporary social existence that has latterly become markedly politicised and that this has a range of important implications that warrant the most careful and sceptical scrutiny.

When we engage the resources of social and political theory to think about a topic like the changing character and scale of the penal realm, we embark on a project that is both explanatory and diagnostic or interpretive. We instantly encounter a variety of tricky empirical questions. What range of tasks are now undertaken in the name of punishment and what justifications are provided for them? How has the range of those activities shifted, extended or diversified and to what effect? Who (if any particular actors can be identified) willed this, and in response to what pressures or demands? Why, say, has the prison population in the United Kingdom risen steeply (but jaggedly, not smoothly) in the last ten years while those of some of its near neighbours (such as Ireland) have remained essentially stable? Are such rises – or more rarely falls – in the population under sentence basically driven by changes in workload (more crimes, more prosecutions) or do we need to cast a wider net, one that captures shifts in culture or disposition or other wider dimensions of social relations?

But the moment we admit the latter possibility we begin to play a rather different game for different stakes. We open a distinctly disconcerting vista crowded with more perplexing questions. What if the stated objectives of a penal system are not the only aims that animate its practices? What if the desire to reduce crime or enhance safety is clouded by class antagonism or ethnic hostility? What then if the scale of punishment is produced by sectional interests or driven by the intensification of fears that have an imaginary or symbolic component? Wouldn't this require that we not only explain what goes on (in the sense of reporting, cataloguing and quantifying) but also that we interrogate our current ways of punishing for clues about the way we live now and about how differently we might hope or fear to live in future? How then do penal practices intersect with other spheres of the culture, politics or economic structures of the social formations in which they arise? Is it fanciful to suggest that we can interpret some wider features of our contemporary social and political predicaments through the prism of the penal?

These questions are not in essence new. Commentators as diverse as Fyodor Dostoyevsky and Winston Churchill have at different times come quite separately to the conclusion that the condition of a society's penal institutions provides a measure of its magnanimity or meanness, its self-assurance or anxiety – its 'mood and temper', as Winston Churchill put it. At least since the political and intellectual revolutions of the later eighteenth century, and with them the idea of subjecting human institutions to disciplined study for the purposes of their improvement, the urge to examine and to compare penal systems and institutions has been evident. This was at the basis of John Howard's arduous journeys through the prisons of Britain and Europe in the 1770s. It animated the writings-home from the United States of French intellectuals like La Rochefoucauld-Liancourt in the 1790s and Beaumont and de Tocqueville in the 1830s. In the fervent excitement of revolutionary

France, Mirabeau articulated the dream of 'a special kind of prison, for which humanity need not blush'. This is not an historical essay, and many of the visions and revisions of the penal realm that have come and gone since the eighteenth century already have their historians. Suffice to note that reactionaries, revolutionists and reformers have all at some point sensed a connection between the ways in which their societies punished and the moral or political character and constitution of the times. In contemplating the penal they have glimpsed – sometimes with satisfaction, sometimes with shame and dismay – the fugitive reflections of their own faces. What do we see now when we look into that magic mirror? Can we bear the sight with equanimity?

Yet even if many of the questions retain a degree of constancy, times and contexts change, sometimes abruptly and disruptively. Moreover, the sense of living through a period of wrenching social upheaval – when formerly accepted traditions, practices, relationships and assumptions are placed in question – itself often provokes doubts and anxieties that connect in a fairly direct fashion to the problem of punishment. At such times, as the sociologist Robert Nisbet once eloquently put it: 'fears run over the landscape like masterless dogs … it is then that men's (sic) minds turn to the problem of authority'. One effect of such conditions is to engender doubt as to the capacity of states to deliver on those historic promises of order and social pacification on which their claims to legitimacy have traditionally depended. On one hand we might expect to see major technical and organisational innovations, as agencies of social control struggle to identify new means of regulating behaviour and governing everyday existence. But at the same time we may see a more impassioned politics of order as lobbies and interest groups contend for more vigorous and visible responses to their insecurities and sense of precariousness and as governments seek to provide overt demonstrations of strength, power and command. In other words, although many aspects of the practical conduct of affairs, including the governance of crime and its associated risks to property and safety, may lie far outside the ambit of the penal system (perhaps indeed increasingly so), the state may nevertheless experience an insuperable pressure to, in Jonathan Simon's telling phrase, 'govern through crime'.

In the remainder of this chapter I will argue that over the last 20 to 30 years the penal politics of many Western societies (though by no means all, or at least not in equal degree) have indeed exhibited many of the tensions just outlined. The economic and cultural dynamism of the United States and United Kingdom in particular over this period has produced multiple effects. The high-energy, mobile, wired world of 'turbo-capitalism' is a frequently exhilarating but by no means always comfortable one to inhabit. Our experience of living in this world generates many paradoxes. For many of us it delivers unprecedented levels of affluence and apparent possibilities for self-realisation through consumption and the conscious cultivation of 'lifestyle'. For others it generates new patterns of exclusion and marginality; and for the many who live close to the cusp between prosperity and precariousness, the fear of falling is hard to dispel for long.

The endless multiplication of media of communication produces in some ways far greater mutual awareness (the consciousness of living among a multitude of diverse lives and fortunes) but this by no means signals a general enhancement of the sense of amity or intimacy across social boundaries. Indeed, what comes at us through our multi-channel, multi-media encounters is just as likely to be a series of disconcerting reminders of, as the great anthropologist and anatomist of cultural responses to risk Mary Douglas puts it, 'danger on the borders'. Yet in an ever-more globally interconnected world, the sense of just exactly where our borders lie and how they can feasibly be defended and by whom is itself increasingly unclear. One consequence can be an anxious re-focusing on our *personal* boundaries – on the safety and integrity of our bodies and possessions and those of our intimates, on the inviolability of the home, street and neighbourhood against incursion from others whom we mistrust and who seem to carry with them the dangers and contagions of an endemically uncertain world. Another effect may be a renewed concern over our leaky and dubious political and territorial borders. Nation-states can look decidedly defensive and beleaguered in the face of historical shifts that escape their planning and control. Moreover, they face new problems. The drastic arrival of a 'war on terrorism' is one obvious ratchet to the insecurities of the times. Similarly, the recent intensification of controversies over mass migration and asylum-seeking further menaces the credibility of states' claims to sovereign potency. Small wonder then that Nisbet's 'problem of authority' remains a besetting one for us.

Punishment has perhaps always held its fascinations and tempta-tions. The lure of being part of an ecstatic crowd at an execution, of having our enemies at our mercy, proffers a seductive sense of potency. Demagogues and dictators have long understood the heady thrill of circuses, lynchings and show-trials. What we are grasping after here, though, is the particular emotional economy of punishment in the culture and politics of our own time – the affluent, agitated, self-absorbed world of late-modernity. We, for the most part, eschew the obvious barbarities that we associate with the archaic past. As modern people we expect effectiveness, accountability and, usually, some degree of parsimony from the relevant authorities, and not just the grim satisfactions of revenge. Yet neither have these themes been banished from the contemporary scene, and in some respects they can be argued to have made something of a comeback. The proposition that we live now in a late modern world does not imply that everything has simply become 'even more modern' if by 'modern' we mean what the leading figures of an earlier generation tended to mean – humane, pragmatic, rational, undemonstrative. Rather, I will argue that the best accounts we have of the place of punishment in late modernity identify some highly paradoxical developments. In some respects punishment shows signs of becoming *hyper-modern* (calculated, instrumental and relatively untroubled by strictly moral considerations) while in others it reaches back to *pre-modern* themes and exemplars for its contemporary appeal. In order to understand what Pat O'Malley has styled this 'volatile and contradictory' situation, we need to elaborate a bit further some of the connections I have begun to sketch here.

The often-fevered penal politics of the last quarter-century become more intelligible, I suggest, when understood in light of what Giddens calls the 'generalized risk climate' of late modernity. In this environment responsible authorities, principally in this case the crime-control agencies of nation-states, face enormous pressures to be seen to do something to manage and reduce risk. Risk, therefore, is not morally neutral or emotionally empty. It brings with it urgent and controversial questions about who provides security and who is to blame when it is compromised. The 'game-space' of penal politics is thus potentially very crowded. There are many contenders for which risks are gravest or most acute; for which perpetrators are most dangerous or most blameworthy; for which control strategies are most effective or most gratifying. This noisy and contentious arena tends, as some public-policy scholars say, to 'raise the bar' of public expectations. The scene is set, we might think, for political drama in which there are gestures as well as strategies, postures as well as policies, passions as well as practicalities.

From modernist to late-modern crime control

David Garland has argued that we are today living out the consequences of a 'crisis of penal modernism'. For much of the twentieth century, especially in the period of social reconstruction in the decades following the Second World War, the dominant tenor of much social science and public policy was to bring the penal system within the ambit of the welfare state. What Garland has elsewhere called the 'penal-welfare complex' sought to align the aims of penal (or 'correctional') institutions and practices with those of other state agencies with which their work intersected, such as education, social work and mental health. It is admittedly a simplification but not in essence a mistake to argue that an ambition that took root in the nineteenth century reached a certain mature flourishing in the mid-twentieth, namely to tame the more unruly passions that punishment has historically invoked and to subject it to the demands of rational administration. The vocational principles to which many public servants in the penal system adhered were deeply shaped by the 'psy-disciplines' – developmental and abnormal psychology and psychiatry. Their characteristic aims had a practical and often an expressly clinical tone – to treat abnormalities of mind and character and defects of behaviour, to correct deficits of upbringing and education, to train for useful work, to 'resettle' and to supervise.

Elements of this ambitious undertaking remain visible today. It has not simply ceased. On occasion, particularly for special groups such as children, addicts or the flagrantly mentally ill, one sees clear reassertions of the rehabilitative programme. The concerns that punishment be deployed in ways that are useful and constructive, or that its more alarming potentialities be moderated by considerations of decency and regard for human rights, continue to be important aspects of the contemporary field. For this reason 'the state' rarely speaks with a single voice and high public officials often pick an uneasy path between competing principles. Yet, at least in the United Kingdom and United States, it is difficult to argue that the conception of punishment as answering to clinical need or welfare assistance is the dominant one now. Often, the welfarist 'voice' rings more like an echo from a world we have lost. In terms of its place in our public culture, punishment today has largely escaped the modernist attempt at domestication. The view of crime that we receive from electoral platforms or through the unending buzz of electronic media is not in general that of a marginal problem, amenable to specialised intervention. Neither is our view of offenders primarily that of needy clients. To the extent that these constructions of the criminal question persist at all they jostle against, and frequently seem overwhelmed by, a different current that is harder, more alarmist, more demotic.

No passably alert observer of the recent British or American political scene, and certainly no student of penal politics, can fail to note these sightings. What is striking is how focal the problem of punishment has latterly become to our societal conversation about order, security and the direction of social change – the things that the Brazilian political theorist

R.M. Unger calls 'the basic terms of social existence'. Issues of crime and punishment have assumed a higher, more insistent and more fevered public profile. At different moments the spotlight has hesitated upon sentencing controversies, sex crime and other varieties of persistent and/or dangerous offending, drugs, prison security and regimes, policing, public order, youth crime and latterly, in Britain at least, an inchoate category known as 'antisocial behaviour'. Each of these and a variety of other issues has enjoyed its hour upon the stage of media attention and political enterprise, and at least some of them have left lasting marks in legislation and criminal justice practice.

Moreover, it is in the nature of contemporary politics, given the global reach of mass media and the extent of their infiltration of everyday life, that these questions come at us in the form of discrete stories, episodes, scandals and *causes célèbres* (and I will say more about the role of the media shortly). There is a certain pattern in the frequency and regularity with which are exposed to such stories and the ways in which they speak to our fears and feelings. These days when we want to suggest that an issue is politically significant we often say that it is 'sensitive' or 'emotive'. In so saying we seem to imply that whatever is political (in the sense that it engenders discourse, highlights contention or provides a motivation for collective action) is so in virtue of its capacity to pluck the nerve of our anxieties, to destabilise our confidence in the reliability or orderliness of things, or to menace our faith in the future.

In this process, as Garland and I have argued in a mildly controversial essay, 'the rules of political speech' have changed. It has become permissible, even at times seemingly obligatory, for governments and candidates for public office to invoke a sense of emergency. For example, the commonplace use of a militaristic metaphor – the 'war on crime' – sanctions measures that would have appeared quite excessive to the sensibilities of many influential people a generation earlier. This, we argue, is indicative of a 'reactionary thematisation of late modernity'. By this we mean that many of the ideas about government and politics that have predominated since the late 1970s, especially those associated with leaders such as Reagan and Thatcher and their successors, consciously distanced themselves from the gradualist, meliorist and socially inclusionary priorities of welfarist social policy. Where once the post-war political 'settlement' had envisaged a future founded on a mixed economy, the moderation of inequalities through redistributive taxation and a preoccupation with social planning and intervention, the Reagan–Thatcher 'restoration' offered instead a headier mix of free-market economics, anti-welfare social policy and cultural conservatism. Late modernity brought with it new freedoms, new levels of consumption and new possibilities for individual choice. But it also brought in its wake new disorders and dislocations – above all, new levels of crime and insecurity. The political reaction of the 1980s and 1990s has shaped the public perception of these troubling issues, persuading us to think of them as problems of control rather than welfare; as the outcome of misguided welfare programmes; as a result of an amoral permissiveness and lax family discipline encouraged by liberal elites who were sheltered from the worst consequences; as the irresponsible behaviour of a dangerous and undeserving underclass – people who abused the new freedoms and made life impossible for the rest of us.

The new political dispensation claimed to be better able, as Giddens puts it, to 'ride the juggernaut' of social change and economic volatility by stripping down the role of the state to its essentials, namely superintending the operation of a dynamic free market and restoring, in Margaret Thatcher's words, 'freedom under law'. There was thus no contradiction between a 'minimal' state and one that was to be more vigorous and effective in pursuit of its proper tasks, including a renewed and more robust emphasis on crime control. This novel 'state regime' with its potent confluence of neo-liberalism in economic affairs and its techniques of governing and neo-conservatism in social and cultural matters thus came to dominance by representing the accumulation of problems of the Keynesian welfare state as a twin crisis of 'ungovernability' and uncompetitiveness. This in part explains why governments on both sides of the Atlantic since the 1970s have staked much of their claim to legitimacy on tough-mindedness in crime control.

Risk and political culture

In the responses of criminologists and other social observers to the stew of developments sketched above, one term seems to recur with increasing insistence and frequency (and hence, arguably, with less and less dependability as to the consistency and precision of its uses): 'risk'. In our attempts to grasp the peculiar features of the present, whether on the levels of states' actions in choosing to 'govern through crime'; or that of private corporations selling 'security'; or of local criminal justice agencies engaging in 'partnerships' to audit and manage losses and threats to individuals, households and businesses; or indeed of people's everyday practices and decisions about housing, consumption and leisure, this protean and seemingly limitlessly adaptable notion presses itself on our attention. Risk has become a central idea and crime one of its emblematic forms.

The potted political history sketched so briefly and inadequately above suggests that crime-risk has become pivotal to the legitimation claims of governments. But this emphatically does not mean that governments are the sole, or even in practical terms the principal, actors in risk management. In many respects the actual conduct of crime control has seeped away from the nation-state to be taken up by a baffling constellation of local authorities, non-governmental agencies, corporate interests and private initiatives. Whereas in the welfare era of the post-war reconstruction, prime responsibility for intervention in crime control seemed to most people to lie decisively with groups of professionals who were clearly in the direct employ of the state (police officers, social workers, clinicians, prison governors), these practitioners now share that domain with a more diverse array of consultants, contractors, entrepreneurs and volunteers. Moreover, we as citizens and consumers (of housing, cars, insurance, schooling, tourism and so on) have also come to regard a certain wary preoccupation with the security of our own persons and property as being entirely normal (and to regard unconcern with these matters as feckless and negligent). The management of danger no longer has – if indeed in practical terms it ever had – one single source or centre. Governance has become, to borrow from recent work by Johnstone and Shearing, 'nodal'. Yet, and paradoxically, it has become if anything more rhetorically central, and more politically explosive, for governments in the process. How can this paradox be unravelled?

In the last 20 years or so risk has moved from the periphery to the core of criminological theorising and crime-control practice. Until relatively recently it held a relatively specialised and limited, though respectable, place somewhere on the margins of criminological research and policy discussion. For those who explicitly used the term at all, it arose in the context of certain determinate and particular questions – could early intervention reduce the chances of 'at-risk' youth embarking on criminal careers?; was the extended incarceration of some individuals on grounds of 'dangerousness' justified?; were parole boards good enough at predicting future behaviour?; did deterrence have any measurable bearing on crime rates?

In some cases of its use, the increasing centrality of 'risk' just means in essence that such discussions have become more intensive and more technically sophisticated. In that process, long-standing professional concerns with judgements about ways of anticipating and forestalling future harms (concerns that have their origin in nineteenth-century preoccupations with 'moral statistics' and twentieth-century innovations in preventive detention, among other places) have evolved and extended to incorporate new methods, statistical models and the availability of previously unimagined computational power.

It is important to note that in criminal justice as in other domains (industrial safety, pollution and environmental policy, food hygiene, fire prevention, medicines management – this list could go on, and on) attention to risk assessment and risk management does not arise arbitrarily. The ascendancy of risk-based reasoning derives in large measure from the fact that probabilistic models based on large data samples do provide more efficient and pragmatic guides to intervention in many spheres of activity than previous methods did. Just as we no longer expect the licensing of, for example, new pharmaceuticals to proceed without rigorous testing, numerous contemporary fields of criminological enquiry (such as, classically, criminal careers research and attempts to scale the probability of reconviction after release from prison but also, especially latterly, attempts to estimate the risks of victimisation experienced by given categories of people or those living in particular localities) are increasingly unimaginable without reference to such methods.

Yet, this is very far from being the whole story. On the one hand, the fact that risk management in crime control bears such close technical similarity to other fields and practices of governance poses the question of how far specifically criminological varieties of expertise can remain immune from colonisation by new cadres of versatile technician-managers for whom crime is just one species of manipulable risk among others. In this respect the stage is set for various as yet unresolved struggles for predominance between risk-based reasoning and other resources of knowledge, influence and prestige (for example, between judicial wisdom and actuarial prediction in sentencing; between clinical judgement and algorithmic scaling in parole decisions; and between 'personalist' social-work values and 'craft' skills versus numericised risk inventories in probation). In other words, 'risk' may be seen, as Mark Brown and John Pratt suggest, as a 'cognitive habit' whose origins lie outside the criminological field as such but which gradually infiltrates its every nook and cranny. The expression 'actuarial justice' famously coined by Feeley and Simon in their account of rise of the 'new penology' nicely and deliberately expresses some of the internal tensions that result.

On the other hand, the very fact that every one of the fields that 'actuarial' thinking enters is already occupied by existing practitioners and their associated specialist discourses, conversely suggests that we should not expect 'risk' always to emerge pristine and unadulterated from the encounter. Rather we should expect to see new hybrid or compromise formations ('effort-bargains' as they are sometimes called) between 'actuarial' reasoning properly so-called and other priorities and commitments. In this respect 'risk' may be the paradigm case of rational decision-making or resource-allocation *de nos jours* but it is remarkable how commonly actual practices depart from their prototypical models.

Moreover, and of more pressing concern for us here, the term 'risk' cannot feasibly be restricted only to what happens in specialist, technical arenas (even if one of its chief properties is precisely that of bringing into being many new arenas of quasi-technical intervention). Rather risk 'seeps out' from such protected spaces to become part of the very idiom of our contemporary moral and political conversations. Increasingly, and undoubtedly at much cost in terms of precision as to when it is or is not being used appositely, risk is part of the common currency of cultural exchange (creeping into the language of everything from weather forecasting to the control of bovine diseases). For this reason Mary Douglas wonders at the 'innocence' of those professional risk analysts who evince surprise when the increasing sophistication of their collective wisdom fails to put an end to public controversy over nuclear power, biotechnology or indeed crime, policing and public safety. Quite the reverse: when we speak now of risk in relation to crime we are plumb in the middle of our topic in this essay, namely how theory and research speak to the moral aspects of the governance of our contemporary insecurities. A risk, Douglas observes, is not a 'thing' but a way of thinking – not just the probability of an event 'but also the probable magnitude of its outcome, and everything depends on the value that is set on the outcome'. Douglas's 'cultural theory of risk' thus brings into special focus the way in which the identification of particular sources of threat and danger (and by extension whom we blame for them) refracts a given community's dispositions towards order and authority. This provides a clue as to why amidst the proliferation of technical means of risk assessment in the administrative culture of modern societies the social discourse of crime and punishment still, as Douglas eloquently puts it, 'falls into antique mode' and refuses to shed 'its ancient moral freight'. Douglas here nails a point that in some degree clarifies a number of the diverse developments already noted in this chapter. Crime and punishment have consequences both for the very texture of personal life and for some embedded features of social organisation. And they are Janus-faced phenomena – they have both novel and archaic dimensions. Once they have been named and identified, risks demand responses from the appropriate bodies even though it may exceed their powers substantially to control, let alone to abolish them. Thus for commentators such as Giddens, thinking about danger *in terms of risk* is a pervasive feature of contemporary life.

In this respect the term 'risk' increasingly does not just denote what happens within specialised expert systems designed to anticipate and manage harm or loss (or the tendency for the familiar institutions of criminal justice to be reconfigured into risk-managing agencies of this kind). Rather it also concerns the often fevered politics that swirl around questions of risk and the battles that determine which risks are selected for particular attention, which categories of person and which places come to be regarded as bearers or containers of intolerable levels of risk, and so on. At the same time the problem of risk is critical to the restructuring of the criminal justice state that we have sketched above. It does appear that in certain senses the state has latterly tended to lose some of its former centrality and authority and that power leeches out and passes to other actors. Yet in other respects this very process engenders a refocusing on certain 'core' activities and a more heated politics of crime and punishment, precisely because the state's capacity to deliver 'security' is so much in question. To this extent there is a narrowing of the grounds on which the state can claim legitimacy and every failure of propriety or competence in risk management is potentially a scandal. Two primary consequences result. First, risk is never the dry, technocratic matter that it initially appears. Instead each system of risk management creates as its counterpart a *blaming* system. Second, the 'minimal' state of neo-liberalism – the state which is, as we shall shortly see, in some degree 'hollowed out' by globalisation – is also, in Loïc Wacquant's term, a *penal* state in ways that are often more intense and more politically central than was the case for its predecessor 'state regimes' of the post-war period.

The media and penal populism

In her important book *Making Crime Pay*, Katherine Beckett begins appropriately with a dramaturgical metaphor, albeit a familiar and somewhat overworked one: 'Crime and punishment sit center stage in the theater of American political discourse.' The argument runs roughly as follows. There is an apparently remorseless tendency for crime and punishment to assume an ever more central position in electoral campaigns and domestic policy agendas, and for soundings of public opinion to provide ostensible endorsement for punitive strategies, including the death penalty and other tokens of severity along with their similarly well known slogans and sound-bites. As is also well known, the period in question has seen a massive expansion in criminal-justice expenditure (even while demands for fiscal prudence and stringency have become the norm in other sectors) and a drastic increase in the prison population and other forms of penal control. Reviewing this so-far, so-familiar story, Beckett begins by countering one proffered line of explanation which, she says, does not work well. This she terms the 'democracy-at-work thesis', or the view that 'the current approach to the crime problem reflects the worsening of the crime problem and the public sentiment to which this trend naturally gives rise'. Along the way Beckett is similarly sceptical of the view that it is principally the fear of victimisation that motivates public endorsement of 'get-tough' measures. In Beckett's view, both 'democracy-at-work' and the argument from 'fear' over-simplify the variability and equivocation detectable in public sensibilities and, moreover, take as given what needs to be shown, namely the 'ideological accomplishment' inherent in the predominance of the view that rising crime is 'a consequence of insufficient punishment'.

Among the reasons why 'democracy-at-work' (or to put it another way, bottom-up populism) is inadequate, Beckett argues, is that recorded crime rates shift gradually but measures of public concern fluctuate jaggedly. Moreover, expressed public concerns map more neatly onto overt and well-publicised state anti-crime initiatives than onto crime rates as such, or indeed onto the overall volume of media coverage. In other words, decisions by political elites to highlight particular issues (and inherently to do so in particular terms) play a crucial role in mobilising public concern, even if the latter is already in some sense latent in popular feeling. One thus sees a reciprocal relation between public receptivity, political initiative and overtly expressed public concerns. The importance of this is that it is not simply fear of crime but rather the mobilisation of receptive feelings in the service of particular initiatives that provides the sort of ideological closure necessary to 'identify enhanced punishment as the best response to this problem'. In other words, what is at stake here is something of central significance for political culture, namely the power to inform common sense. This concern recalls Hall *et al.*'s diagnosis of the media politics of crime and punishment in Britain in the 1970s in *Policing the Crisis*, in which they examined 'the ability of the conservative discourse on crime to address social and personal troubles *in a compelling manner*' (emphasis added).

Race has been an endemic feature of the politicisation of crime and punishment in their modern guise since the 1960s, most notably in the United States but by no means exclusively so. The notion of a 'culture of poverty' and Moynihan's allegation of a 'tangle of pathology' surrounding the black family (with his simultaneous coinage of the term 'welfare dependence') both reached back into a long history of racially coded censures, and concomitant efforts to differentiate the deserving from the undeserving poor, and provided a point of departure upon which subsequent laminations of ideology concerning the habits and propensities of what came to be known as the 'underclass' could be laid. At the same time the dealignment between party affiliation and social class provided the New Right with an opportunity to discover a new fractional alliance for whom law-and-order discourse and conservative interpretations of 'the social issues' were powerful rallying points. From this point the key elements of the right's communication strategy on crime (the centrality of the family, the futility and perversity of welfare interventions, the remoteness of liberal elites from popular virtues and sound common sense, the refocusing of crime control on street crime and especially on drugs) developed with notable success. Beckett illuminatingly documents two aspects of this in particular. One is the increasing prominence of 'respect for authority' in officially sponsored 'package displays', especially in respect of youth crime and drugs. The other is their increasingly *volitional* character – a refocusing on decisions and choices that lends itself powerfully to blaming and demands for retributive accountability. The issue here is how easily and frequently the reporting or dramatising of crime – coming to us as it does in the form of a flow of emotionally captivating particular *stories* – elides with an alarming and pessimistic interpretation of social and cultural change – a meta-story, as it were.

A similar point is made by the journalist David Anderson in a compelling and troubling account of the effect of the Willie Horton scandal on American presidential politics. Horton came suddenly to public notice during the 1988 election campaign. The fact that Horton had committed serious crimes, including the rape of a white woman, while on temporary release from a Massachusetts prison, was used to great effect by Republican campaigners to besmirch the reputation of Michael Dukakis, Governor of Massachusetts and Democratic candidate. Anderson expresses a concern that the inflation and hyperbolic over-investment of the Horton story (Horton's translation 'from lowlife to ghoul' as he puts it) came to be framed in a way that *presupposed* 'a wholesale meltdown of morality, values and social control'. Such pessimism, he argues, conduces towards precisely the kind of culture that 'ventilates the resulting anger with vengeful laws'. Anderson thus points to what he terms 'a new expressiveness' in public life. This poses, he suggests, 'no less an issue than how Americans are to think of themselves, what kind of people they are to be'.

The frequent irruption through the media of certain powerfully emotive themes and images associated with crime and punishment into political culture, and the tactical uses to which they can then be put, works powerfully to the advantage of certain political positions and the detriment of others. It is tempting to see this as a peculiarly American, or to some extent Anglo-American, problem. The exceptional nature of the American prison population encourages this view, as does the disparity between the recent criminal justice histories of, say, America and Canada. Conversely, one might discover that the hyping of the penal was a temptation to which all advanced capitalist countries were subject and that they differed only in degree or in the particular targets to which their anxieties and enmities attached. But if that were so it would mean that the media politics of punishment were implicated in a set of transformations that were being felt in some way *everywhere*.

This of course is exactly the conclusion that much recent social theory urges. Consider for a moment what is entailed in this regard by the arguments about globalisation. For example, Manuel Castells suggests that we live in a world that is shaped by conflicting trends of globalisation and identity. In this world, Castells says, power (in the sense of 'strategically decisive economic decisions') moves more fluidly and more freely than ever before, yet the locus of our political attachments and demands remains firmly stuck at the traditional level of the nation-state. That state, Castells argues, still 'looks very nice in its shiny buttons' but is structurally incapable of vindicating its claims to sovereign authority and hence of meeting the demands for cohesion and security that we repose in it. Power therefore moves in 'the space of flows' but we are fated to inhabit the 'space of places', and for most of us those places become one form or another of 'defensive trench'. Leviathan has no clothes, but is nevertheless compelled to robe itself in whatever shreds and patches of authority it can stitch together to hide its nakedness and emulate its former terror and magnificence. Zygmunt Bauman explores a similar thesis with more express reference to the fear of crime and the politics of punishment. In his view there is an intrinsic potentiality for the unholy meeting of media hyperbole, the 'ambient insecurity' under which we the audience live, and the willingness of political actors and moral entrepreneurs to promise the kind of strong medicine that will palliate our symptoms:

> In an ever more insecure and uncertain world the withdrawal into the safe-haven of territoriality is an intense temptation; and so the defence of the territory – the 'safe home' – becomes the pass-key to

all doors which one feels must be locked to stave off the ... threat to spiritual and material comfort ... It is perhaps a happy coincidence for political operators and hopefuls that the genuine problems of insecurity and uncertainty have condensed into the anxiety about safety; politicians can be supposed to be doing something about the first two just because being seen to be vociferous and vigorous about the third.

Perhaps we could term this the 'Wizard of Oz' theory of penal politics. It is one whose complex practical as well as psychic consequences have already begun to be explored by various authors. For example, Anderson acutely notes that the rise of 'the new expressiveness' in American penal politics had something to do with 'helping an angry, anxious public manage its feelings'.

This is not simply to repeat the loose but not infrequently made assertion that fear and anger about crime are just inventions got up by the wicked media to bamboozle and exploit us. Yet the recurrent invocation through the media of an interlocking array of anxieties and rebarbative passions makes these a theme in political culture whose significance is hard to overstate. What is really at issue here is how in our kind of society, in which political process and media discourse can hardly meaningfully be separated, certain resonant themes and images address, channel and give form to otherwise inchoate concerns, around which discussion and action congregate. This in turn points back to the major connection that this chapter seeks to specify between, on one hand, the personal and cultural habitats in which we, as late-moderns live and move and, on the other, macro-structural context within which what Loïc Wacquant calls the 'penal temptation' arises for those who would claim political authority over our lives. This latter question is not one that can in the end adequately be explored only from within criminal justice (nor hence one that falls only within the ambit of criminology). Crime and punishment constitute only one theme within the ascendancy of conservative political outlooks. In that it is a particularly important one, we need also to ask why this issue occupies such a prominent position in letting us know what kind of people we are being encouraged to be, and what sort of governance we are persuaded to accept.

Populism in retrospect and prospect: beyond the New Right?

I have argued above, in common with others (some of whose works are listed at the end of this essay), that punishment was one important theme in the successful recapture of political initiative and ideological hegemony by a revitalised conservatism from the 1970s onwards. History did not end, however. In staking so much of its capital on something as intrinsically contentious, and in many respects uncontrollable, as crime, the neo-liberal project was arguably a self-limiting and defensive one. It remains open to us to ask what further mutations in penal politics are taking place now. Here it may be helpful to focus briefly on the case I know best, namely that of Britain, and to sketch some of the continuities and changes that have occurred between the heyday of Thatcherite neo-liberalism and its 'New Labour' successor.

In Britain in recent times the shifting fortunes and ideological dispositions of key political actors in respect of the penal realm have been quite complex. The assertive and somewhat authoritarian rhetoric characteristic of early Thatcherism gave way (especially during its years of greatest economic optimism and political dominance around the end of the 1980s) to a period during which the penal question was less overtly politicised. Indeed, as Vivian Leacock and I have argued elsewhere, it was the conjunction between a number of unpropitious events and a declining swing in the political-business cycle, that signalled a return to a crude politicisation of penal severity from the early 1990s onwards. The events in question included the abduction and murder of a toddler, James Bulger, from a shopping centre on the deprived outer edge of Liverpool by two older children in early 1993. This hideous incident, etched into public consciousness by the grainy image from a CCTV camera of James walking away unsuspecting, hand in hand with his killers, pitched the country into a paroxysm of unhappy self-examination. Other episodes, in other parts of the criminal justice woods, included a series of high-profile prison escapes in 1995–96, most notably those of a number of Irish Republican inmates from the nominally impregnable special security unit at Woodhill prison. These are only two sightings from among many. Although causally unconnected, they contributed to a climate in which a major reversal of political fortunes took place. What interpretations for these developments are most plausible?

John Gray is a commentator (indeed himself an angry refugee from the New Right) who sees the dissolving legitimacy of Thatcherite neo-liberalism in Britain in the 1990s as intrinsic in its choices. In its radical form, he argues, British neo-liberalism always was a work of creative destruction. Thatcherism was, in Gray's view, a 'brutal and unconscious agent of modernisation'. What Gray observes is 'the self-destruction of British conservatism by New Right ideology'. In its 'doctrinaire pursuit of a general theory of minimal government', its 'long march through British institutions ... has emptied them of much of their ethos and legitimacy'. In Gray's view, British neo-liberals never confronted the central point of contradiction in their thought and policy, namely 'the contradiction between endorsing the permanent revolution of the global market and the preservation of stable forms of family and community life'. Unable to accept that disastrous social consequences may ensue from the unchecked reign of market forces, neo-liberal conservatives engage in a high degree of vindictive projection – 'the atavistic fantasies of cultural fundamentalism'. This is invective, of course, but of a high order. It crystallises some of the more uncongenial and unattractive features of the recent period. It clarifies, for example, some ways in which Thatcherite authoritarian populism was distasteful to some traditional Tories, just as it helps in specifying some of the challenges, opportunities and threats that its legacies bequeathed to its New Labour successors.

Thatcherism always was in some part a 'strategy of inequality' and the 1980s and 1990s saw a further dispersion of incomes and a hardening of poverty in Britain. Moreover, the recasting of poverty in the favoured language of neo-conservatism (especially the terminology of 'under-class') presaged slender patience with the excluded, especially the misbehaving young. Moreover, the coincidence between these experiences of polarisation and a state regime experiencing deepening legitimation problems has had marked and particular consequences for the tone and content of criminal justice policy and politics in this period. Gray points to reasons for the self-subversion, indeed the implosion, of Conservative hegemony. The very promises that served the Tories so well in 1979 (the 'smack of firm government', the restoration of 'freedom under law') had become unredeemed debts against their political mortgage by 1993. Rising crime rates and rising measures of public insecurity (both peaking according to official measures in 1994) had themselves become – to reverse the polarity of Downes and Morgan's narrative of post-war penal politics – 'hostages to fortune'. Thus, when in 1993 the Conservatives launched a new drive towards penal austerity under the slogan 'Prison Works!' it was, in purely electoral terms, a spectacular failure. In this sense the two primary 'moments' of authoritarian populism in recent British political history call to mind Marx's dictum about historical recurrences, namely that they come once as tragedy and again as farce.

So, for example, it is by now a matter of record that in Britain in the 1990s, despite a flagrantly populist campaign, the Conservative Party were completely unable to wrest back political advantage from a resurgent Labour Party, in matters of law and order as on virtually every other political issue of consequence. On that occasion the very conditions that made the populist strategy politically necessary – the terminally declining legitimacy of an incumbent party – also ensured that it would 'fail'. At the same time the then new New Labour leader Tony Blair moved coolly to reposition his party in such a way as to neutralise any lingering suspicion of 'softness' on law-and-order issues. His celebrated 1993 sound-bite 'tough on crime, tough on the causes of crime' (enunciated within a month of the Bulger murder) allowed him at one and the same time to compete on the Conservatives' ground while designedly accusing the Tories of having a narrow 'one-club' agenda, remote from voters' everyday concerns with youth offending, drugs, low-level public order problems and other incursions on their security and 'quality of life'.

David Garland has influentially argued that there are two distinct and contrary tendencies in the way that contemporary nation-states respond to crime under contemporary conditions. Chief among those conditions is that high volumes of crime have become chronic and are becoming normalised. A dominant response (which Garland terms the way of 'adaptation') is therefore to adopt various strategies for managing, coping and ameliorating, including multiple varieties of delegation to, responsibilisation of, and partnership with local authorities, individuals, voluntary bodies and companies. A second response (which Garland styles 'denial' or 'hysterical counter-reaction') is to engage in display, an 'archaic' 'show of punitive force' which 'seeks to reassert the state's power to *govern* simply by displaying its power to *punish*' (emphasis in original). In Garland's view, these 'schizoid' and 'ambivalent' tendencies are both now deeply entrenched – with predictably dismaying consequences for the demonisation of 'othered' and outcast populations – those who are imprisoned, tagged, surveilled, ghettoised. In arguing thus, Garland stands within a major current of contemporary social analysis that emphasises the frailties, the 'hollowing out' of the nation-state by globalisation. Thus, as strategically decisive economic decisions increasingly escape its influence; as flows of capital and information become uncontrollably mobile; as the great corporations come to rival or exceed it in scale and geopolitical significance; so the state cleaves to such levers of influence and prestige as remain under its exclusive control. Moreover, facing a political culture that is marked by, in Bauman's phrase, 'ambient insecurity', and a public discourse that is, as Nikolas Rose has it, 'individuated and demotic', there is rich scope (as we have seen above) for media and political campaigns that are emotivist and charged with vicarious victimisation, anxiety and resentment.

Under such conditions it may readily be argued that Wacquant's 'penal temptation' is one to which all advanced societies are subject, especially at moments of political or social crisis. Yet it may also be wise to entertain certain riders to these lines of argument. One such is comparative and empirical, namely that the predominance of 'populist punitiveness' is very much more marked in certain countries than in others, and for complex reasons to do with religion, trust in and/or mistrust of elites, legal culture and judicial processes, the survival of socialised welfare systems and so on. In other words, Garland's argument applies much more fully to the United States (and somewhat more fully to the United Kingdom) than to many other contemporary states. But why would the United States or United Kingdom (in many respects among the most potent political entities ever to stalk the earth) find their sovereignty so much more menaced now than, say, Switzerland? The answer might seem to lie not so much in the objective erosion of sovereignty by globalisation as in just how far a given political order stakes its authority on crime control, and by what means, and under what kinds of pressure from internal divisions, interest groups and political contests – a question in other words of political legitimacy rather than pure sovereignty.

It seems beyond doubt that there have been long-run and perhaps irreversible infrastructural changes taking place in both professional practice – for example, in the redefinition of institutions such as probation and parole primarily as techniques for managing risk rather than as delivery systems for welfare services – and in everyday culture and consciousness. On the other hand, it is simply not the case that the politics and practices of punishment over this period have been entirely consistent either in their intensity or their content and justificatory rationales.

How can we best explain these instabilities? There is of course a rich tradition in the sociology of punishment that associates variations in penal severity with economic and political crises. Thus, to return to the British case, we could argue for the period in question here that there have been two major moments of 'structural politics' (around the elections of 1979 and 1997) with one more contingent episode (the run on the popularity of the incumbent party starting in 1993) sandwiched between them. I regard this view as distinctly plausible, as I hope is by now clear. However, such accounts still leave the specific ideological content and penological consequences of such moments of politicisation to be fleshed out. O'Malley proposes that some of the 'volatile and contradictory' features of recent penal politics become intelligible when we understand them in 'a more substantively political light'. So, if we remind ourselves of the coalition within New Right politics between neo-conservative themes (a form of statecraft favouring strong government, the restoration of social and moral order) and free-enterprise neo-liberalism (with its preference for market mechanisms, responsibilisation of individual choice, risk-taking entrepreneurship, disdain for state welfare and the 'dependency culture' of its clients', we can readily see how an array of diverse penal strategies can co-exist, to be drawn upon in promiscuous and tactical ways: 'Thus within a New Right penality the repertory or range of available sanctions is expanded in contradictory directions, namely the innovative and the nostalgic.' O'Malley nicely captures here the oscillation (and sometimes conflation) between managerialist innovation and punitive rhetoric that I take to characterise recent British and American penal politics.

However, if we continue in the same 'more substantively political vein' we may also see that such unstable alliances are not always indefinitely sustainable. Plural strategies that at one time look supple and smart, at others may look merely incoherent. John Gray's argument, introduced above, is not merely that British neo-liberalism has advocated a punitive 'authoritarian individualism' but also that it has been a 'self-limiting' project, foundering in part on the very insecurities that its drive towards flexibilisation, de-layering, down-sizing and ceaseless mobility ('the pulverizing force of labour market deregulation' as Gray puts it) has engendered. Among the ironies of this political experiment that Gray identifies are the delegitimation both of market fundamentalism itself and of the neo-Conservative nostalgism that has accompanied it. In this context students of penal politics are well advised to avoid the slippage involved in presupposing that every attempt by a political actor to flourish a punitive big stick for populist effect will work (or conversely that every expression by members of the public of unease, anxiety or resentment about crime is best described under the notion of 'punitiveness'). Public sensibilities, it turns out, are plainly not simply politicians' modelling clay. Moreover, if, as Garland plausibly suggests, the propensity to reach for punitive rhetoric is indeed characteristic of political weakness, there may be good reason to presume the failure of such gambits in the absence of evidence to the contrary, since they may arise precisely at the point of terminal corrosions in the legitimacy of state regimes in public esteem (either in point of their competence, or their variance from widely held beliefs, or both).

Envoi: populism and penal strategy

It may no longer be the case that the major actors in British or American politics can meaningfully be ranked as more or less 'populist', or indeed as more or less 'punitive'. Rather, populism can reasonably be regarded as one of the inevitable modes of late-modern politics; while 'punitiveness' is a stance that no serious politician can safely disavow. Such attempts at scaling (how much?) slice less deeply into the strategy than do more practically and institutionally specific questions (what? to whom? how? on what terms?). Viewed in this light, students of penality confront important challenges in grasping the nature of the interactions between changes that occur on the public stage of political competition and opinion-formation and those that take place in the infrastructure of the processing, management and surveillance of offenders. Indeed, as Margaret Canovan suggests, it may be generally the case for contemporary political culture that the very complexity and hence 'opacity' of those backstage practices are among the conditions that favour politicians' recurrent tendency to resort to populist gestures. Thus:

> Ideology, which reduces the complexity of politics to dogmatic simplicity, is ill-fitted to deal adequately with [these] intricacies, and yet ideology is indispensable in mass politics … The paradox in other words, is that while democracy (more than any other political system) *needs* to be comprehensible to the masses, the ideology that seeks to bridge the gap between people and politics misrepresents (and cannot avoid misrepresenting) the way that democratic politics necessarily works. This contradiction between ideology and practice is a standing invitation to raise the cry of democracy betrayed, and to mobilise the discontented behind the banner of restoring politics to the people.

This observation seems highly redolent of some observed features of the penal realm in recent times – colonised by 'managerialist' systems and 'actuarial' procedures of opaque sophistication yet quite unable to break free for long from the pull of emotivism and sloganising. Sometimes these are 'just politics', moments of populism pure-and-simple when politicians 'jockey' for position or 'play to the gallery'. Some such gambits enjoy some success and some fail dismally. At other times a new posture on crime and punishment arises in alignment with a moment of social and political change of more far-reaching kind. Observers of politics and students of punishment need to remain equally alert to this distinction since transitions between state regimes and changes in the practices and politics of punishment are intimately connected. It is for this reason an important civic and intellectual responsibility to continue to scan the horizon for the emergence of new configurations in the relations between the social and the penal faces of the state.

Bibliographical review

The sociology of punishment is now a thriving sub-field of the wider discipline. So it should be, my essay might be read as proposing, in view of the indicative importance of this topic in the culture and politics of our time. As attentive readers may have noticed, this means that as well as preoccupying a quite large number of academic specialists the area also attracts the attention of a diverse range of commentators (including social theorists, political philosophers and journalists) even if their main interests sometimes lie elsewhere.

Here I note the main works on which I have drawn directly in preparing this essay as well as providing some suggestions for further reading that may be of interest to those who would like to follow up specific issues.

The term 'crisis of penal modernism' comes from David Garland's influential book *Punishment and Modern Society* (Oxford: Clarendon Press, 1990). In that work Garland provides succinct and accurate accounts of the implications for the social analysis of punishment of a number of key thinkers (Durkheim, Marx and later marxists, Weber, Foucault and Elias) before going on to explore a variety of aspects of punishment in contemporary culture. Garland's subsequent work *The Culture of Control* (Chicago: University of Chicago Press, 2001) has if anything been yet more widely referenced and discussed. This is perhaps the most ambitious statement available of the sorts of problems with which I also deal here and must provide a starting point for anyone developing a serious interest in the field. Although my essay shares a lot of common ground with Garland and draws fairly heavily on his account, I am rather more interested in the relation of punishment to explicit political conflict and competition than I take him to be. Also Garland is perhaps somewhat less concerned than some others (see below) with the question of risk. The essay that Garland and I wrote together, and part of whose argument is summarised here, is called 'Criminology, Social Theory and the Challenge of our Times' and forms the introduction to our co-edited volume *Criminology and Social Theory* (Oxford: Oxford University Press, 2000). That collection also includes contributions by authors including Douglas and Rose whose views are touched upon in the essay. Another source, ranging over some of this ground and a bit beyond, is a piece by Ian Loader and Richard Sparks called 'Contemporary Landscapes of Crime, Order and Control: Governance, Risk and Globalization' in *The Oxford Handbook of Criminology*, third edition (edited by M. Maguire, R. Morgan and R. Reiner (Oxford: Oxford University Press, 2002).

My views on recent penal politics in Britain are explored more fully in various places including (with Vivian Leacock) 'Riskiness and At-riskness: Some Ambiguous Features of the Current Penal Landscape' in N. Gray, J. Laing and L. Noaks (eds) *Criminal Justice, Mental Health and the Politics of Risk* (London: Cavendish, 2002). Some readers may also be interested in my 'Perspectives on Risk and Penal Politics' in T. Hope and R. Sparks (eds) *Crime, Risk and Insecurity* (London: Routledge, 2000). Quite a few of us have been wrestling with the strange twists and turns of crime control and penal policy in Britain over the last few years, though in my view the definitive account remains to be written. I refer readers (for a highly informative treatment of the critical period of the early 1990s) to Lord Windlesham's *Responses to Crime, vol. 3: Legislating with the Tide* (Oxford: Clarendon Press, 1996). There is also useful material in Ann James and John Raine's more concise *The New Politics of Criminal Justice* (London: Longman, 1998). Critical responses to 'New Labour' crime policies exist in diverse places but have not at the time of writing been drawn together in an accessible form. Some of the contributions to K. Stenson and R. Sullivan (eds) *Crime, Risk and Justice* (Cullompton: Willan, 2001) offer useful starting points, but this is a fast-moving field and academic insight is all too soon overtaken by events.

The key source, in my view, on the problem of risk and political culture is Mary Douglas's magisterial *Risk and Blame* (London: Routledge, 1992). This is not mainly a book about the penal system, however. Another influential thinker who addresses the general implications of risk for contemporary social organisation, and whose views I refer to *en passant* here is Anthony Giddens. Giddens's writings are voluminous and widely available. A succinct statement of some relevant points, and to my mind one of his most interesting books, is *The Consequences of Modernity* (Cambridge: Polity Press, 1990). Among other general social theorists referred to here, and one with whom I would recommend anyone to engage – provided that they have a large slice of time at their disposal – is Manuel Castells, whose three-volume *magnum opus The Information Age* is one of the most ambitious and exciting attempts to get to grips with living in a 'network society' yet undertaken. I refer primarily to volume II, *The Power of Identity* (Oxford: Basil Blackwell, 1997).

John Gray's controlled anti-New Right polemic is in his book *Endgames: Questions in Late Modern Political Thought* (Cambridge: Polity Press, 1997). Although they began in quite different academic traditions, and with very different political affiliations, Gray's views have much in common with the later writings of Zygmunt Bauman. Bauman's remarks cited here come from his paper 'The Strangers of the Consumer Era' in his *Postmodernity and its Discontents* (Cambridge: Polity Press, 1997) and from his remarkable little book *Globalization: the Human Consequences* (Cambridge: Polity Press, 1998).

Among authors working more expressly on the uses of risk in penal practice, the contributions of Jonathan Simon and Malcolm Feeley (writing both separately and together) and Pat O'Malley are of central interest. Feeley and Simon originated the term 'actuarial justice' in their 1992 article 'The New Penology: Notes on the Emerging Strategy for Corrections and its Implications' (*Criminology*, vol 30(4)). This must be one of the most widely cited and much-anthologised academic papers ever published, though it should be acknowledged that it is cited almost as frequently by its critics as its admirers. One place in which it is reprinted is in O'Malley's comprehensive (but correspondingly expensive) collection *Crime and the Risk Society* (Aldershot: Ashgate 1998). O'Malley's works on this topic are, as readers will have gathered, ones that I especially admire. I would draw particular attention to his article 'Volatile and Contradictory Punishment', *Theoretical Criminology*, 3(2), 1999, and his essay 'Policing Crime Risks in the Neo-liberal Era' in Stenson and Sullivan (eds) *op. cit.* I also refer readers both to O'Malley's essay 'Risk Societies and the Government of Crime' in M. Brown and J. Pratt (eds) *Dangerous Offenders* (London: Routledge, 2000) and to the editors' own insightful contributions. For me, however, the key source and the book that makes most clear the relationship between incarceration and risk-based reasoning is Jonathan Simon's *Poor Discipline* (Chicago: University of Chicago Press, 1993).

A persuasive and readable overview of the issues of race and 'the underclass' in American penal politics, with special reference to political campaigns and mass-media influences, is provided by Katherine Beckett in her *Making Crime Pay: Law and Order in Contemporary American Politics* (New York: Oxford University Press, 1997). I also refer admiringly to David Anderson's *Crime and the Politics of Hysteria: How the Willie Horton Story Changed American Justice* (New York: Times Books, 1995). Other sources relevant to the race-imprisonment nexus include John Hagan and Ruth Peterson (eds) *Crime and Inequality* (Stanford: Stanford University Press, 1995) and Michael Tonry *Malign Neglect: Race, Crime and Politics in America* (New York: Oxford University Press, 1995). For these authors the racial disparities in both 'underclass' membership and imprisonment are major causes for concern. For Tonry in particular the language and prosecution of the 'war on drugs' has been primarily responsible both for the acceleration of the growth of imprisonment in the United States and for the racial disproportions therein. The recent writings of Loïc Wacquant are also particularly provocative on this topic and are about to become more widely available in English. See on this his contribution to the special issue of *Punishment and Society* on 'Mass Imprisonment' (3(1), 2001). That issue contains numerous informative essays on this central topic and has also been published as a book under the same title, edited by David Garland (London: Sage, 2001). In general, *Punishment and Society* is a useful place in which to follow these debates.

Chapter 6

Penal theory and penal practice: a communitarian approach

Nicola Lacey

This chapter examines the relationship between penal philosophy and penal practice. Why have the practical fruits of theories of punishment been so modest, and could this be otherwise? In the main body of the chapter, I suggest that once penal theory moves beyond certain parameters that have bounded it during the past century, it may be able to offer a richer set of substantive ideas about how penal practices might be improved. I argue that a modified version of what I have described elsewhere as a 'communitarian' account, which emphasises the collective aspects of punishment and, in particular, the role of punishment in expressing shared values and commitments, can escape some of the limitations of other approaches. I also note, however, certain difficulties with the communitarian approach – difficulties that appear especially acute once one considers the possible moves from theory to practice. In conclusion, I raise some further questions about the potential for philosophical theories to contribute to social analysis and policy construction. My aim here is to point out the further intellectual resources that need to be drawn upon in the construction of theoretical frameworks that might truly speak to social practices.

Contemporary ideas about the justification of punishment

Recent philosophical debate about the justification of punishment has charted a course between two dialectical extremes. The debate sets out from a definition of punishment as the infliction of what would generally be regarded as unpleasant treatment on an offender in response to his or her breach of criminal law. Utilitarian theories argue that punishment is a prima-facie evil which has to be justified by its compensating good effects in terms of human happiness or satisfaction achieved through mechanisms such as deterrence, reform or incapacitation. Retributive theories, on the other hand, insist that punishment is justified solely by the offender's desert and blame-worthiness in committing the offence. Each approach has serious limitations. Utilitarian theories struggle to provide adequate limits on the amount and distribution of punishments: if a penalty of life imprisonment for parking offences were so effective a deterrent that it would almost never have to be inflicted, the utilitarian moral calculation might well regard it as justified. Purely retributive theories struggle (but ultimately fail) to provide a positive argument for punishment that is distinct from an unappealing principle of vengeance. They also fail to deliver a convincing 'algebra' that could translate the desert for a particular crime into a specific sentence: how are we to judge whether a particular rape or theft deserves a certain punishment? And how do we calculate the gravity of different types of offence?

Over the last 50 years, something approaching a consensus has emerged among liberal philosophers that this apparent deadlock may be broken by adopting a pragmatic theory of punishment which accommodates the virtues of each of the utilitarian and retributive theories. Controversy continues to rage over just what these virtues are and how they may be combined in a 'mixed' theory. Essentially, most mixed theories adopt the strategy of distinguishing between different questions about the justification of punishment: what is punishment?; why should people be punished?; who should be punished, and by how much? They then give different answers to each of the questions. Each answer is, however, still constructed along utilitarian or retributive lines. For example, one influential mixed theory argues that people should be punished because punishment has good social effects, but that only those who deserve it should be liable to punishment. So although the advocacy of mixed theories constitutes a real advance, it is a limited one, because the underlying assumptions and values employed are much the same as those underpinning the unsatisfactory theories which the mixed theories combine. The advance is in terms of the number of values that can be accommodated by any one theory rather than any novelty in the sorts of arguments being introduced to the debate or any genuine synthesis of the available arguments. At a practical level, this means that where retributive and utilitarian arguments conflict with one another, the mixed theories are of little help. Take, for instance, the case of liability without fault. In both Britain and the United States, criminal law often imposes liability on people for conduct in relation to which they were not at fault in the usual sense. Thus, someone whose factory discharges pollution into a river may be held criminally responsible even though he or she was unaware of the circumstances leading to the emission. Utilitarian principles support this kind of 'strict' liability wherever it maximises favourable outcomes – for example, where it is effective in motivating people to take stringent measures to prevent such 'accidents'. Retributive theories, on the other hand, oppose strict liability in principle: those who are not responsible or at fault do not deserve to be punished. Mixed theories provide no mechanism of translation – no common terms in which one could balance up the arguments that proceed from the two fundamentally opposed moral visions. They therefore take us little further forward.

Methodological and political individualism in penal theory

In considering the best way forward from this apparent impasse, it is worth examining certain assumptions that underlie the philosophical debate. Amid the apparently irreconcilable conflict between retributive and utilitarian principles, there can nevertheless be discerned some important common themes, at least among recent versions of these traditional theories. Such shared presuppositions help to explain both the unsatisfactory nature of some of the policy prescriptions of recent penal philosophies, and also their failure to offer such prescriptions in certain key areas.

I shall focus on two main assumptions underlying penal philosophy of the latter half of the twentieth century. In the first place, I want to examine its assumptions about human nature. Modern Western societies, touched as they are by liberal political ideas, are distinguished by the central place they accord to the moral claims of the human individual. This means that contemporary penal theories are primarily exercised by the moral problem of how to explain the justice of the state's imposition of penal sanctions on free individuals. In penal philosophy, this individual is typically conceived as entering society endowed with a set of pre-social needs, interests, preferences or rights, which must be respected by subsequent political arrangements. This person is, moreover, conceived as a rational, responsible individual, capable to a significant extent of shaping his or her behaviour to chosen ends and of controlling and understanding that behaviour. This means that questions about the social causes and conditions of criminality – questions that play a central role in both criminological and political debate – tend in penal philosophy (with the important but partial exception of rehabilitative theories) to drop out of view. This focus on the individual offender and his or her relationship with the state also means that contemporary penal theories have little to say about victims of crime and their moral claims in the debate about punishment.

At a theoretical level, penal philosophy's strongly individualistic presuppositions about the nature of human beings and social relations are open to challenge. An obvious objection is that human nature – our needs, identities, attitudes, preferences and outlook – indeed, the very idea of what it means to be a person – is in a fundamental sense the product of the particular social and political environment in which we live. This is not to say that human nature is entirely socially determined, nor is it to deny the possibility of people acting on their environment and exercising choice and autonomy. It is rather to observe that given the inevitably social conditions of human existence, the assertion of a set of 'pre-social' rights or interests is an eminently unsuitable starting place for reflection on the proper content of political values and human needs. When those rights or interests are defined through hypotheses about entitlements assumed to exist in a 'state of nature', it is hard to see how the connection between the ensuing theory and actual social practices is to be made. Since human needs, interests and values are worked out in concrete historical settings, these socially constructed ideas provide a firmer starting point for social theory (including penal theory) than do hypotheses about the nature of an imaginary pre-social individual.

A second set of assumptions implicit in much contemporary penal philosophy has to do with political values. The particular version of liberalism that informs current penal theory tends to be individualistic not only in its conception of human being but also in its political commitments. This particular form of liberalism is characterised by a relative lack of interest in the existence or development of collective, social or public goods. Goods that cannot be reduced to the sum of their value to individuals, and values that have to be pursued and enjoyed collectively or in relation to other community members, have not been a central focus of this influential strand of political philosophy. This is particularly curious given the salience of public goods – witness the current preoccupation with public morality – to political debate, notwithstanding the intensely individualistic political complexion of governments in Britain and the United States over the last 20 years.

How are these individualistic assumptions played out in the theories of punishment, and what problems do they create? Let us look first at the implications of the individualistic conception of human being. The retributivist typically sees the individual as a holder of moral rights. This vision sets up an intractable problem of justification for punishment, which prima facie violates the offender's rights. Thus the argument for punishment must be capable of defeating individual claims of right. This results, in some versions of retributivism, in the assertion that the offender has *a positive right to be punished*. Although this has some attractions as a principle that might limit state power, the right to be punished is one for which, as we shall see, retributivism can produce no comprehensible moral explanation. The utilitarian, on the other hand, sees the individual as a being engaged in the rational pursuit of self-interest; punishment is therefore justified by its contribution to the aggregated interests of individuals. This means, as we have seen, that the utilitarian approach sets up rather weak limits on the treatment of individual offenders. A penalty that would generally be regarded as disproportionately harsh, or otherwise unfair to an individual offender, is nonetheless justified on a utilitarian approach if its overall effect is to maximise social happiness: an exemplary deterrent sentence would be such a case. This weakness explains the concern of liberal utilitarians to develop principles that act as individual liberty-respecting limits on the pursuit of utility. The most famous example is John Stuart Mill's 'harm principle', which stipulates that the only justification for the use of coercive power to limit individual freedom is the prevention of harm to others. But since the harm principle is rooted in intuitions about justice and the value of liberty which cannot be explained in purely utilitarian terms, its introduction subverts rather than merely qualifies a utilitarian approach. As in the case of the mixed theories of punishment, we are left with no guidance as to how the demands of justice and utility are to be balanced in cases in which they conflict.

Next, let us consider the implications of the lack of focus on public goods and collective values for theories of punishment. In the case of retributive theories it might be argued that the ideals of 'doing justice' or meting out an offender's 'just deserts' do in fact appeal to precisely such a conception. Retributivism, in other words, might be understood as arguing that punishment contributes to some intrinsically valuable feature of the social order which can be understood in terms of the public good or collective values. But if we press further in an attempt to identify what the value or good appealed to consists in, we meet what can only be described as a retreat into metaphor, in the form of claims that deserved punishments are required to 'restore the moral equilibrium' or to re-establish the 'relationships of justice' which existed before the offence was committed. The impoverished conception of the public and of civil society underlying many modem expositions of retributivism prevents them from developing these metaphors into a comprehensible, let alone a concrete, vision of either the proper substance of, or even the upper moral limits on, punishment.

Utilitarian theories of punishment can incorporate what might be considered public goods and collective values such as moral education and the promotion and maintenance of a peaceful and law-abiding society into their stated penal goals. But given the structure of utilitarian theory, with its ultimate value of happiness or preference-satisfaction, these social values, like other goals such as deterrence or rehabilitation, can only be accommodated instrumentally: in other words, not as goods in themselves, but as means to the ultimately valuable end of utility. For example, the good of a peaceable society is only valued by pure utilitarians in so far as it contributes to the maximisation of the average or aggregate sum of happiness or preference-satisfaction. Such a valuation falls short of any distinctive focus on the potential contributions of criminal justice to the social good. Yet it is just such a focus which, I shall suggest, an adequate conception of the rationale of punishment needs to develop. For without a proper exploration of the impact of punishment on the social good, it seems unlikely that we can come up with a convincing justification for the social practice of punishment.

Penal theory and criminal justice policy

How have philosophical ideas about punishment affected the debate on criminal justice policy? It is instructive to consider two specific policy arguments: that of the rehabilitative movement influential in the 1960s, and the 'just deserts' model of the 1970s and 1980s, which developed largely as a reaction to the excesses of the rehabilitative ideal and the treatment model that it generated in penal practice.

A rehabilitative approach to punishment belongs most obviously to the utilitarian tradition in penal philosophy. Rehabilitative approaches aim to maximise utility by means of crime reduction, but do so through potentially more intrusive and paternalistic means than are implicit in the utilitarian strategies of individual and general deterrence. Notwithstanding the treatment model's affinity in principle with the view that criminality is socially produced, a certain individualism is clearly at work in its understanding of crime as personal pathology. Although the rehabilitative approach of the 1960s and 1970s was informed by a deterministic view of human nature and was hence less in tune with that of a free, rational and responsible person than modern versions of retributivism, its penal response was focused primarily on the offending individual abstracted from his or her social environment.

The goal here might be seen as one of restoring the offender, through rehabilitative measures, to the group of rationally calculating and law-abiding citizens. On this view, the interim loss of freedom is justified by the end in view, and as such, rehabilitation theory can be seen as a genuine version of utilitarianism applied to punishment.

The theoretical and practical limitations of the individualist assumptions that I have already described are inherent in these rehabilitative arguments. The construction of crime as individual pathology dictates a punitive/treatment response which focuses primarily on the individual offender and his or her attitudes, rather than on the situational or environmental aspects and antecedents of the offending behaviour. Rehabilitative ideology therefore legitimated attempts to 'reform' the individual in conditions of incarceration and hence in an institutionalised setting far removed from that in which the offence was committed. It entailed judging (often with wide and unaccountable discretion) the offender's suitability for release in terms of his or her performance in and adaptation to that institutionalised environment. Clearly, the extent and abuse of professional discretion to which rehabilitative schemes gave rise, and the poor conditions pertaining in many of the custodial institutions in which rehabilitation was avowedly sought, were important problems in their own right. But, even leaving these aside, the rehabilitative approach was fractured in principle by a deep tension between individualist and determinist impulses.

In the light of both its perceived ineffectiveness in reducing reoffending and civil libertarian fears about the implications of the rehabilitative ideal, it was hardly surprising that the next emerging theme in penal policy would veer away from both determinism and utilitarianism. This is not to say that rehabilitative ideas have been completely abandoned in penal practice. Nonetheless, throughout the 1970s and 1980s there were several influential restatements of a retributivist approach, rendered more palatable to modern tastes in the guise of 'just deserts' or 'the justice model'. These restatements have been accompanied by a range of practical changes such as a move to determinate sentencing and the promulgation of sentencing guidelines which seek to ensure consistency of treatment in the courts.

The modern 'justice model' locates retributive ideas within a liberal political framework. Typically, the social order is seen as being based on some form of social contract; a mutuality of political obligations flowing from hypothetical or actual agreement. It follows that someone who voluntarily commits an offence takes an unfair advantage *vis à vis* other law-abiding citizens, and, in particular, in relation to victims of crime. Hence many recent retributive theories accommodate principles of compensation or reparation within their conception of punishment.

According to the justice model, the offender's unfair advantage in failing to restrain themselves from committing an offence creates a moral disequilibrium in society by upsetting pre-existing relationships of justice, reciprocity and fairness; punishment must be imposed so as to remove the unfair advantage, thereby restoring the moral equilibrium. Alternatively, some versions of the justice model speak in terms of a forfeiture of the offender's rights until the deserved punishment has been served, so allowing the offender to be restored to full citizenship. On this view, distributive justice as between rational, responsible individual citizens provides the moral underpinning of political society. Crime is understood as individual wickedness and transgression. Once again, the social context of both offence and offender is ignored. This creates a vacuum in which the assertion that any offence (petty shoplifting by a very poor person, for example) gives rise to a moral disequilibrium that has to be righted seems unproblematic. The morally crucial link between retributive justice and social justice, and between the justice of the criminal law and the justice of punishment, is subtly severed. This moral isolation of the question of punishment facilitates the political espousal and social legitimation of the increasingly severe approaches to punishment that characterise current British and US penal policy.

If individualistic assumptions about human beings have had adverse effects on contemporary penal theory, the same can be said of the failure to engage in debate about public goods and community values. This is especially clear in the rehabilitative approach, whose basic goal, as we have seen, is the reform of individuals as a means of maximising utility. Such a structure of value allows no place for any intrinsically valued public goods or community values. For although values such as the good of a peaceful and mutually supportive community may be recognised by utilitarian theories, this recognition is indirect: it is measured in terms of punishment's contribution to aggregated or averaged individual utility – to the total, or average, sum of individual happiness. In the debate about rehabilitation, there was little space for political argument about the values underlying the conception of 'social health' to which reform programmes were oriented, or of the kind of society for which those programmes sought to make their subjects fit. While retributive judgments confine themselves to desert for breaches of criminal law, the discretion inherent in the indeterminate sentences of rehabilitative policy invited broad judgements about antisocial conduct and attitudes – judgements which were seldom made explicit and which were outside the sphere of political accountability.

Modern retributivism, however, does little better than the rehabilitative approach in terms of recognising the kinds of public goods that the practice of criminal justice might foster. Certainly, the values of a moral equilibrium and relationships of justice might be elaborated so as to express comprehensive social goods; interestingly, the closest approaches to such developments have come from explicitly non-liberal proponents of retributivism. Yet rather than any explication and discussion of the public goods and social values that might underlie these ideas, retributivists simply offer us assertions about the value of 'doing justice' and giving offenders their 'just deserts'. Such assertions hardly serve to illuminate or unpack the original retributive metaphors, the obscurity of which the modern statements claim to resolve.

From theories of punishment to theories of justice

What of the relationship between political espousal of these two penal ideologies and actual reforms of penal institutions such as imprisonment? It is incontrovertible that each of these ideologies has been associated with specific trends and reforms. The rehabilitative ideal, especially in the United States, led to a redistribution of power to criminal-justice officials with discretion to 'diagnose' and make decisions about 'cure'. It also led to changes in regimes in many penal establishments. Courts handed down indeterminate sentences more frequently, and offenders sentenced to both custodial and non-custodial penalties found themselves required to participate in 'therapeutic' programmes, their response to which had a direct influence on the length of their sentence. The 'just deserts' movement led to legislative sentencing reforms in several jurisdictions including, albeit late in the day, England and Wales. These reforms formally curtailed the discretion of both sentencers and other officials at the post-conviction stage, and led to a far greater degree of determinacy in sentencing. The 'just deserts' movement also, contrary to the intentions of a substantial section of its proponents, went hand-in-hand in many countries with a rise in the overall severity of sentencing. Governments on both sides of the Atlantic have exploited the political popularity of tough 'law and order' policies by amending sentencing legislation to provide for harsher penalties. Retributivism's lack of any determinate formula for translating particular crimes into particular deserved penalties has left it unable to mount any critique of the drift to severity, while its language of guilt and desert has proved a remarkably welcoming rhetorical framework for the expression of law-and-order politics.

None of this is to deny that many proponents of both rehabilitative and retributive penal philosophies have had broadly humanitarian and reformist aspirations. What it does suggest is that, in terms of progress towards these aspirations, the practical realisation of rehabilitative and retributive ideas has often been counterproductive. This is, at least in part, because the humanitarian ideals that motivated both the treatment and the justice movements were contingent rather than necessary features of the penal theories themselves. Hence those ideals were not fully argued for within the theories. Examples include the rehabilitative aspiration to humane, positive and respectful treatment for offenders, and the hopes of civil libertarian supporters of the justice model that greater determinacy in sentencing might also lead to reductions in sentencing levels and, in particular, in the use of imprisonment. The theories' failure to engender real progress towards these goals – failures that have often been more spectacular than their successes – are attributable, I would argue, to a number of features of penal philosophy. One is the individualism which I have already discussed, and which made a distinctive contribution to the narrow framing of questions of penal philosophy. A second, flowing from the first, is penal philosophers' method of abstracting questions about punishment from broader moral and political questions about social justice and democratic structure. State punishment is, after all, merely one among a number of interrelated social practices. Once this is recognised, it becomes apparent that a just and progressive criminal justice policy is utterly dependent upon a broader commitment to social justice and the existence of an adequate set of political institutions stretching far beyond the penal sphere.

Although penal theories abound with arguments about whom we should punish, why they should be punished, and to what end, penal philosophy has made little useful contribution to debate about the forms and amount of punishment that should be imposed. Leaving aside the detailed plans that Jeremy Bentham, the utilitarian thinker, developed for the 'Panopticon' – a prison designed to allow for the constant surveillance of inmates – utilitarian theories simply offer us the prescriptions implicit in the utilitarian calculus. This is a test that is enormously difficult to apply: how are things such as happiness or preference satisfaction to be measured? Moreover, utilitarianism presupposes a theory of human motivation substantially at odds with our (albeit limited) understanding of criminal behaviour. While the model of the rationally calculating offender who weighs up the expected costs and benefits of a particular offence may be plausible in some areas – for example, property crime – it is implausible in relation to many others – for example, violent and sexual offences.

Retributive theories, once we abandon the crude *lex talionis* with its prescription of 'an eye for an eye', offer us the apparently determinate idea of proportionality or commensurability between penalty and seriousness of the offence. This proportionality is judged in terms of the offender's culpability and the harm done. But since there are no common units in which we can measure any such relationship of 'equivalence' between crime and punishment, we are thrown back on other criteria in trying to work out just what penalties proportionality directs. These other criteria are likely to consist in estimates of the consequences of different punishments, intuitive judgements of one kind and another, and arguments from custom and convention surrounding existing penalty scales. These criteria do merit careful consideration, but many retributivists have tended to shy away from their analysis, presumably because any such exploration might lead to a muddying of the pure waters of retribution. Recent writers have attempted to give substance to retributive principles by developing a 'living-standard analysis' of the harms caused by particular crimes. But nothing in the analysis can determine the political equation between a certain perceived harm and its 'equivalent' or 'deserved' penalty: the retributive promise of a formula equating particular crimes with particular penalties remains illusory. This explains the constant vulnerability of retributive ideas to exploitation by politicians who see electoral advantage in severe penal policy.

In general, penal philosophers have been preoccupied with the theoretical details of their models, and relatively uninterested in questions about the institutional framework within which their ideas might be realised. Small wonder, then, that even where theoretical arguments about the justification of punishment have been directly or indirectly influential at the policy level, they have tended to have little impact on important matters such as the extent of the use of imprisonment, or its nature, or the nature of other penalties. For given the vagueness of penal theories' ideas about proper forms and amounts of punishment and the consequent difficulty of equipping theoretical arguments with any practical cutting edge, the force of inertia and public consensus has tended, at best, to favour the status quo. At worst, the vacuum of principle has conduced to a situation in which penal practice becomes a political football, vulnerable to the vagaries of popular demands for severity. In this context, a tough stance on 'law and order' becomes an attractive strategy for governments which, given the globalisation of world markets, find it increasingly difficult to present themselves as effective managers of the economy, and which are therefore in search of more favourable terrain for the propagation of a powerful image.

Because of their understanding of crime in terms of *individual* criminal responsibility, the political ideas inspired by penal philosophies avoid the need to focus on *patterns* in either crime itself or the use of penal measures such as imprisonment: they maintain their theoretical integrity and force by limiting their vision. The growing prison population can be written off as a straightforward consequence of increased 'lawlessness', while the increased state control that underlies and accompanies the expansion of the prison system is not identified as a moral issue. The high level of imprisonment among certain social groups – in both Britain and the US, young black men are the most striking example – is regarded as a straightforward reflection of criminality, and the broader moral and social implications of this pattern all but ignored. Although all but the most extreme policy-makers recognise the need for non-custodial as well as custodial penalties, the former too develop without regard to their implications for civil liberties: the best example here is the growth of electronic tagging not only of offenders but also of those on bail.

Beyond the individualist framework?

How, then, might penal philosophy modify the individualistic assumptions that I have described, and what would it mean to move instead towards a communitarian approach? The communitarian conception of the person is one that recognises human identity as a fundamentally social construction and acknowledges the extent to which we discover and develop our personhood, personality, preferences and needs in particular social contexts. This vision entails a distinctive commitment to human freedom according to which importance is attached not merely to freedom in the negative sense – as the absence of external coercion and constraint – but also in the positive sense – as the capacity to discover and develop ourselves as members of a community, including a capacity to act on and shape, at least within limits, our own environment. Positive freedom implies a commitment to the creation and maintenance of facilities and the provision of resources necessary to the realisation of personal autonomy for all members of society. It goes hand-in-hand with a commitment to democratic and participatory forms of government both as a means of realising the conditions of autonomy and as a sphere in which citizens express and develop their autonomy. Such a political vision embraces a fundamental concern with the welfare of all members of society, and conceives welfare in terms of realisation not only of preferences but also of socially acknowledged interests and values which transcend the preferences of individuals. Implicit in this vision is the recognition that personal autonomy and welfare can only be realised in a social context – in the context of our relationships with each other and our interactions with social institutions. This recognition leads naturally to a focus on democratically determined social goods and collective values and on the background public culture that supports their realisation and development.

This communitarian vision points the way towards a modified theory of punishment: one which would integrate penal theory with broader political and moral issues. Identifying penal practices as one important expression of public culture, such a theory would focus on the social functions of punishment in terms of its contribution to underpinning fundamental community values enshrined in criminal law (a much more minimal one than is currently the case). This ideal vision would depend on criminal law having a relatively equal potential impact on all citizens, and on its being invoked in circumstances in which a person's behaviour has expressed an unequivocal rejection of or hostility or indifference towards the norms of that law. Although deterrent, incapacitory, rehabilitative or other similar effects might be accounted incidental benefits of punishment where they could be shown to exist, they would have the status of side-effects. For the principal functions of punishment would rather be to provide a necessary underpinning to the norms of the criminal law: to ensure that the community's adopted values are taken seriously by expressing and symbolising, unambiguously, those defining social values. The symbolic dimensions of punishment would therefore be regarded as central to its justification.

The demotion of the instrumental effects of punishment in favour of a focus on punishment as a symbolic expression of the community's judgement has important implications, I would argue, for the form of punishment. Like utilitarianism, the communitarian approach entails a strong principle of parsimony; but it is in a better position to realise parsimony in practice because it opens the way for penalties to take a predominantly symbolic rather than material form. It thus provides arguments for substantial mitigation of the present severity of the scale of punishments in the UK and, particularly, the USA, which increasingly regard substantial terms of imprisonment, often under very harsh conditions, as the standard penalty even for crimes generally acknowledged to be among the less serious. Furthermore, such an approach would focus not exclusively on individual but also on social responsibility for crime. Thus adjudication of breaches of a more minimal criminal law would be seen as providing an occasion for reflection on social responsibility for that law and its impact on citizens, as well as on the offender's responsibility. The approach would prompt questions about whether criminalisation can be justified; whether the kind of conflict or infraction in question can be tolerated without real danger to the community; or indeed whether this instance of offending reveals injustice or discrimination in the substance or operation of the criminal law. Public deliberative institutions such as courts and legislatures would find a framework here within which a broader set of questions about crime and society could be addressed.

However, before this argument can be pursued, we must address the obvious fact that the nature and meaning of criminal justice in our society in many respects falls far short of the ideal from which the theory I have sketched proceeds. Of what relevance is such a theory in real societies which are, to varying degrees, unjust and inegalitarian? Ultimately, this must depend on whether we feel that an analogy, even if a weak one, can be drawn between the legitimate functions of criminal justice in an ideal society and its actual or potential functions in our own society. In so far as contemporary penal practice reflects the sorts of principles that I am advocating, it does so in the area of juvenile justice. Here, for much of the last century, the demand for retributive punishment has been tempered by a concern for the broader social implications of youth crime and by a recognition of the need to ensure that the penal process does not reinforce young people's disposition to break the law by taking an unduly stigmatising approach. In recent years, this has often taken the form of initiatives inspired by ideas of restorative rather than retributive justice or deterrence. Such relatively progressive areas of actual practice provide a foothold for penal theory which operates in what might be called an 'interpretive' way. Rather than speaking from some Olympian point outside any actual system, interpretive theory fixes on the ideals immanent, but imperfectly realised, within particular social practices, and seeks to unearth them and to effect their practical re-evaluation. In other words, ideals to which the criminal justice system already aspires yet which it realises inadequately are used as resources for criticism and reformist prescription. The approach implies, of course, that sometimes no analogy between the actual and the ideal can be drawn: that no appealing immanent framework can be unearthed. Where penal politics have moved too far in the direction of vengeance and are driven by the impulse to quell anxieties about social dissensus through excluding and stigmatising penalties, the promotion of a more temperate debate about punishment may be impossible. Arguably, this is the current position in the US, and is fast becoming that in the UK. Once offenders and ex-offenders are viewed as being outside the community or polity, the critical bite of a communitarian or restorative vision is lost. But, at least in the UK, areas such as juvenile justice do provide a small foothold for the kind of immanent and constructive criticism that an interpretive approach advocates.

If we conclude that there is any value in current conceptions and practices of criminal justice from a communitarian perspective – for example, in acknowledging wrongs to victims, and in creating, as in certain parts of the youth system, a genuine possibility of reintegration – we can use the critical tools provided by the communitarian approach. They can furnish arguments and ideas for radical changes in our practices of criminalisation; that is, both in the criminal law and in social responses to its breach. They emphasise the interplay between general social (in)justice and (in)justice in the construction and implementation of criminal law and punishment. Taken in this way, a communitarian approach could recognise the political importance of research that explores, demonstrates and underlines phenomena such as links between recession and crime; socio-economic, racial and gender bias in the impact and enforcement of the criminal law; and the lack of humanity which all too often characterises the treatment of those on the sharpest end of both criminal justice and general social policy.

Communitarianism and imprisonment

It follows from the communitarian approach to punishment that has been sketched that certain aspects of the current practice of imprisonment in Britain and the US fly directly in the face of the very values that communitarian punishments would exist to promote. These include those prisons with inhumane and overcrowded conditions, institutions where there is minimal respect for the interests of prisoners in maintaining relationships outside the prison or even occupying their time usefully within it, complaints and disciplinary procedures which are of dubious efficacy and fairness, and an alarming growth in the size of what is inevitably, if partially, a repressive system. For if the proper social functions of punishment have to do with the maintenance of and respect for fundamental community values, then any inhumanity in a prison system must be seen as directly, both symbolically and instrumentally, counterproductive. At least some of the existing inhumanities of imprisonment could be mitigated by practical reforms. Yet a communitarian approach would lead us further, and would prompt us to question the extent of the use of such a draconian measure. The communitarian approach could provide a basis for the development of detailed critical and reformist arguments about the use and nature of imprisonment.

It is relatively easy to identify the features of imprisonment that would have to be addressed by such an analysis. They include the freedom-restricting coercion inherent in the fact of custody; the inevitable disruption of personal, social and employment relationships for the prisoner; the impact on the prisoner's family and associates; the implications of the existence of a prison service and the sorts of jobs it creates; the depression, discomfort, stress, mental disorder and general unhappiness inevitably caused to prisoners and their families during imprisonment; the continuing disabling effects of institutionalisation in terms of ability to resocialise and consequent criminogenic effects; the social and economic costs and the political implications of the prison system, broadly conceived. Clearly, these implications vary with conditions both within and outside the prison. Communitarian arguments do not hold that imprisonment is wrong in all circumstances: its effects in assuaging the well-founded fear of victims is just one obvious example of the arguments for custody which have to be fed into the moral equation. Nonetheless, each of the features of imprisonment that I have noted raises issues to which the communitarian critique may be applied, and for which it has direct implications.

Communitarian analysis also directs attention to a number of issues that have been curiously neglected by penal philosophers. In the first place, a communitarian approach implies that serious attention should be paid to the facts of crime and disorder *within* the prison, in terms not only of riots, or assaults on prisoners and staff, but also of the violence inherent in the reality of coercive incarceration, the inevitable impact this has on relations within the prison institution, and the means whereby that inherent coerciveness can be mitigated. It would therefore begin to break down the pervasive attitude that crime and violence within or implicit in the prison is somehow 'not society's concern,' or simply calls for further measures of repression and control within the institution.

Second, the communitarian perspective would lead us to question the efficacity of an approach to reforming prisons which focuses principally on 'prisoners' rights'. In the UK, for example, it has been argued that prisoners should retain all civil rights which are not implicitly or explicitly removed by the fact of custody. What this argument ignores is the possibility that incarceration inevitably puts inmates in a peculiarly powerless position in which the notion of rights can have only an attenuated meaning. At the very least, we need to consider whether the approach to reform through individual prisoners' rights begs prior questions: can we say what rights could be left intact by the fact of custody until we have answered some fundamental questions about the nature of the custodial regime and its implications for human autonomy?

Third, a communitarian approach directs our attention to evidence, from both empirical research and common sense, about the criminogenic effects of imprisonment. If the impact of imprisonment on many offenders is to make it more likely that they will offend again, imprisonment is prima facie a counterproductive institution. Imprisonment would therefore be ruled out in the majority of cases by the communitarian approach, even leaving aside the latter's commitment to parsimony in punishment.

A fourth focus of communitarian critique would be the invisibility of the prison in contemporary societies. Both geographical location and design are relevant here: high-security prisons tend to be situated away from major population centres, and the architectural structure of many prisons emphasises the exclusion of the community and the inward-looking nature of the institution. Also relevant is the extent to which non-prisoners – families, friends and other visitors drawn more widely from the community – have access to the prison. Physical and human isolation allows the prison to function as a kind of internal exile, which in turn allows the broader community to disavow or ignore our responsibility for the existence of the prison system. This situation is reinforced by the geographical and social isolation of prison staff. If we are to examine the conditions under which imprisonment is justifiable in the context of a recognition that crime raises issues of social as well as individual responsibility, we have to accept social and political responsibility for prisons, and to open them up to community scrutiny and accountability. Although it does not in itself rule out all forms of privatisation, the communitarian emphasis on shared social responsibility for prisons certainly generates severe restraints on the degree to which, and the conditions under which, delegation of state responsibility for incarceration is legitimate.

Fifth, a communitarian approach would prompt us to consider how prison life might be democratised. 'Prisoners' rights' might be reconceived in terms of genuine participation and empowerment, not least by means of proper education, training and employment within the prison. By these and similar means, prisoners' status as citizens could be properly recognised; something which a serious appreciation of the social functions of punishment suggests should be emphasised rather than denied.

Sixth, democratisation would have to extend outside the prison to embrace the issue of accountability of those running prisons to the wider community. Again, this could be furthered by opening up prisons to broader inspection, but the possibility of local government involvement and setting up interested community support and contact groups would also be explored on a communitarian approach. These changes would operate as means both of increasing accountability and of securing the place of prisons as part of the community.

Seventh, communitarian analysis would give real consideration to the inevitable suffering of those who are materially and emotionally involved with prisoners: people whose position is generally ignored in both theoretical and policy debates. In abandoning a totally individualistic perspective, we become aware of the nature of imprisonment as a penal measure that inevitably leads to punishment of innocent parties.

Eighth, a communitarian approach to punishment would also dictate a radical reappraisal of what would count as an acceptable role for those who work in prisons, and in particular for those who currently have major responsibility for security and control: prison officers. Questions would be raised about the conditions under which a civilised society should ask its members to engage in work that is primarily oriented to repressive means of control of other human beings. Current proposals that clearly offend such values are the extension of 'boot camps' in which the central role of prison officers is to ensure that young offenders under the special regime find the experience thoroughly unpleasant. This is tantamount, I would argue, to an invitation to brutality in an already repressive context. A communitarian approach would look carefully at the possibilities of retraining prison staff so as to integrate security, educational, welfare, therapeutic, working and other activities inside the prison, dismantling the current perceived hierarchy between different jobs. This would have the benefit of removing one important source of conflict and, one might hope, of facilitating a wider social revaluation of work in the prison service.

Dangers of a communitarian approach

The adoption of a communitarian approach to punishment therefore suggests a number of areas for radical reappraisal, many of which would have an important impact on the use and forms of punishment. Communitarianism as I have defined it dictates that punishment be imposed only where necessary to, and in a form that respects, the maintenance of the social values that the law exists to protect. This would mean resort in the first instance to symbolic forms of punishment such as formal statements of judgement and warning in courts and possibly apologies and other means of restoration where direct victims are involved. These are forms of punishment that can only have any meaning within a polity that regards its framework values enshrined in criminal law as defining a minimal shared identity. In cases of serious and persistent crime, one might envisage community service or restitution as the major type of non-symbolic punishment. Imprisonment, given its draconian nature, would only be imposed in very serious cases where the behaviour in question directly violates some of the community's most fundamental values and where the impact of imprisonment on the offender and his or her associates is not disproportionate to the harms caused or threatened by the offence. Obvious examples would include serious violence against the person and the grave violations of sexual integrity such as rape–areas in which both the unequivocal violation of framework values and the fear and horror created in victims justifies a stringent social response.

Inevitably, judgements such as these will be influenced by current social conceptions of the relative seriousness of different kinds of harm. It is the political duty of any community to reflect carefully upon the implications of using imprisonment as a penal measure, and to make this judgement in an informed and conscientious way. This raises what I now see as a difficulty with the communitarian approach and necessitates a modification of the argument. The principal danger is that because of its appeal to prevailing social values, communitarianism in punishment may slide into the legitimation of an authoritarian populism; one whose force in the criminal-justice area we see only too clearly in contemporary Britain and the US. If the automatic legitimation of this reactive, punitive climate is to be avoided, the values and commitments that inform and structure penal practices must themselves proceed from a process of deliberation which is at least less unreflective and pragmatic than is the case in Britain or the United States today. This means that the broad question of legitimate democratic processes is central to the agenda of penal philosophy, and gives the lie to the idea that penal philosophy is in any sense separate from broader political philosophy. A full discussion of this refined communitarianism falls beyond the scope of this chapter, but I do want to emphasise the importance of the distinction between critical communitarian positions such as those which Antony Duff and I have defended and non-critical communitarianisms. Critical communitarianism is marked by a continuing commitment to the civil libertarian values that have occupied a central place in liberal theories of punishment, as well as to the filtering of decisions about punishment through deliberative

processes informed by constitututional standards. It must be acknowledged, however, that a critical communitarian debate about
punishment can only proceed on the basis of a shared commitment to the
(re)integration of offenders in the political community. To the extent that
this goal has been abandoned in the divisive law-and-order politics of
contemporary Britain and the US, I am driven to the bleak conclusion
that no possibility of a constructive political debate about punishment
exists and that, as David Garland has recently argued, punitive
pragmatism is the inevitable order of the day.

There are, however, intellectual as well as political preconditions for
the development of a critical communitarian approach. The romanticism
and naivety that are a constant risk of communitarianism can only be
avoided if penal theorists concern themselves with actual social
practices. This means accepting the interdependence of their own
enterprise and political history and sociology. For only if one has a deep
appreciation of the role that criminal justice practices play within
particular social orders – at an institutional level as well as a symbolic
level – can one begin to work through the actual implications of
philosophical arguments in particular worlds. All penal philosophies are
implicitly shaped by their authors' intepretive grasp of the nature of
crime and punishment in their own societies, or in societies of a
relatively similar nature. Only if this grasp is secure will the
prescriptions of penal philosophy be able to realise the potential for
immanent critique, and to speak effectively to the practical issues of
reconstruction that should concern them. Without such a grounded
knowledge, theoretically inspired reforms are always likely, as in the
case of the 'just deserts' movement in the US, to miss their original goals
or even to put those goals yet further out of reach. The penal theorist
cannot, therefore, be purely a philosopher: he or she must also be
concerned with the insights of disciplines such as sociology, political
science, economics and social history.

Conclusion

In sketching the nature of a communitarian approach to punishment, I
have argued for a renewed focus on collective goods such as a humane
and peaceful environment and conditions of solidarity and mutual
support between citizens. For these provide the public culture necessary
for the development and expression not only of human autonomy and
the realisation of adequate levels of human welfare but also of a genuine
respect for the civil liberties that are properly central to the liberal

tradition. A communitarian approach to criminal justice, I have argued, could suggest a wide set of policy initiatives, many of which can already be recognised as both attractive in principle and politically feasible. However, I have also noted the dangers inherent in the appeal to 'community': the populist conservatism of an insufficiently reflective reliance on 'community' standards. Such populism is, of course, a salient feature of contemporary criminal-justice politics in Britain and the US. It poses what is probably the greatest current challenge to progressive penal politics. In the light of the proven capacity of conservative political forces to exploit appeals to popular sentiment or community feeling in engendering law-and-order policies, a communitarian approach needs to be carefully crafted so as to preserve the critical advantages of civil libertarian approaches that emphasise the claims of individuals, albeit, crucially, of individuals understood in terms of their social relationships.

Ultimately, our theories must be set to the test of practical situations. Penal philosophies cannot, without substantial supplementation, fulfil their promised role in relation to policy analysis and prescription. This supplementation must come from a variety of disciplines in the social sciences, and from a recognition of the interdependence of penal and social justice. I hope to have done enough in this chapter to indicate that a communitarian approach could point us in the direction of values and issues currently insufficiently considered. But I do not believe that the full potential of any evaluative theory can be realised unless it is developed alongside a historical and social-scientific analysis of the development of particular societies and, in particular, of the role of discourses of crime and punishment in specific political cultures. In moving from the ideal to the actual, in other words, we need an interpretive account of the role of crime and punishment in particular social orders. Without this, penal philosophy risks both naivety and misdirection. Only by building bridges between the levels of critical social analysis and interpretation and that of utopian vision can we ensure that penal theories will speak to penal practices in ways which can be heard.

Bibliographical review

Further bibliographical details of the works cited can be found at the end of this review. The philosophical theories of retributivism and utilitarianism discussed in the early part of this chapter are the subjects of a voluminous literature. The classic statement of utilitarian penal philosophy is Jeremy Bentham's *An Introduction to the Principles of Moral and Legislation* (1789; ed. J. Burns and H.L.A. Hart, Methuen, 1982). Retributivist positions are set out in Immanuel Kant's *The Philosophy of Law* (trans. W. Hastie, Edinburgh, 1887); J.D. Mabbott, (1939) 'Punishment' (*Mind*, 48, 152); and John Finnis's *Natural Law and Natural Rights* (Oxford University Press, 1980). Statements of the modern 'just deserts' approach may be found in the report of the American Friends Service Committee, *Struggle for Justice* (Hill and Wang, 1971) and Andrew von Hirsch's *Doing Justice* (1976). The most persuasive case for a 'mixed' theory of punishment is made in H.L.A. Hart's *Punishment and Responsibility* (Oxford University Press, 1968), particularly Chapter 1. Antony Duff's *Trials and Punishments* (Cambridge University Press, 1986), John Braithwaite's *Crime, Shame and Reintegration* (Cambridge University Press, 1989), John Braithwaite and Philip Pettit's *Not Just Deserts* (Oxford University Press, 1991), Andrew von Hirsch's *Censure and Sanctions* (Oxford University Press 1993), my own *State Punishment: Political Principles and Community Values* (Routledge, 1988) and Antony Duff's *Punishment, Communication and Community* (Oxford University Press, 2001) all develop mixed theories that seek to do more than merely to combine the strengths of utilitarianism and retributivism and which emphasise the symbolic aspects of punishment. For a good general discussion of modern theories of punishment, see Ted Honderich, *Punishment: the Supposed Justifications* (Penguin, 2nd edn, 1984).

The backcloth to much of my argument in this chapter is liberal political philosophy. The particular liberal tradition to which I am alluding finds expression in John Stuart Mill's *On Liberty* (1859; Penguin, 1974); its most influential modern exposition is to be found in John Rawls' *A Theory of Justice* (Clarendon Press, 1972). The communitarian critique of liberal political theory, and in particular of its conception of human individualism, has taken a variety of forms. Important contributions include Michael Sandel's *Liberalism and the Limits of Justice* (Cambridge University Press, 1982), Alasdair MacIntyre's *After Virtue* (Duckworth, 1981), and Charles Taylor's essay, 'Atomism', in his *Philosophy and the Human Sciences* (Cambridge University Press, 1985). My *State Punishment* (see above) explores the relevance of communitarian ideas for punishment. The potential dangers of communitarian approaches, which are canvassed in this paper, are explored in greater depth in Elizabeth Frazer and Nicola Lacey, *The Politics of Community* (Harvester Wheatsheaf, 1993).

The practical questions thrown up by theories of punishment have also generated a large literature. The difficulties in assessing the (utilitarian) effects of punishment are discussed in K. Bottomley and K. Pease, *Crime and Punishment: Interpreting the Data* (Open University

Press, 1986). Nils Jareborg's and Andrew von Hirsch's 'Gauging Criminal Harm: A Living-Standard Analysis'(*Oxford Journal of Legal Studies*, 11) attempts to develop a system for translating particular crimes into deserved punishments. Andrew Ashworth's *The Criminal Process: An Evaluative Study* (OUP, 1998) explores the relevance of normative principles for the detailed design and conduct of criminal justice practices. The Woolf Report, *Inquiry into Prison Disturbances* (HMSO, 1991) into conditions in English prisons applies several 'communitarian' principles in its critique of the current prison system and its argument for prison reform, as does the Prison Reform Trust's Committee on Women's Imprisonment in its report, *Justice for Women* (PRT, 2000). For a stimulating (and depressing) account of the impact of political culture on penal policy, see David Garland, *The Culture of Control* (OUP, 2001).

References

Ashworth, A. (1998) *The Criminal Process: an Evaluative Study*, 2nd edn. Oxford: Oxford University Press.

American Friends Service Committee (1971) *Struggle for Justice*. New York: Hill and Wang.

Bentham, J. (1789) *An Introduction to the Principles of Morals and Legislation* (J. Burns and H.L.A. Hart, eds, 1982). London: Methuen.

Braithwaite, J. (1989) *Crime, Shame and Reintegration*. Cambridge: Cambridge University Press.

Braithwaite, J. and Pettit, P. (1990) *Not Just Deserts*. Oxford: Clarendon Press.

Duff, A. (1986) *Trials and Punishments*. Cambridge: Cambridge University Press.

Duff, A. (2001) *Punishment, Communication and Community*. Oxford: Oxford University Press.

Finnis, J. (1980) *Natural Law and Natural Rights*. Oxford: Clarendon Press.

Frazer, E. and Lacey, N. (1993) *The Politics of Community*. New York: Harvester.

Garland, D. (2001) *The Culture of Control*. Oxford: Oxford University Press.

Hart, H.L.A. (1968) *Punishment and Responsibility*. New York: Oxford University Press.

Honderich, T. (1984) *Punishment: the Supposed Justifications*, 2nd edn. Harmondsworth: Penguin.

Jareborg, N. and Von Hirsch, A. (1991) 'Gauging Criminal Harm: A Living-Standard Analysis', *Oxford Journal of Legal Studies*, 11, 1.

Lacey, N. (1988) *State Punishment: Political Principles and Community Values*. London: Routledge.

Lacey, N. (1994) 'Government as Manager, Citizen as Consumer', *Modern Law Review*, 57, 534.

Lacey, N. (2001) 'Social Policy, Civil Society and The Institutions of Criminal Justice', *Australian Journal of Legal Philosophy*, 26, 7–25.

Maguire, M., Morgan, R. and Reiner, R. (2002) *The Oxford Handbook of Criminology*, 3rd edn. Oxford: Oxford University Press.

Mill, J.S. (1974) *On Liberty* (originally published in 1859). Harmondsworth Penguin.

Prison Reform Trust (2000) *Justice for Women: The Need for Reform*. London: Prison Reform Trust.

Rawls, J. (1972). *A Theory of Justice*. Oxford: Clarendon Press.

Raz, J. (1986). *The Morality of Freedom*. Oxford: Clarendon Press.

Taylor, C. (1985) *Philosophy and the Human Sciences*. Cambridge: Cambridge University Press.

Von Hirsch, A. (1976). *Doing Justice*. New York: Hill and Wang.

Von Hirsch, A. (1993) *Censure and Sanctions*. Oxford: Clarendon Press.

Lord Woolf (1991) *Inquiry into Prison Disturbances*. London: HMSO.

Zedner, L. (1994) 'Reparation and Retribution', *Modern Law Review*, 57, 228.

Chapter 7

Restorative justice and punishment

Richard Young and Carolyn Hoyle[1]

As we write this chapter, the prison population of England and Wales stands at over 70,000 and is increasing at a rate of 400 inmates per week. Since 1993, when prison numbers hit a low of 42,000, this rise has been relentless. The inevitable result is overcrowded cells and worsening regimes, prisoners placed far from their families, and a much greater risk of violence, riots and suicides. Throughout this era of rampant jail expansion, crime rates have fallen steadily; the British Crime Survey suggests an overall decrease since the mid-1990s of 22 per cent. Similar trends of declining crime rates and expanding prison populations have occurred in various other countries, including the United States, Canada, Australia and New Zealand. The lack of evidence to suggest that the increasing use of imprisonment has contributed to a reduction in crime has led to a widespread questioning of custodial sentencing.

In the United Kingdom, ministers and senior judges, not to mention prison reformers, urge the criminal courts to use imprisonment sparingly, cautioning against the negative effects of prison over-crowding. Yet sentencers seem reluctant to heed this warning, perhaps reflecting a perception of public punitiveness, perhaps believing that in many cases there is no other option. The rise of restorative justice has coincided with this period of expansionism and its advocates have argued vehemently that for many offenders it can provide a viable alternative to prison. At the same time, some restorativists have resisted considering restorative justice as a form of punishment. Unless we tackle the vexed question of the appropriate role of restorative justice within state punishment, we are unlikely to persuade judges and magistrates that restorative justice has anything more to offer the criminal process than the possibility of diversion for young, petty offenders.

199

The bulk of the literature on restorative justice was for many years theoretically unsophisticated, containing a mixture of uncritical description, aspirational advocacy, and critiques that paid little attention to empirical reality. While publications of this ilk are still commonplace, they are beginning to be overshadowed by more thoughtful writings. In particular, the sociological roots and philosophical underpinnings of restorative justice are now the subject of much debate and analysis. It is our view that the maturing of the literature is important to the future prospects of restorative justice. As we shall see, the development of a thorough understanding of the relationship between punishment and restorative justice may be an important factor in determining whether the latter is able to sink foundations that will be deep enough to resist the winds of penal fashion.

Defining restorative justice

The term 'restorative justice' as yet has no settled meaning, but for the purposes of this chapter we will take it to encompass values, aims and processes that have as their common factor attempts to repair the harm caused by criminal behaviour. Most restorative justice advocates agree that its core values include: mutual respect; the empowerment of all parties involved in the process; accountability; consensual, non-coercive participation and decision-making; and the inclusion of all the relevant parties in dialogue. The inclusion of victims as 'relevant parties' is generally agreed to be an extremely important value. There is disagreement over what it means to participate, with some arguing that participation can be indirect – through a mediator, for example, or through a representative at a meeting.

Restorative justice embraces multiple aims. While some argue that it should aim at such outcomes as a reduction in the risk of re-offending, the lessening of the fear of crime and a strengthening of a sense of community, others focus more on the restorative process itself. The latter argue that this should seek to restore all three groups who are recognised as having a legitimate interest in determining the response to an offence – offenders, victims and those making up the wider society – and that restoration should address their material and emotional loss, safety, damaged relationships, dignity and self-respect. The key aim for many is to give a voice to both victims and offenders. Restorative processes should hold offenders accountable by requiring them to explain how they think their actions might have affected others. Through dialogue it is hoped that victims' feelings of anger or fear towards 'their' offender, or crime more generally, will be alleviated, and that offenders will experience genuine remorse and develop a greater sense of victim empathy. As with sentencing, it is important that these aims are ranked in some order of priority if undesirable incoherence and inconsistency are to be avoided. Currently, there are deep divisions in the literature concerning what this ranking should be.

Many definitions of restorative justice emphasise the importance of a dialogic process. They make clear that victims and offenders, together with their respective 'supporters', must come together in a face-to-face meeting and between themselves must determine the outcome of that meeting. This model fits with the forms of restorative justice known as 'conferencing', direct mediation (as opposed to 'shuttle' mediation) and 'circles', and allows for restorative justice to work alongside the established criminal process rather than positing it as a wholly new, alternative system. The necessity for dialogue, however, is sometimes seen as being too restrictive. Wider definitions include judicially imposed reparative measures such as community service and compensation orders (as long as the intent is to bring 'healing' to victims and the offended 'community'). A 'restorative response' is thus enabled, even in those cases where a face-to-face meeting is not possible either because the parties are unable or unwilling to enter into dialogue or because there is no identifiable victim of the offence. As a way out of the definitional divergence, the majority of commentators concede that, regardless of the appropriateness of 'lesser' alternatives, the best outcomes are achieved when victims and offenders are brought together in a face-to-face meeting by someone trained in facilitating the kind of dialogue that promotes the repair of harm. The question of who should take on the role of facilitator is another point of some controversy.

Restorative justice generally presupposes that the offender has acknowledged responsibility for an offence. In other words, it is not concerned with fact-finding but with an appropriate response to an admitted offence. Within the criminal justice process its concern is therefore sentencing and not the trial itself. Early restorativists shied away from considering their own forms of victim–offender mediation as having anything to do with sentencing as traditionally conceived. By contrast, we think there is much to be said for thinking about restorative justice in terms of sentencing and punishment. In what follows we consider the development of restorative justice, its applications, its relationship with state justice, its relationship with vengeance and punishment, and some interconnected philosophical issues.

The birth, infancy and maturation of 'restorative justice'

The modern Anglo-American professional and bureaucratic criminal justice system, with decisions on whether to prosecute concentrated in the hands of the state, did not emerge until the latter part of the nineteenth century. Although this system has, at different times, swung to and fro between rehabilitative and retributive models of punishment, it has always focused primarily on the offender. The consequence has been the marginalisation of both victims and communities from the day-to-day workings of the criminal process.

The 1970s and 1980s saw the start of diversionary initiatives that tried to embrace victims. The first 'victim–offender reconciliation programme', founded in Kitchener, Ontario, in 1974, was followed by various American community-based programmes which brought together victims and offenders, usually after a court had passed sentence. By the mid-1990s, over 300 such mediation schemes in North America, and many similar schemes in England and Wales, were promoting individual reparation and reconciliation.

The first attempts to include 'the wider community' (however defined) in such programmes emerged in the 1980s. Indigenous Canadian peace-making processes, for example, provided the inspiration for 'sentencing circles' – group mediation involving offenders, victims, their families and other community members – which focus on the harms resulting from offences and seek consensus on their redress. These local models began to catch the attention of criminal-justice agents, academics and policy-makers throughout the English-speaking world. Although they encompassed a broad range of aims and practices, most were classified under a new umbrella label: 'restorative justice'. While many of these localised models struggled for survival on the margins of the established system, aspirations that it could become a fully functioning alternative to established criminal justice began to be voiced.

The jurisdiction that has gone furthest in this regard is New Zealand, where 'family group conferencing' has become the standard way of dealing with serious offences committed by youths. In this model, offenders and their family members meet with victims and their supporters to discuss the offence and its aftermath. The offender and his or her family are given some private time to formulate suggestions for an appropriate reparative outcome, which are then discussed by the reconvened conference. Subsequent to its adoption in New Zealand, the conferencing model has become popular in Australia, the United Kingdom, the United States and elsewhere. The precise form that conferencing takes differs from jurisdiction to jurisdiction. Australian practices were initially strongly influenced by the criminological theory of reintegrative shaming; early models were police-led, and included no provision for private family time. In the United Kingdom, the police-led model proved influential in the late 1990s and restorative justice accordingly took root primarily within pre-court diversionary practices, particularly police cautioning. In both Australia and the United Kingdom the ideological dominance of the police-led model has now declined somewhat as other agencies entering the field have influenced ideas about best practice.

Restorative justice schemes are usually targeted at young offenders, particularly those at an early stage of their criminal career who have not committed a serious offence. In England and Wales, for example, the 46 'restorative justice programmes' funded by the Youth Justice Board in the early 2000s all dealt with relatively minor offences committed by young people. The same emphasis can be seen in the systemic reforms that have taken place in this jurisdiction since the current government came to power in 1997. These have focused sharply on youth justice. Thus, guidance has encouraged the adoption of a restorative ethos among those responsible for delivering pre-court cautions, reprimands and warnings; measures used primarily for youths committing relatively petty offences. A more fundamental transformation of youth justice practices was achieved by legislation requiring the criminal courts to refer the vast majority of young people convicted for the first time to a youth offender panel. These referral orders envisage that the panel (made up of two community volunteers and one youth justice professional) will operate in accordance with the principles of restorative justice. In practice this means that victims should be invited to take part in a discussion with the panel members, the offender, and his or her supporters aimed at settling a programme of reparative and rehabilitative activities. If this 'contract' is fulfilled, the offender's conviction is regarded as spent, meaning that it does not have to be declared in response to questions about one's background except in limited circumstances.

Important as these various developments are, they are all sited in the shallow end of the penal system. However, there are a number of different schemes in this and in other countries which use restorative interventions for adult offenders and for more serious crimes. Programmes in Thames Valley, England, and Canberra, Australia, both deal with adult offenders as well as juveniles, and both can deal with moderately serious offences. Since the establishment of these programmes, the government has set up experiments in England and

Wales to evaluate the effectiveness of restorative justice for adults convicted of fairly serious offences, and in South Australia conferences are now being held for such offences. As discussed further below, in recent years restorative justice has been used selectively for crimes involving severe violence, including those where death resulted. In some of its manifestations restorative justice is clearly well past infancy and could be more appropriately likened to a rebellious teenager co-existing uneasily with established authority. Until restorative justice reaches full maturity, its implications for routine criminal justice practices will remain somewhat uncertain.

Explaining the rise of restorative justice

Most of the many accounts of the development of restorative justice go little further than highlighting the successive inception of particular forms of novel practice in a variety of jurisdictions. This chronology is typically accompanied by a descriptive account of how practices have spread and mutated internationally. Our own abbreviated chronological understanding is set out above. Deeper analyses, which seek to identify the social forces that might explain why restorative justice arose at this particular moment of penal history, are now starting to appear.

For some writers, a crucial impetus was the prominence of social movements of the 1960s and 1970s. These included: feminist campaigns concerning violence against women and children, and the inept and often damaging response of criminal justice systems to such crimes; the civil rights movement in the United States (partly inspired by racist justice practices); and protests by indigenous groups in the United States, Canada, Australia, New Zealand and elsewhere about the historical segregation and over-imprisonment of native peoples. Other forces at work were the growth of consumerism in the sphere of public services and a decline in trust of professionals. The criminal justice system was increasingly seen by key groups of offenders and victims as in need of reform, supplementation or replacement, and a variety of new practices and organisations began to emerge: advocacy of prisoners' rights and alternatives to or abolition of imprisonment; neighbourhood-based conflict resolution processes; victim support and advocacy groups; and the various forms of restorative justice to which we have already referred. Contrary to the oft-heard claim that restorative justice has been a practice-driven movement, these writers also point out that much relevant theoretical work preceded and informed practice. Literatures on informal justice; abolitionism; reintegrative shaming;

psychological theories of emotion (particularly affect theory) and perceptions of legitimacy; the philosophical underpinnings of criminal justice; and religious and spiritual reflections on the criminal process all played a part in shaping practices. At the same time as identifying some common roots, emphasis is placed on the need to examine in each jurisdiction the unique constellation of factors (cultural, historical, legal, institutional, political and so on) that help explain the particular forms and meanings that characterise restorative justice at a particular point in time and space. The plea, in short, is for a much 'thicker' account of the rise of restorative justice that pays proper attention to its global, social and historical context as well as local variation and flux.

This story of 'bottom-up' pressure for transforming justice practices should itself be set in the context of other changes in the field of punishment. When one takes into account 'top-down' developments in contemporary penality (the ideas and practices of punishment), restorative justice can appear something of an anomaly. The growth of the 'risk society', in which the key theme is 'public protection' through the management and segregation of threatening individuals and groups (involving the use of situational crime prevention, risk-assessment tools, CCTV, child curfews, sex-offender registration, electronic tagging, indeterminate custodial sentences, mass imprisonment and so on) has preoccupied some scholars to such an extent that restorative justice has been relegated to the status of a dismissive aside or footnote. The 'criminology of the other' that modern penality encompasses, in which offenders are defined as the predatory, callous 'them', quite separate from the law-abiding, victimised 'us', and the 'criminology of everyday life' in which crime is accepted as a constant threat that must be guarded against routinely through situational crime prevention, has little in common with restorative justice's inclusionary emphasis on promoting mutual respect, empathetic exchanges and restoration of relationships. Nor does restorative justice's emphasis on responding to crime through community dialogue and consensus (a form of communitarian crime control) cohere well with the growing significance of individualistic legal protection under the European Convention of Human Rights and other international charters. This raises two related questions. First, how can one explain the flourishing of restorative justice in such an apparently inauspicious context? Second, how and where is restorative justice succeeding in carving out space for its operations and what concessions are being made along the way? Put another way, how are the tensions between the paradigms of risk management, human rights and restorative justice resolved in practice?

At a general theoretical level, the questions can be addressed together in the following way. While human rights norms now provide a safety-net beneath which protection for individual liberty cannot fall, there remains plenty of scope for laws and legal processes oriented towards the promotion of social welfare. Such laws might either operate through organic communitarian processes, in which social groups and institutions respond to deviant behaviour by mobilising shared norms and other forms of informal social control, or through bureaucratic-administrative arrangements characteristic of the risk-management approach. In contemporary societies the latter have achieved pre-eminence because the conditions for communitarian control (in particular, the presence of interdependent communities with shared values) are perceived to be largely lacking. But restorative justice remains an attractive prospect for those who do not subscribe to the 'criminology of the other', who believe that communitarian control is still a viable option in at least some cases, and who yearn for a more humanised response to crime. Accordingly, we should expect to find restorative justice carving out a space for itself in spheres where this kind of moralising, relational social control seems most apt.

The traditional subjects of moral pedagogy are the young, and it is noticeable that the sphere most often colonised by restorative justice is the youth justice system. We may also note that within a morally pluralistic (and socially divided) society it may be harder to persuade offenders (especially the young) of the legitimacy of criminal-law norms than it is to encourage empathy and remorse for the suffering of flesh-and-blood victims. Thus the rise in concern for victims of crime combines with a shift away from moralising based on abstract criminal norms to produce the emphasis, within restorative justice, on harm to people. Nonetheless, under contemporary conditions many offenders (and others) do not have a strong stake in making or mending co-operative relationships. Moreover, while the young may be more impressed by concrete harms than abstract ones, adolescents are less likely than adults to think through issues from someone else's perspective. It would thus be naive to expect 100 per cent rates of participation in restorative programmes, or to anticipate that empathetic exchanges leading to genuine apology and repair of relationships will routinely occur within conferences. No doubt weaknesses in implementation can be blamed in part for the low rates of victim participation and restorativeness seen in many restorative justice programmes, but contemporary social structure is likely to be another important explanatory factor.

This leaves open the question of why the state has provided top-down support for restorative justice in youth justice and some other spheres. It might be argued that this support is consistent with the bifurcated approach to crime control evident in many advanced capitalist societies. On the one hand, the state has adopted a 'responsibilisation' strategy in which private firms, voluntary agencies and citizens and communities are required to bear more of the burden of routine crime control, especially for the relatively minor offences that form such a high proportion of the 'crime problem'. On the other hand, the state has buttressed its claims to residual sovereign power by pursuing coercive risk-focused measures for those labelled as the most serious and persistent offenders. This helps us to understand why those agitating for change in criminal justice have succeeded primarily in the lower reaches of the system. In addition, while purporting to do things for victims is politically popular, for the state to support the idea that victims should meet with serious or persistent offenders would appear a much riskier strategy. Indeed, one might argue that the adoption of a low-key or reparative approach to minor offending increases the pressure on the state to respond much more punitively to those crimes that excite public emotion.

The possibility remains, however, that the impressive bridgehead now established by restorative justice may provide a basis for a more comprehensive challenge to established criminal-justice routines. In the United Kingdom the prospects for this have been bolstered by the government's enthusiasm for rehabilitation programmes and evidence-based policies, but weakened by that same government's avid pursuit of managerial efficiency and risk-based policies. For example, the insistence that criminal-justice practitioners must, efficiently and economically, produce reductions in re-offending carries the danger of distorting key values and principles of restorative justice. Pressures on practitioners from central government focus not only on crime rates, but also on *apparently* unacceptable delays in the system. Many commentators have noted that the emphasis on speedy disposal within modern criminal justice works against the time needed to prepare and facilitate meetings between victims, offenders and their respective supporters. The 15-day limit set for youth offender panels to hold their first meeting following a referral from the courts, for example, has contributed to the very low rate of victim attendance at these meetings. Moreover, the emphasis on reducing offending may lead to restorative justice becoming offender-focused in day-to-day operation, with the inevitable result of marginalising other key players in the process. These kinds of tension between competing policy strands are becoming ever more evident as restorative justice practices spread beyond the youth justice terrain.

Moving beyond youth justice: wider applications of restorative justice

The use of restorative justice as a response to domestic and sexual violence is controversial. Many feminists have campaigned for years in favour of 'tough' arrest, prosecution and punishment policies for men who commit violence against women. Only relatively recently have their efforts begun to bear punitive fruit. From this perspective, a restorative justice response to gendered violence can be seen as undermining these reforms by sending the wrong symbolic message about the seriousness of such offences. This assumes, however, that restorative justice would operate by diverting violent men away from the courts and by treating their offences as expressing a civil dispute or conflict requiring a reconciliatory response. Both these assumptions are incorrect. The more serious the offence, the more likely it is that restorative justice will operate as part of court sentencing and with a clear sense among the participants that the behaviour in question must be authoritatively condemned in order to express solidarity with the victim and to reinforce an important societal norm. Moreover, as we will argue below, it is a serious mistake to regard restorative justice as a non-punitive practice. It is likely to be seen by many victims as a more punitive response than relatively small fines and conditional discharges – typical responses of the courts to the majority of domestic violence offences.

Some feminist critics argue that when restorative justice is used for offences of domestic and sexual violence it brings with it the dangers of intimidation, emotional pressure and re-victimisation. They question the assumption that vulnerable victims are able to assert their own needs and promote their own interests in the presence of the perpetrators of violence against them. In other words, rather than empowering such victims, restorative justice might further traumatise them. Others, conversely, see restorative justice processes as increasing women's choices as well as promoting their safety. The hope is that within a restorative process female victims will be supported by their family and friends and helped to express their stories, their emotions and their hopes and fears for the future. It is argued that restorative justice can allow equal representation of parties and consequently a hearing for victims who would otherwise be powerless, excluded or silenced. The empirical record is currently too thin to allow conclusions to be drawn about the degree to which these potential dangers or benefits materialise in practice.

In terms of practical outcomes, it can be argued that restorative justice, with its mobilisation of informal social control mechanisms, and its emphasis on inducing empathy to change attitudes and behaviour in the offender, can provide more effective justice for female victims of male violence than the existing court-based system. At present many prosecutions fail because victims, seeing more risks than benefits in pursuing the matter, withdraw their complaints. Victims of domestic violence are much more interested in securing an end to the violence they suffer than in the symbolism of traditional state punishment. It is possible that a greater proportion of female victims would co-operate with the criminal justice system if it took their interests – in participation, respectful treatment and safety – more fully into account. While a great deal of preparatory and follow-up work would be required in cases of domestic and sexual violence where victims and offenders wished to meet, restorative justice might play a useful role in responding to offences that would otherwise receive inadequate or no statutory attention. Similar points to those made above about domestic violence are applicable when considering racially motivated offending, although space precludes further analysis here.

Corporate and 'white-collar' criminals are rarely discussed in the restorative justice literature despite the suggestion of leading reintegrative shaming theorists that the regulation of corporate crime in most countries is implicitly somewhat 'restorative'. Communitarian regulation is argued to have achieved considerable success in securing a more responsible approach to compliance with the law by institutions as diverse as coal-mining firms, nuclear power plants and nursing homes. However, the extent to which white-collar criminals may be beyond the reach of the techniques of reintegrative shaming is beginning to be debated. Moreover, critics consider that it may be premature to assume that a deterrent strategy is relatively ineffective in controlling corporate and white-collar crime, when the agencies responsible for the detection and prosecution of such offences have typically been chronically under-resourced. Even some of those advocating restorative justice for white-collar offenders concede that deterrence and, ultimately, incapacitation, may be needed for the recalcitrant. A separate question is whether the heavy use of compliance strategies for white-collar crime under-mines the symbolic power of the law. If there were a shift towards an explicit use of restorative justice principles, such crime would be more authoritatively (and in our view, appropriately) condemned than at present. Currently, the securing of future compliance with the law is given so much weight that the issues of restoration and justice for victims of white-collar and corporate crime are woefully neglected.

Probably the most serious cases dealt with by way of restorative practices have occurred in North America, where victim–offender mediation and dialogue are increasingly used for cases of homicide and sexual assault. Indeed, there have been mediation sessions between families of murder victims and their killers, shortly before the murderer's execution. It has been argued that this experience helps both parties to develop a sense of 'closure' and resolution, although it seems to us grotesque that any involvement with the state's taking of a further human life could be described as restorative. A reintegrative state execution is surely a contradiction in terms. Such practices provide a stark illustration of the way in which restorative justice principles can become compromised by too close an engagement with the exclusionary aspects of criminal justice.

Restorative practices are increasingly being used in response to behaviours which, although not brought within the criminal justice system, are harmful either to the offender or to others. For example, restorative techniques are used in some schools to deal with cases of bullying, truancy, and with conflict between staff and pupils as well as for some minor offences committed in school. Part of the rationale in such situations has been to reduce suspensions and exclusions of pupils from school, responses which are now seen as likely to promote crime. Paradoxically, this inclusionary approach has been supported by the government in England and Wales at the same time as it has advocated the punitive and exclusionary use of Anti-Social Behaviour Orders (ASBOs) for minor offences or disorderly behaviour. In some areas, lurid naming-and-shaming campaigns have followed the imposition of ASBOs, with local news coverage, posters and leaflets informing communities of who is subject to an order and what its conditions are. Both restorative justice practices and the naming and shaming of youths subject to ASBOs are examples of the devolution of crime-control responsibilities to local communities, but they are informed by very different principles and values. The former seek to reduce harm and repair relationships by bringing together those who are perceived to have wronged with those who consider themselves to be damaged by these behaviours, whereas the latter seek primarily to exclude, under the justification of protecting the public. Rather than bringing people together and finding common ground and paths to recompense, they further dichotomise communities into 'victims' and 'offenders'.

Another example of naming and shaming is provided by the treatment of some people released from prison for sex offences. There has been a series of notorious cases where people who have already been punished by a term of imprisonment are then further punished by national and local media campaigns to 'name and shame', with the justification of protecting communities apparently at risk. Such responses may well undo any rehabilitative work done with the offender in prison and, by forcing ex-prisoners to keep on the move to escape such publicity, could make more likely further offending. Contrast this with Canadian 'circles of support', which are formed (mainly of lay volunteers) to help plan for and deal with the release of serious sexual offenders (often guilty of paedophilia) into the community at the end of their prison sentence. Circles agree on a reintegration plan to reduce the fears within the community, and to try to reduce the likelihood of re-offending, by holding the released prisoner accountable to the plan and by providing him with the necessary community resources.

Now that restorative justice is being used to respond to such a wide range of offences and other behaviours, the question of the state's role in restorative practices cannot be ducked. On the one hand, there is the view that the state must play an active role in regulating restorative justice through state-funded facilitators and legal advisers, as well as by establishing proportionality limits and procedural safeguards. On the other hand, there is the view that state involvement will contaminate restorative values and lead to the widening of the nets of formal social control (with the result that more people find themselves defined as offenders in need of intervention) and to the dominance of professionals over the community. This is a complex debate and we confine ourselves here to a brief discussion of three key questions: who is best placed to facilitate restorative processes?; is the provision of legal advice desirable?; and, what is the appropriate relationship between state justice and localised justice?

The state's role in facilitating restorative justice

One of the key requirements of a restorative process is that the facilitator remains respectful of all participants and dispassionate in approach. By asking the right questions of the right people at the right time, they should be able to facilitate the recounting of multiple experiences and explanations within a safe environment, almost regardless of the seriousness or sensitivity of the offence and the biographical details of the offender or other participants. They should have no personal agenda in the questions they ask or in who they invite to participate.

This raises the question of whether any professional state representative can be true to the values of restorative justice. Do they all come to the process with an intrusive amount of professional baggage? Fears about police officers facilitating restorative conferences are more often voiced than concerns about other state agents, for example, social workers. Some argue that the police are exploiting the vogue for restorative justice to expand their punitive function, and that it is wrong in principle (from a checks-and-balances perspective) for an investigatory body to play such an influential role in the finalising of a case.

The United Kingdom and New Zealand provide two different models of state involvement in restorative justice. Conferences in the Thames Valley Police area of the UK, which take place at the pre-court level (as part of a caution or warning), are usually facilitated solely by police officers although occasionally co-facilitated by a police officer and a social worker. The training the facilitators receive requires them to use a script that charts a course towards a genuinely restorative process and outcome. In theory, therefore, it should matter little who facilitates the process. However, research in the Thames Valley area observed conferences where police facilitators did use their power in an unacceptable way. In some cases, for example, the conference process took on the structure and tone of a police interview. In others, police facilitators lapsed into stigmatic or deterrent language, or became defensive when participants raised concerns about how the police had arrested or otherwise dealt with the offender. This points to the importance of strategies for securing full implementation of restorative blueprints. Criminological theories and criminal justice research alike tell us that police 'agendas' are highly likely to result in middle-class participants being treated more fairly and more respectfully than those lower down the social scale, disparities which contradict restorative values. This established understanding of policing practices has provided the basis for powerful critiques of police involvement in community conferencing within indigenous communities. Central to these critiques is the view that it is deeply problematic for a police service that is not seen by indigenous people as legitimate to play such a central role in restorative processes. This concern seems also to be applicable to the position of marginalised communities within Western countries. For example, many of those living in disadvantaged areas with a high proportion of unemployed, immigrant or ethnic-minority residents may see the police in predominantly negative terms – as part of the problem rather than as part of the solution.

In New Zealand, the role of facilitator is taken by a 'youth justice co-ordinator', normally a social worker. Conferencing, led by social workers, like police conferencing, is not without its problems. Research in New Zealand has found that social welfare and restorative justice values are not necessarily reconcilable, and where conferences have met restorative objectives and reflected restorative values, this has happened despite being placed in a social welfare setting rather than because of it. In the few cases in the authors' Thames Valley research where social workers acted as co-facilitators there was similarly a pronounced drift away from a focus on restoration for all the stakeholders and towards assessing and responding to the offender's problems and needs.

From this discussion it might seem prudent to set up an independent agency specialising in restorative justice facilitation. This, however, would have enormous cost implications and it seems unlikely that the state would be willing either to provide the necessary funds or to provide sufficient referrals. Furthermore, the majority of participants seem to welcome state involvement in the process. In particular, police officer facilitation in a number of jurisdictions has been found to have lent legitimacy to the process. Participants appear to expect and want an authoritative response to criminal offences and police facilitation is seen as achieving this. It is worth noting, however, that this desire might be satisfied in other ways. In the UK, for example, the volunteer members of the youth offender panels could take on the role of facilitator with minimal additional training. A secondary advantage of police involvement is that it encourages a community-policing ethos in which crime prevention through restoration of relationships and moral persuasion takes priority over a simple deterrence model of policing and punishment. This point should not be overstated, however, for this educative effect has been found to be largely confined to those acting as facilitators rather than permeating throughout a police service.

As a matter of practical politics, police facilitation in pre-court justice seems set to continue for the foreseeable future and the pressing question is how this should be regulated. It would seem desirable, at a minimum, for police facilitators to have played no part in the investigation of a case. Additional strategies are needed, however, to guard against the risk that facilitators may allow the agendas of the agencies in which they are based to dominate the restorative process. Such strategies could include a requirement that representatives of state agencies co-facilitate with a volunteer drawn from the local community (an arrangement that seems to work well in the running of youth offender panels); the monitoring of practice by other agencies, peers, or supervisors; the use of feedback forms from participants; occasional top-up training; and the encouragement of independent research into practice 'on the ground'. In addition, police services should consider whether they are likely to be regarded as legitimate facilitators by the communities in which they work. If not, reform of policing more generally should be secured prior to, or alongside, the use of police facilitators in pre-court justice. An alternative is for legal advice and representation to be provided to the participants as a check on any potential unfairness or abuse of the power of the facilitator. While this introduces another possible way in which the state could regulate the restorative process, it also carries the potential for its distortion.

Safeguarding restorative justice through the provision of legal advice

Most people who are concerned about police and prosecution powers are in favour of suspects' and defendants' rights. They approve of legal frameworks that provide 'equality of arms'; in other words, they welcome the role of legal advisers in the justice system. Some restorative justice advocates, however, do not wish to see lawyers involved in the restorative justice process, or at least wish to see that role greatly restricted. Their fears are that rights-based forms of representation fail to confront offenders with the impact of their actions on others, that lawyers will monopolise the process, and that professional advice will fail to give sufficient weight to the interests of participants other than the offender. These fears appear to be rooted in the assumption that criminal lawyers typically act as a 'mouthpiece' for offenders, mitigating and thus minimising their personal responsibility by using ploys, exaggerations and untruths in order to secure low penalties. While this assumption is something of a caricature of how defence lawyers operate in the criminal courts, it is nonetheless right to acknowledge that pure adversarial ideology calls for lawyers to put the interests of clients above all others, and that this sits uneasily with restorative values.

One might argue that if restorative justice is being used in a diversion scheme, with no risk of re-entry into the criminal process, then legal representation is less crucial. However, if restorative schemes are, in effect, being used to sentence people, legal representation should be encouraged, if not mandated, as otherwise the guarantees against unfair processes and disproportionate outcomes are too weak. The key functions of lawyers in terms of obtaining and clarifying information, advising on procedures and options, and acting as advocates where defendants are unable to speak effectively for themselves, may be as pertinent to restorative justice as to the criminal courts. However, most restorativists who concede a role for lawyers argue that they need to be trained to act in a manner different to that envisaged by pure adversarial ideology. In other words, rather than be combative, they need to act in a way that furthers restorative values. In the same way that defence lawyers already owe duties to the court as well as their client, in a restorative forum they should be seen as owing duties to other participants – such as to treat them with respect and to help in the search for restorative outcomes that are fair to all concerned.

At present, in England and Wales, there is no requirement for young people who are given a reprimand or a warning to have access to legal advice. Similarly, offenders sentenced to a referral order by the courts will rarely be legally represented in their dealings with youth offender panels. Indeed, the proposition that offenders should have legal representation during a conference or other restorative process has provoked some government hostility. Hence the original *Guidance for Youth Offender Panels* insisted that young people should not be legally represented at a youth offender panel meeting. This was in clear conflict with Article 6(3)(c) of the European Convention on Human Rights, which provides that a person who is the subject of criminal proceedings is entitled to employ a lawyer of his or her choice for each stage of the criminal process, with free legal assistance where justice so demands. Concern raised over the guidance resulted in the government deciding that legal representatives should be allowed to attend youth offender panel meetings. However, since at present legal aid is not available for panel meetings, this change is unlikely to have much impact in practice. The government could reasonably be accused of paying mere lip-service to the protection of the human rights of minors in the criminal process.

The relationship of the state to restorative justice

Perhaps the greatest tension in restorative justice is to be found in the question of whether it should be integrated into the mainstream state justice system, and if so, to what extent. Some restorativists have argued that restorative processes should largely or entirely replace the established criminal justice process, partly because they see that process as irredeemably flawed. The wisdom of this aspiration may be doubted. One of the ostensible and significant benefits of a restorative approach is that it brings about a genuinely dialogic approach which, empirical evidence suggests, satisfies all parties involved. If the high case-loads currently processed by the criminal courts were handled *en masse* by a restorative justice system, there would be little hope of facilitating meaningful discourse in the majority of cases. Restorative conferences achieve high levels of satisfaction with the communicative aspect of the process partly because the facilitators generally have the luxury of time to prepare for and negotiate the process. If restorative justice were to assume a significantly larger case-load, which it would have to do if mainstream criminal justice were sidelined or even dismantled, it too would be likely to take on some, if not all, of the routinised features of the court process.

Arguments for a purely communitarian, restorative approach to crime partly stem from a rejection of the established criminal justice system and all its perceived ills. Restorative justice is held up as the fairer, more accountable alternative; rooted in the local community and taking into account the contexts within which people commit or experience crime. As such, it is argued that restorative justice has the potential to empower indigenous peoples and other marginalised groups by taking seriously their distinctive cultural norms. This argument is sometimes underpinned by a romanticised understanding of indigenous justice and a concomitant blindness to the potential virtues of state justice. Indigenous justice is not always and everywhere restorative in orientation. And local, individualised justice can be disproportionately punitive (whether through 'negative shaming' or through particularly harsh reparation agreements) and tainted by gendered, racial and other forms of prejudice. Any process that purports to change behaviour, and to facilitate agreements between people who might ordinarily be assumed to be opposed to one another, needs to be accountable and subject to safeguards designed to protect the rights and interests of all participants. As a minimum, courts are needed for those offenders who do not accept guilt or who do not wish to accept an outcome proposed by other participants during a restorative intervention.

An institutionalised response to criminal offences, in particular to the more serious offences, ultimately requires some input from one or other of the criminal-justice agencies – even if only for societal recognition of the legitimacy of the process. Criminal justice cannot be a merely private affair but necessarily involves a public dimension. If offences are not seen to be dealt with effectively, vigilantism becomes more likely and there is even a danger of undermining the general deterrent effect of the criminal law. It is certainly the case that some communities do not perceive state justice to be either legitimate or effective. It is equally beyond doubt that state justice often fails to deliver on its promises of safeguarding rights, promoting equality of treatment and securing fairness in the distribution of punishment. But the question is whether the appropriate response to this situation is to set up an alternative justice system as opposed to seeking to reform state justice. In practice, this may be a false dichotomy, as the very act of introducing a stand-alone system is likely to galvanise the established criminal justice system into whatever degree of reform is thought necessary to secure renewed legitimacy.

More pragmatically, purely community-based restorative justice schemes with no statutory basis tend to receive only a small number of, usually non-serious, referrals. In our view it is better for restorative justice advocates to seek to engage with, and transform certain aspects of, established criminal justice (even in the knowledge that their efforts will, at least in the short term, result in partial failure and questionable compromises) than to insist on an independent and thus marginalised setting for restorative interventions.

Most informed commentators are now in agreement that the state must retain a role in safeguarding the public interest (including the protection of basic rights) within restorative processes, however 'informal' and 'benign' these processes are alleged by their advocates to be. There is much less agreement about how extensive those safeguards should be, or what form they should take. Naturally, those who adhere to liberalism tend to advocate strong safeguards, including tight proportionality constraints and a ban on non-restorative outcomes (such as an agreement that the offender should observe a curfew), while those more attracted by communitarian or utilitarian ethics place greater value on the promotion of 'creative' and 'flexible' outcomes, with some accordingly accepting only minimal constraints and safeguards (such as a ban on penalties greater than a court could impose).

'Just deserts' theorists are particularly concerned that the influence of victims or the wider community could result in disproportionate outcomes. Even where those outcomes are purely reparative in nature, this concern remains. The potentially poor fit between reparation and desert can be seen in the example of a destitute offender who is asked to pay extensive compensation to a victim for all the harm caused by an offence, including harm that was not foreseen and perhaps not even reasonably foreseeable. Fears over disproportionate reparation agreements might be ignored if restorative justice were being used solely for diverting from court low-level cases involving minimal losses where victims sought no more than an apology. However, as soon as restorative processes are used within the mainstream system for offences of any seriousness (as with referral orders), arguments about proportionality and consistency in sentencing become harder to disregard.

One interesting synthesis of just deserts and restorative justice values starts from an acceptance of the desirability of conveying correct moral messages about the relative wrongfulness of different actions. This calls forth a general principle of proportionality in the amount of punishment imposed on individual offenders. However, since there are other important interests in play, such as the right of the victim to positive freedom, the principle of proportionality need not be strict. Instead, the state should set upper and lower limits on the amount of reparation to which an offender should be liable so that a degree of flexibility can be left to the conference participants when discussing what the outcome should be. Within retributive limits, victims and offenders would be encouraged to agree on forms of reparation that they considered to be appropriate. Guidelines on forms of appropriate reparation would also be necessary in order to guard against counterproductive agreements, such as one that presented an impoverished offender with the choice between using illegitimate means to get the money necessary to pay compensation to a victim or face the consequences of failing to comply with the agreement. In most cases the process and outcome would be enough to satisfy the public interest in seeing offences appropriately censured. Where this was not so, the state, rather than the victim or the community, would be responsible for determining any additional punishment necessary. Proportionality could also be a fallback for those cases where the various parties cannot agree on reparation or an agreement remains unfulfilled.

Restorative justice and proportionality are not always regarded as being compatible concepts. Indeed, the theory of reintegrative shaming was developed in critical opposition to a just-deserts model. For its leading proponents, the limits of restorative justice are to be found in international human-rights instruments rather than in any philosophical commitment to proportionality. However, it is questionable whether a human-rights safety net could protect offenders from excessive punishments such as were witnessed by the rehabilitation movement of the 1960s, which fell out of favour partly because of concerns about disproportionate sentences.

Restorative outcomes should not be judged only by the standard of proportionality (whether that standard be broadly or narrowly defined) but also in the light of core values of restorative justice, such as mutual respect and empowerment. Hence the *amount* of reparation should not be the only issue. Offenders should not be asked to perform degrading or stigmatising tasks as part of a reparation agreement. The now notorious example from the Canberra restorative conferencing programme of participants in a conference agreeing that the young offender would wear a T-shirt in public stating 'I am a thief' contradicts the fundamental values of restorative justice. Such outcomes appear to be infrequent, partly because the presence of a range of stakeholders and the involvement of a properly trained facilitator are usually enough to guard against them. Nonetheless, under a purely communitarian model the involvement of victims and community representatives poses significant threats, including the possibility that some offenders will be subjected to exclusionary processes and outcomes. Critics of restorative justice fear that individual victims may enter restorative processes bent on humiliating and stigmatising offenders. The recent victim- and community-led campaigns resulting in 'Megan's Law' in the United States, and the fight for 'Sarah's Law' in the United Kingdom, suggest that this concern should be taken seriously. Against this backdrop it can scarcely be plausibly suggested that there is no need for the state to oversee communitarian forms of justice. Below, however, we argue that it is equally implausible to argue that the involvement in restorative processes of victims and other members of the public will typically result in the humiliation of offenders.

The vengeful victim

Many harsh, exclusionary measures, such as mandatory minimum sentences and indeterminate sentences for those deemed dangerous, have been justified by reference to 'public opinion' and the demands of victims. If the public generally, and victims specifically, really were in favour of harsh punishments across the board, then the arguments against providing victims and their supporters with any decisive say in responding to an offence become overwhelming, for that way lies the lynch mob. In fact, however, the evidence from a variety of jurisdictions is that the public is much less vindictive than is commonly supposed, and that the more people know about the circumstances of an offence and an offender, the less punitive they tend to become.

Opinion pollsters have repeatedly found that a large majority of the public will respond that sentencing is much too lenient when asked for their views about this issue. But analysis shows that this is largely because the public has in mind the most serious types of crime and criminal when answering this type of question, and because they substantially underestimate the severity of actual sentences. In other words, they have in mind social constructions of crime, criminals and sentencing rather than actual representative phenomena. The media, ably abetted by politicians, bear the main responsibility for the formation of these constructions through their focus on the atypical, the sensational and the cruelly vicious. Given that the public get their information about crime and punishment primarily from the media, one should expect to find that shifts in penal policy and sentencing levels make little difference to public opinion, and this is indeed what empirical inquiry finds.

Informed public opinion is very different from the 'gut reactions' tapped by general opinion polls. When asked to specify a sentence for a hypothetical offender in a given set of circumstances, the public 'sentences' broadly in line with actual court practices, and those who have recently been victims of the type of offence used in such exercises generally prove to be no more punitive than non-victims in this regard. The 1998 British Crime Survey (BCS) found that, while victims predictably varied in their views concerning an appropriate response to the crimes they had actually suffered, the relatively lenient option of a caution or discharge was the most popular choice across the board, suggested as an appropriate disposal in a quarter of all crimes. About two-thirds of victims were prepared to consider either a mediation meeting with their offender (41 per cent) or receiving reparation from them (58 per cent). The 1984 BCS had found a similar level of support, thus casting doubt on the thesis that the public has become increasingly punitive in recent years. When members of the public take on a decision-making role within criminal justice, as jurors or magistrates, their behaviour again contradicts the image of a universally punitive public. Other things being equal, juries are more likely to acquit where the probable (or mandatory) penalty is perceived as disproportionately severe, and lay magistrates (the part-time volunteers responsible for most of the sentencing that takes place in the UK's lower tier of criminal courts) are often more lenient than professional magistrates. More broadly, research has shown that local communities can be resistant to, and successfully mobilise against, the imposition of state-favoured 'risk-management' policies of policing and punishment. So what philosophy of punishment does the public subscribe to? When their views are unpicked carefully, the great majority seems to favour individualised responses to offending that mix a large degree of respect for proportionality with a desire to see sentencing achieve some rehabilitative or restitutionary 'good'.

We might therefore expect to find that when offenders and victims and their respective supporters come face-to-face in a setting that encourages respectful dialogue, the social distance between the participants narrows and demands for punishment become even more moderate – perhaps even to the point where lower proportionality limits are breached. Consistent with these expectations, a survey of 25 restorative justice programmes in five countries found that restorative processes generally acted in such a way as to preclude dispro-portionately harsh outcomes, and that external review mechanisms (such as judicial oversight of conference outcomes) were typically used to prevent outcomes that were too lenient. Such oversight is also needed, of course, to cater for the occasional vengeful victim or community, or the conference agreement that is based on erroneous assumptions about the effectiveness of a proposed penalty or programme (whether judged in terms of deterrence, rehabilitation or incapacitation). Examples include the infamous case mentioned in the preceding section where it was agreed that a young offender should wear an 'I am a thief' T-shirt, and a less well-known conference which required an offender to wash ten police cars in a case involving a personal victim.

The great bulk of research into public views on sentencing has focused on the opinions, knowledge and preferences of individuals. A large proportion of victims within the criminal justice system are, however, corporations. Here there may be pronounced tensions between the inclusionary ethics of restorative justice and the exclusionary logic of risk management favoured by many corporate bodies. In particular, business victims are often more interested in keeping offenders away from their property (through situational crime prevention, banning policies, and by seeking deterrent or incapacitative measures through the formal criminal justice system) than in empathetic exchanges, apology and reconciliation. Moreover, corporate victims typically operate through representatives who must act in accordance with corporate policies. This may inject a degree of rigidity into conference processes which is at odds with restorative values. Thus two large retail stores in one United States programme regularly asked for 40 hours of community service to be written into the conference agreement. A 13-year-old girl is reported to have completed this amount of community work for the theft of one candy bar. The need for upper proportionality limits to be set for restorative processes could scarcely be made more obvious.

In general, research has found that people participating in restorative conferences bring to bear a mix of penal philosophies. In particular, retributive, restorative and rehabilitative principles and terms have been observed to be intermingled in the interactions that take place within the process. In successful conferences (measured by the satisfaction of the participants and the sense of relational repair that results) there can be discerned a core sequence of shifts in penal focus. When participants, including the offender, begin a conference by talking about the offence, the harm it caused and the feelings it engendered, the principle most in play is one of retributive censure. When they move on to discuss what can be done to put right the offence, the emphasis shifts to restoration for the victim and others. As part of this discussion, the prevention of future offences through the rehabilitation of the offender often becomes salient, not least because many victims are keen to see that something good for others comes out of their own bad experience. In less successful conferences this sequence will tend to be lacking. For example, where participants perceive that retributive censure has failed to bring forth some acknowledgement of remorse or shame by the offender, the shift to the reparative stage may not occur. Instead participants may resort to deterrent or incapacitative language and strategies in order to inflict a lesson on the supposedly recalcitrant offender. Similarly, victims are likely to resent any talk of rehabilitation and reintegration for the offender when the issue of their own losses has yet to be addressed. In practice, it seems that most conferences leave most participants fairly or very satisfied with the fairness of the process and the outcome. At the same time, it is only in a minority of conferences that one finds evidence of offenders and victims coming to deep, empathetic understandings of each other's position and a strong sense of relational repair and reintegration.

The empirical evidence on the effectiveness of restorative justice in reducing offending is also somewhat mixed, with some evaluations suggesting positive results for certain types of offender but not for others, and with one well-designed study finding that, when compared with court-handled cases, restorative processes made offending worse among drink-drivers. For many restorativists any reduction in re-offending should be seen as a useful side-effect of a conference rather than its central aim. Victims and policy-makers, however, appear to hold higher expectations and may lose faith in restorative justice once the relatively modest level of its success in reducing the likelihood of re-offending is appreciated. Government ministers in the UK may find it difficult to maintain their support for restorative justice if politicians from rival parties begin to trumpet its failures. That would be a pity because in most contexts restorative justice seems at least as effective in achieving reductions in recidivism as other penal measures. And it might be a good deal more effective if the exclusionary elements in wider penal and social policies were to be eliminated. If restorative justice is not to become a casualty of competitive party politics, it is important that expectations of its ability to reduce re-offending are moderated while at the same time its comparative advantages over other penal measures are publicised.

We have already touched on the safeguards needed to cater for situations when restorative justice fails to work as intended. But an important normative question that arises from this empirical evidence is the moral justification for processes and outcomes that, even when everything goes to plan, seem to exhibit such a mix of penal theories. This brings us to the question of the philosophical justification for restorative justice, and its relationship to other theories of the appropriate purposes of punishment.

Acknowledging the punitive bite of restorative justice

The question of whether restorative justice involves an alternative to punishment or is an alternative form of punishment has become keenly contested. Many leading advocates of restorative justice from the outset drew a sharp distinction between restorative justice, with its focus on dialogue and repairing harm, and retributive justice, which they associated with adversarial relations and vindictiveness. More recently, a number of writers have challenged both the usefulness of this dichotomous understanding and the misleading image it paints of retribution as a penal philosophy. Retribution, it is pointed out, is concerned with the issue of treating the offender with the respect owed to those capable of exercising autonomy. Thus retributivists typically include forms of moral communication (such as censure) into their theories and insist that the burden of punishment should not be disproportionate to the degree of harm and culpability involved in a crime. Given that the process and outcome of restorative justice can be characterised as a form of moral communication involving the imposition of burdens on offenders, it is evident that retributive and restorative practices are likely to overlap.

While some restorativists have accepted this argument up to a point, they maintain that restorative justice does not fall within their (restricted) definition of punishment as there is no direct intent that the offender should suffer. The analogy is drawn with parents who require their children to pay compensation to a neighbour whose window they have broken. It may be that these children will find paying the compensation burdensome, but it is not part of their parents' direct intention that they should suffer, only that they should repair the harm caused by their act. This argument has been found to be unconvincing on the ground that it is the intentional and authoritative imposition of a burden (viewed objectively) on the offender as a response to the wrong represented by the breach of a criminal-law norm that qualifies a process as punitive. Whether that burden is motivated by a wish to cause the offender to suffer or experience pain is not determinative, nor is it a necessary quality of punishment that it actually be experienced as painful. Thus, when it comes to sentencing, probation orders and other rehabilitative measures, as well as compensation orders and other reparative measures, can all properly be called punishments.

One retributive theory of recent origin explicitly argues that restorative justice and retributive justice are not merely overlapping concepts but are integrally interlinked. Offenders are seen as having damaged their normative relationships (as fellow citizens) with the victim and community members. The appropriate (desert-based) response, and one that shows concern to offenders, victims and others, is to confront offenders with their wrongdoing and encourage them to recognise and repent the culpable wrong they have committed. This will inevitably involve a process of retributive censure which, when it involves offenders and victims (or other citizens) coming together, can be termed criminal mediation. Within this process of criminal mediation, repentance must be demonstrated by the offender seeking to restore the bonds of community damaged by the offence. An apology (to the victim and to others) is the minimal reparative requirement here, but this must be supplemented by an agreement to make monetary compensation or carry out work for the victim or wider community in order that the reparation is commensurate with the seriousness of the offence. Finally, this process of secular penance involves a commitment not to repeat the offence and to seek or accept help that might be needed in order to fulfil this. Thus the end result of criminal mediation may be entry into some kind of rehabilitation programme or process. Having completed criminal mediation, other citizens owe it to the offender to offer reconciliation and restoration of the bonds of community.

The linkage between restoration and rehabilitation within this theory mirrors the empirical evidence (summarised in the preceding section) that the rehabilitation of the offender is often important to a victim's sense of repair. Thus it seems that the analytical distinction between restoration and rehabilitation in the work of some theorists cannot be sustained in practice. We have already adverted to the dangers in allowing victims to have a say in determining a rehabilitative programme for offenders. It is perhaps fortunate that, in practice, restorative justice appears to work with a different notion of rehabilitation to that favoured by the currently dominant 'what works' agenda, in which it is the thinking and behaviour of the offender that is the focus for corrective, psychological 'interventions'. By contrast, conferences tend to find and exploit the rehabilitative potential inherent in the creation or strengthening of informal bonds, ties and relationships between the offender and other participants or the broader society. Thus, reparative discussions seem frequently to slide quite naturally into dialogue concerning how to build on an offender's strengths and maximise their opportunities, whether by getting them back into school, into a job, or out of drug dependency or poor housing. This relational form of rehabilitation is likely to be attractive to those who argue that a disadvantaged offender may have a right to restoration from society.

The process of secular penance is intended to be painful and burdensome and so qualifies as punishment even under the more restricted definition noted above. That being so, the process of secular penance shares with 'just deserts' theory the feature that it may achieve a certain amount of individual and general deterrence but only as a side-effect of an essentially retributive process. Secular penance also echoes in certain respects the theory of reintegrative shaming, which calls for offences to be censured through processes that avoid the stigmatisation of offenders and which terminate with gestures of reintegration. But whereas reintegrative shaming supports a basically utilitarian conception of restorative justice, the process of secular penance is unashamedly retributive in its emphasis on individual desert and proportionality.

One key virtue of the theory of secular penance is that it focuses attention on the penal bite of the restorative process. Many opponents of restorative justice have, by contrast, paid almost no attention to the process, confining their critique to the potential for inconsistency in the outcomes arrived at. More generally, it can be argued that sociological analyses of the fragmentation and diffusion of punitive practices in the late twentieth century have been given insufficient attention by most philosophers of punishment. The rise of community justice and mediation schemes challenges the stock assumption of penal philosophers that crime and punishment are exclusively or primarily matters of state power. But the assumption that the only thing calling for justification in restorative justice is the outcome of such practices (such as an agreement to compensate a specific victim) is equally questionable. This is because restorative justice typically operates through mobilising pre-existing norms and discourses, seeking to hold offenders accountable and change their attitudes and behaviour. Offenders are expected to talk about their feelings, to acknowledge harm to others, to listen to the views of friends, family members and victims about what they have done, and to apologise and make offers of restoration. This can be seen as a form of moral disciplining and offenders typically find the experience somewhat intrusive, uncomfortable or difficult. Analysts have only just begun to consider the disciplinary nature of restorative processes and the normative questions it raises. The potential for abuse of the powerful role of the facilitator, the power imbalances a restorative process may perpetuate, and the counterproductive resentments that interpersonal moral communication may engender are all matters for philosophical reflection as well as empirical inquiry.

More obviously, in a society which, from a variety of political standpoints, can be seen as unjust, the penal theories associated with restorative justice raise many thorny issues concerning the legitimacy of censuring, shaming, or seeking repentance for, offending behaviour. The legitimacy of restorative justice, as with all forms of punishment, must ultimately be located within some coherent and defensible political theory. While a criticism sometimes made of restorative justice is that it lacks any such anchoring theory, it is more accurate to say that restorative theorists differ on the appropriate moral and political basis for restorative practices. As might be inferred from the above discussion, some find their basis through exploring the well-worn links between penal theory and political theory, whereas others seek to distance their political support for restorative justice from the concept of punishment.

At a more pragmatic level, acknowledging the overlap between punishment and restorative justice is important for a number of reasons, of which we mention just three here. First, it may help win public acceptance for restorative processes. We have noted that the public are attracted by backward-looking desert-based thinking as well as by forward-looking crime-preventive measures. The punitive bite of restorative processes and outcomes, and their potential for securing a measure of deterrence and individual reform, should thus be publicised (but not given more weight than is merited) rather than denied. Second, it alerts us to the need for procedural safeguards (e.g., against the possibility of the wrongful punishment of the innocent) and for proportionality limits, limits which might not seem so important if it were accepted that restorative justice is an alternative to punishment. Third, if one accepts a blurring of the distinction between punishment and restoration then it becomes crucial to identify and protect those elements that nonetheless distinguish restorative punishment from other forms of punishment. Otherwise, there is a danger that any distinctive elements will be downplayed in practice in favour of other modes of punishment. For us the most distinctive value lies in the equal respect shown to offenders, victims and others as fellow citizens with a shared interest in retribution, restoration and reintegration. Punishment is properly thought of as something we should engage in with regret, as something that at best is a necessary evil. From that perspective restorative justice looks to be the lesser evil of those currently on offer in the penal marketplace.

Bibliographical review

A number of excellent collections and monographs deal with the various relevant issues and debates in restorative justice. Were we to list just three, we would choose Gerry Johnstone's *Restorative Justice: Ideas, Values, Debates* (Cullompton: Willan, 2002) for its concise but thoughtful overview of theoretical issues; John Braithwaite, *Restorative Justice and Responsive Regulation* (Oxford: Oxford University Press, 2002) for its comprehensive analysis of empirical findings allied with advanced theoretical discussion (including a welcome focus on the application of restorative justice to the crimes of the powerful); and A. von Hirsch, J. Roberts, A.E. Bottoms, K. Roach and M. Schiff (eds) *Restorative Justice and Criminal Justice: Competing or Reconcilable Paradigms?* (Oxford: Hart, 2003) for cutting-edge thinking from a variety of theoretical and empirical perspectives. These sources provide rich material on the definitional issues raised in the introductory section of this chapter; but see also issue 3 of the journal *Contemporary Justice Review*, published in 2000. The rest of this narrative bibliography is organised according to the subheadings used in the main text.

The birth, infancy and maturation of restorative justice

Jim Dignan deployed the metaphor of the infant struggling for survival in his insightful writings on the development of restorative justice in England and Wales. See his article 'The Crime and Disorder Act and the Prospects for Criminal Justice' (1999) *Criminal Law Review*, 48, and the chapter he co-authored with Peter Marsh: 'Restorative Justice and Family Group Conferences in England' in A. Morris and G. Maxwell (eds) *Restorative Justice for Juveniles: Conferencing Mediation and Circles* (Oxford: Hart, 2001). Other chapters in that book describe developments in Australia, New Zealand, South Africa, Canada and Europe. For details on schemes in North America, see Mara Schiff and Gordon Bazemore, 'Restorative Conferencing for Juveniles in the United States: Prevalence, Process and Practice' in E. Weitekamp and H.-J. Kerner (eds) *Restorative Justice: Theoretical Foundations* (Cullompton: Willan, 2002). The operation of youth offender panels is documented in Adam Crawford and Tim Newburn, *Youth Offending and Restorative Justice* (Cullompton: Willan, 2003).

Explaining the rise in restorative justice

This section begins by drawing heavily on the work of Kathleen Daly and Russ Immarigeon. See especially 'The Past, Present, and Future of Restorative Justice' (1998) *Contemporary Justice Review*, 1(1), 21–45, and a related unpublished 1998 paper by Daly, 'Restorative Justice: Moving Past the Caricatures', which is available from her website: http://www.gu.edu.au/school/ccj/kdaly.html

David Garland's book, *The Culture of Control* (Oxford: Clarendon, 2001) contains an incisive and convincing account of developments in contemporary penality, including the state's 'responsibilisation' strategy and the importance of the 'criminology of the other' and the 'criminologies of everyday life'. However, while Garland notes that the state has justified many of its exclusionary policies by reference to victims, he has little to say about restorative justice. Richard Sparks' chapter in this collection mirrors many of Garland's concerns but takes the argument forward in some interesting ways. For sociological analysis of how the rise of restorative justice can be explained within the contemporary penal landscape, one can do no better than turn to the chapter by Anthony Bottoms, 'Some Sociological Reflections on Criminal Justice' in A. von Hirsch, J. Roberts, A.E. Bottoms, K. Roach and M. Schiff (eds) *Restorative Justice and Criminal Justice: Competing or Reconcilable Paradigms?* (Oxford: Hart, 2003). Kathleen Daly's chapter in the same book, 'Mind the Gap: Restorative Justice in Theory and Practice', presents empirical evidence that the nirvana story of restorative justice is encountered relatively infrequently in practice.

Moving beyond youth justice: wider applications of restorative justice

For an examination of the arguments for and against using restorative justice for domestic violence and sexual assault, see Barbara Hudson, 'Restorative Justice and Gendered Violence: Diversion or Effective Justice' (2002) *British Journal of Criminology*, 42, 616. See also Allison Morris and Lorraine Gelsthorpe, 'Re-visioning Men's Violence Against Female Partners' (2000) *Howard Journal*, 39, 422; John Braithwaite and Kathleen Daly, 'Masculinities, Violence and Communitarian Control' in T. Newburn and E. Stanko (eds) *Just Boys Doing Business: Men, Masculinities and Crime* (London: Routledge, 1994); and Julie Stubbs, 'Shame, Defiance and Violence against Women: A Critical Analysis of "Communitarian" Conferencing' in S. Cook and J. Bessant (eds) *Women's Encounters with Violence: Australian Experiences*, (Thousand Oaks, CA: Sage, 1997). Regarding racially motivated crimes, see Barbara Hudson's 'Restorative Justice: The Challenge of Sexual and Racial Violence' (1998) *Journal of Law and Society*, 25, 237.

For an optimistic view of the role of restorative justice for white-collar and corporate crime, see John Braithwaite, *Restorative Justice and Responsive Regulation* (Oxford: Oxford University Press, 2002) and his essay 'Restorative Justice and Corporate Regulation' in E. Weitekamp and H.-J. Kerner (eds.) *Restorative Justice in Context* (Cullompton: Willan, 2003). Some doubts about the likely success of reintegrative shaming strategies in this sphere are offered by Mike Levi in a so-far rather overlooked essay, 'Shaming and the Regulation of Fraud and Business "Misconduct": Some Preliminary Explorations', in S. Karstedt and K-D. Bussman (eds) *Social Dynamics of Crime and Control* (Oxford: Hart, 2000).

A discussion of research findings on mediation in cases of serious violence is provided by Mark Umbreit, William Bradshaw and Robert Coates, 'Victims of Severe Violence in Dialogue with the Offender: Key Principles, Practices, Outcomes and Implicatons' in E. Weitekamp and H.-J. Kerner (eds) *Restorative Justice: Theoretical Foundations* (Cullompton, Willan, 2002).

The use of restorative justice within school settings where exclusionary impulses are still evident is considered by Lisa Cameron and Margaret Thorsborne, 'Restorative Justice and School Discipline: Mutually Exclusive?' and Brenda Morrison, 'The School System: Developing its Capacity in the Regulation of a Civil Society', both in H. Strang and J. Braithwaite (eds) *Restorative Justice and Civil Society* (Cambridge: Cambridge University Press, 2001). On public forms of stigmatising shaming, see John Pratt, 'The Return of the Wheelbarrow Men' (2000) *British Journal of Criminology*, 40, 127, and John Muncie, 'Institutionalised Intolerance: Youth Justice and the 1998 Crime and Disorder Act' (1999) *Critical Social Policy*, 19, 147.

The use of circles of support to ease the reintegration of ex-prisoners back into society is touched upon in Daniel Van Ness, Allison Morris and Gabrielle Maxwell, 'Introducing Restorative Justice' in A. Morris and G. Maxwell (eds) *Restorative Justice for Juveniles* (Oxford: Hart, 2001) and in John Braithwaite, *Restorative Justice and Responsive Regulation* (Oxford: Oxford University Press, 2002, pp. 75–76). See also the discussion of the Toronto circles working with paedophiles, in Jon Silverman and David Wilson, *Innocence Betrayed: Paedophilia, the Media and Society* (Oxford: Polity, 2002). This is an area in urgent need of more extensive research.

The state's role in facilitating restorative justice

Andrew Ashworth examines the proper division of functions between state, victims, offenders and 'communities', the development of arguments in favour of greater procedural safeguards, and criticisms of police facilitation, in 'Responsibilities, Rights and Restorative Justice' (2002) *British Journal of Criminology*, 42, 578. See also Rob White, 'Shame and Reintegration Strategies: Individuals, State Power and Social Interests' in C. Alder and J. Wundersitz (eds) *Family Conferencing and Juvenile Justice: The Way Forward or Misplaced Optimism?* (Canberra: Australian Institute of Criminology, 1994), and Danny Sandor, 'The Thickening Blue Wedge in Juvenile Justice' in the same book *Family Conferencing and Juvenile Justice: The Way Forward or Misplaced Optimism?* (Canberra: Australian Institute of Criminology, 1994).

For a critique of social workers facilitating restorative conferences, see Gabrielle Maxwell and Allison Morris, 'Family Group Conferences and Reoffending' in A. Morris and G. Maxwell (eds) *Restorative Justice for Juveniles: Conferencing Mediation and Circles* (Oxford: Hart, 2001, p. 267). The issue of police facilitators using their powers in an unacceptable way in restorative conferencing is considered by Richard Young, 'Just Cops doing "Shameful" Business? Police-led Restorative Justice and the Lessons of Research' in A. Morris and G. Maxwell (eds) *Restorative Justice for Juveniles: Conferencing Mediation and Circles* (Oxford: Hart, 2001). The evident popularity of police facilitation among participants in a number of jurisdictions is discussed in Carolyn Hoyle and Richard Young, 'Restorative Justice, Victims, and the Police' in T. Newburn (ed.) *The Handbook of Policing* (Cullompton: Willan, forthcoming).

Safeguarding restorative justice through the provision of legal advice

For a critique of the role of lawyers in restorative processes, see Martin Wright, *Restoring Respect for Justice* (Winchester: Waterside Press, 1999). Joanna Shapland presents a persuasive case for restorative justice to put aside its dislike of lawyers in 'Restorative Justice and Criminal Justice: Just Responses to Crime?' in A. von Hirsch, J. Roberts, A.E. Bottoms, K. Roach and M. Schiff (eds) *Restorative Justice and Criminal Justice: Competing or Reconcilable Paradigms?* (Oxford: Hart, 2003). For a discussion of the government's position on the role of lawyers in youth restorative justice processes, see Caroline Ball, 'The Youth Justice and Criminal Evidence Act 1999 – Part I: A significant move towards restorative justice, or a recipe for unintended consequences?' (2000) *Criminal Law Review*, 211.

The relationship of the state to restorative justice

The view that restorative justice programmes should remain in-dependent of mainstream criminal justice is put forward by Tony Marshall, 'Results of Research from British Experiments in Restorative

Justice' in B. Galaway and J. Hudson (eds) *Criminal Justice, Restitution and Reconciliation* (Monsey, NY: Criminal Justice Press, 1990). The opposing view, that restorative justice should engage with and seek to reform established criminal justice, is developed by Lode Walgrave, 'Restorative Justice and the Law: Socio-ethical and Juridical Foundations for a Systemic Approach' in L. Walgrave (ed.) *Restorative Justice and the Law* (Cullompton: Willan, 2002). Adam Crawford's essay in the same collection, 'The State, Community and Restorative Justice: Heresy, Nostalgia and Butterfly Collecting', considers the scope for a constructive relationship between community and state norms and modes of regulation in which one serves to correct the excesses of the other.

Just-desert theorists who have expressed concern over the potential for disproportionate outcomes in restorative and reparative processes include Andrew Ashworth, 'Victims' Rights, Defendants' Rights and Criminal Procedure' in A. Crawford and J. Goodey (eds) *Integrating a Victim Perspective within Criminal Justice* (Aldershot: Ashgate, 2000), and Martin Wasik, 'Reparation: Sentencing and the Victim' (1999) *Criminal Law Review*, 478. Restorativists who recognise the need for some upper and lower limits on sentencing include Michael Cavadino and Jim Dignan, 'Reparation, Retribution and Rights' *International Review of Victimology*, (1997) 4, 233. Most notable among those who argue that restorative justice and proportionality are incompatible concepts is John Braithwaite. See his chapter 'In Search of Restorative Jurisprudence' in L. Walgrave (ed.) *Restorative Justice and the Law* (Cullompton: Willan, 2002).

A. von Hirsch, J. Roberts, A.E. Bottoms, K. Roach and M. Schiff (eds) *Restorative Justice and Criminal Justice: Competing or Reconcilable Paradigms?* (Oxford: Hart, 2003) contains a chapter that represents the first sustained attempt by just-deserts theorists (Andrew von Hirsch and Andrew Ashworth, writing with Clifford Shearing) to develop a model of restorative justice that might be acceptable from a rights-based perspective: 'Specifying Aims and Limits for Restorative Justice: A "Making Amends" Model?'. The essay (in the same volume) by the leading consequentialist theorist of restorative justice, John Braithwaite, 'Principles of Restorative Justice', indicates that, compared with some of his earlier writings, he is now engaging more fully with just-deserts arguments. Taken together with Jim Dignan's 'Towards a Systemic Model of Restorative Justice' in that work, these chapters indicate that theorists from different traditions are now engaged in a reasoned debate about restorative justice and just deserts rather than, as often seems to be the case in philosophical writing, talking past each other.

The vengeful victim

The implications of invoking public and victim sentiments to justify exclusionary forms of criminal justice are considered in Andrew Sanders, 'Victim Participation in an Exclusionary Criminal Justice System' in C. Hoyle and R. Young (eds) *New Visions of Crime Victims* (Oxford: Hart, 2002). For discussion of the view that the state is a necessary buttress against a modern version of blood-feuds (consisting of outraged victims exacting disproportionate revenge on their aggressors, thus provoking reactions in kind), see the chapters by Neil MacCormick and David Garland, 'Sovereign States and Vengeful Victims: The Problem of the Right to Punish' and John Gardner, 'Crime: in Proportion and in Perspective', both contained in A. Ashworth and M. Wasik (eds), *Fundamentals of Sentencing Theory* (Oxford: Clarendon Press, 1998). Our argument is that informed public opinion is much less hard-line than the media, politicians and some academics seem prepared to admit and that restorative justice both benefits from, and can reinforce and deepen, the widespread support for proportionate and reintegrative responses to offending. We draw in particular on Joanna Mattinson and Catriona Mirrlees-Black, *Attitudes to Crime and Criminal Justice: Findings from the 1998 British Crime Survey, Home Office Research Study 200* (London: Home Office, 2000), and the summaries of international evidence contained in Julian Roberts, 'Public Opinion and Sentencing Policy' in Sue Rex and Mike Tonry (eds) *Reform and Punishment: The Future of Sentencing* (Cullompton, Willan, 2002), and Julian Roberts, Loretta Stalans, David Indermaur and Mike Hough, *Penal Populism and Public Opinion* (Oxford: Oxford University Press, 2003). For a detailed analysis of the integral, informal safeguards within restorative justice, see the empirically informed book by Declan Roche, *Restorative Justice and Deliberative Accountability* (Oxford: Clarendon Press, 2003). The argument that the new penology of risk management may be successfully resisted and reworked at the point of application within local communities is advanced by Lisa Miller, 'Looking for Postmodernism in all the Wrong Places' *British Journal of Criminology*, (2001), 168. The problems posed by non-individual victims are discussed by Richard Young, 'Testing the Limits of Restorative Justice: The Case of Corporate Victims' in C. Hoyle and R. Young (eds) *New Visions of Crime Victims* (Oxford: Hart, 2002). For discussion of the mixture and sequencing of penal ideas and practices within restorative conferences, and a careful unpicking of what these conferences tend to achieve, see Kathleen Daly, 'Restorative Justice: The Real Story' *Punishment and Society* (2002), 4(1), 55. The mixed evidence produced by the leading studies of the impact of restorative justice on re-offending is analysed in Carolyn Hoyle and Richard Young, 'Restorative Justice: Assessing the Prospects and Pitfalls' in M. McConville and G. Wilson (eds) *The Handbook of the Criminal Justice Process* (Oxford: Oxford University Press, 2002).

Acknowledging the punitive bite of restorative justice

In a series of papers, Kathleen Daly has challenged the notion that restorative justice can be sharply distinguished from retributive justice, and has argued that restorative justice includes elements of punishment. See, especially, 'Revisiting the Relationship between Retributive and Restorative Justice' in H. Strang and J. Braithwaite (eds) *Restorative Justice: Philosophy to Practice* (Aldershot: Ashgate, 2000). Lode Walgrave has been equally tenacious in defending the view that restorative justice and punishment are conceptually distinguishable, an argument that is put in its most persuasive form in 'Imposing Restoration and Inflicting Pain' in A. von Hirsch, J. Roberts, A.E. Bottoms, K. Roach and M. Schiff (eds) *Restorative Justice and Criminal Justice: Competing or Reconcilable Paradigms?* (Oxford: Hart, 2003). Jim Dignan's 'Towards a Systemic Model of Restorative Justice' in the same collection critiques Walgrave's position and considers the justifications and limits called for given the punitive nature of restorative justice. The overlapping natures of restorative and retributive justice are considered in Lucia Zedner's 'Reparation and Retribution: Are they Reconcilable?' (1994) *Modern Law Review*, 57, 228.

Antony Duff's theory of secular penance is defended fully in *Punishment, Communication and Community* (Oxford: Oxford University Press, 2001), the relevant elements of which he has set out in accessible form in (among other places) the chapter 'Punishing the Young' in I. Weijers and A. Duff (eds) *Punishing Juveniles* (Oxford: Hart, 2002). On the emphasis within restorative justice on a relational form of rehabilitation, see Gordon Bazemore, 'After Shaming, Whither Reintegration: Restorative Justice and Relational Rehabilitation' in G. Bazemore and L. Walgrave (eds) *Restorative Juvenile Justice: Repairing the Harm of Youth Crime* (Monsey, NY: Criminal Justice Press, 1999). For the argument that restorative justice must encompass the duty of repair owed by the state to socially and politically excluded offenders, see Pat Carlen, 'Youth Justice? Arguments for Holism and Democracy in Responses to Crime' in P. Green and A. Rutherford (eds) *Criminal Policy in Transition* (Oxford: Hart, 2000).

A number of essays by Nicola Lacey argue the case for penal

philosophers to engage more with political theory and sociological analyses of punishment. See, in particular, 'Penal Practices and Political Theory: An Agenda for Dialogue', in M. Matravers (ed.), *Punishment and Political Theory* (Oxford: Hart, 1999), which discusses the analytic importance of taking into account Foucault's notion of disciplinary power. For an analysis of restorative justice that does this explicitly (in relation to police facilitators), see Richard Young, 'Just Cops Doing "Shameful" Business?' in A. Morris and G. Maxwell (eds) *Restorative Justice for Juveniles* (Oxford: Hart, 2001). The disciplinary effects of restorative justice on the parents of offenders are considered (but without reference to Foucault) by Jeremy Prichard, 'Parent-Child Dynamics in Community Conferences – Some Questions for Reintegrative Shaming, Practice and Restorative Justice', *Australian and New Zealand Journal of Criminology*, 35, 330 (2002). The problem of power imbalances within restorative conferences is considered in Barbara Hudson, 'Restorative Justice: The Challenge of Sexual and Racial Violence' *Journal of Law and Society* (1998) 25(2), 237.

For the links between political theory and conceptions of restorative justice, see the differing approaches of Antony Duff, *Punishment, Communication and Community* (Oxford: Oxford University Press, 2001) and John Braithwaite and Phillip Pettit, 'Republicanism and Restorative Justice: An Explanatory and Normative Connection' in H. Strang and J. Braithwaite (eds) *Restorative Justice: Philosophy to Practice* (Aldershot: Ashgate, 2000). The former argues from a liberal position, the latter from a consequentialist perspective. Lode Walgrave has developed Braithwaite and Pettit's arguments in two recent essays: 'Restorative Justice and the Republican Theory of Criminal Justice: An Exercise in Normative Theorising on Restorative Justice' (in the collection just cited) and 'From Community to Dominion: In Search of Social Values for Restorative Justice' in E. Weitekamp and H.-J. Kerner (eds) *Restorative Justice: Theoretical Foundations* (Cullompton, Willan, 2002).

Note

1   We are grateful to Andrew Ashworth, Seán McConville and Hannah Young for their helpful comments on an earlier draft of this chapter.

Chapter 8

The necessity of chance

Seán McConville

Criminal courts so dramatise the human condition that they are themselves subject to endless dramatic representations. Over the years, as observer and participant, I have seen in courts something of the wide range of human capabilities and reactions. Cruelty, duplicity and wickedness in its many ingenious forms sit alongside kindness, honesty and inspiring philanthropy. Anyone watching closely will quickly sense another tension – that between the presence of the accused as a human being and the impersonality with which he is processed. As with any public institution that deals with people in extreme conditions, a degree of separation is a means of getting business done and controlling the wear and tear on staff. But no matter how familiar one is with the scene, a troubling realisation intrudes from time to time: practicalities and a web of working relations marginalise the person who should be the centre of attention. Hemmed in physically, for the most part ignored, and sanitised by the professional disinterestedness of the court, the accused becomes a two-dimensional being, his humanity suspended – paradoxically with the intention of treating him humanely.

There is a similar effect in thinking and writing about punishment. Abstraction omits the particular in order to reach a broader understanding. Applied to punishment, this may produce a particularly unfortunate blind spot. To examine social structures and processes and address the capacities of the law may lead us to overlook the human being who should define and direct our speculations. This chapter examines this asymmetry in the light of current and emergent ways of thinking about offenders, related research and new technologies, and asks whether and how the human, and therefore the moral, element can survive in punishment.

Moral capacity

Freedom is central to any discussion of punishment. Most obviously, punishment involves restriction or loss of freedom. Much of the analysis offered by contributors to this book deals with this side of the equation and considers the place of punishment in a wider social context, as well as its forms, costs, effectiveness and appropriateness. The last forces us to consider who merits punishment, which in turn may cause us to contemplate the nature of justice in an unjust world. It is at this point we find ourselves approaching the concept of freedom from a different direction. Is it possible to justify punishment if the offender cannot be said to have exercised free will? Or to paraphrase Orwell, can there be justice when we assume that all are free to choose, but some are freer than others? Yet without free choice surely there can be no responsibility (or at least it is much diminished); without responsibility no culpability; and without culpability no just punishment. And with this in mind, can there be equality before the law? Palpably, a version of this argument continues, choice is more open to some than others, and many are driven to crime by necessity, psychological and cultural forces, criminogenic social and economic arrangements and the maldistribution of life chances. Society, in other words, of its nature and by its choices, shares in the offender's culpability; crime is one of the costs of the way we live. This line generates furious debate. A consideration of punishment from this angle therefore casts us into the millrace of some of the oldest of philosophical and political discussions.

Analyses of free will take many forms, but one that is particularly germane here is the concept of moral agency or capacity. This is sometimes confused with morality, and morality with ethics. Moral agency or capacity is the ability to make choices. While it is true that morality is inconceivable without the possibility of choices, morality is not synonymous with ethics. A person might choose to follow an ethical code, but that set of rules does not exhaust moral agency; he might be drilled, persuaded or coerced into adhering to a code, but that would not necessarily demonstrate moral capacity. Freedom in this sense of ability to choose is therefore simultaneously a *sine qua non* for certain theories of punishment, and an irresolvable philosophical conundrum. How can we test free will in a universe of causes? Is the notion of moral capacity not another version of René Descartes' body–mind dualism? Indeed, is the concept of personality similarly irreducible to physical components, physiological processes, molecular relationships and external causes, no matter how minute the units and effects which modern science allow us to examine? The human presence, most manifest perhaps when in death it ceases, continues to baffle us. The sense of self, through which we all live, flickers for the individual and remains ultimately unknowable to another.

I take the view that, confronted with an irresolvable philosophical problem, it is open to me to accept a position which, while it cannot be verified in the empirical sense, is justified on some rational grounds, in this case tradition and benignant outcome. More narrowly, I join that fairly general consensus which asserts that the notion of moral agency is an essential building block of criminal justice, and of much else besides, and that when we deny it, however benevolent our motives, we distort justice and injure civil society. Even philanthropic attempts to deal with related inequities may produce outcomes very different to those intended. These questions, however dealt with, are critical in any analysis of relations between the individual, society and the state. An examination of what it means to be a person is therefore inescapable.

As a prelude, we should note that only some schools of penal thought are concerned with the offender's moral capacity. To utilitarians (such as Bentham and his modern followers) who emphasise crime reduction as the primary purpose or sole justification of punishment, it must surely be a matter of some indifference whether the offender is capable of free choice. Deterrence works to the extent that certain behaviours are discouraged. Whether one abstains from crime because of moral choice or because of fear of punishment is scarcely a matter of concern: to borrow from Deng Xiaoping, it does not matter whether a cat is black or white, so long as it catches mice. Bentham's 'calculus of felicity' – that elusively shifting point of balance between effectiveness and oppressiveness, between the gain or pleasure of crime or other undesirable behaviour and the dread of punishment – consciously and resolutely denies the moral. (The unease thereby generated was later addressed by J.S. Mill, but at the cost of hopelessly muddling the theory.) Such an approach could as well be applied in teaching tricks to a circus animal as restraining or improving the citizen. And indeed, in certain spheres – road-traffic law, financial, fiscal, environmental and other regulatory matters – the calculus of felicity offers a shortcut, reduces bureaucracy and lightens the hand of the state. Intention and mental state must on grounds of practical enforcement be excluded.

Similar comments could be made about those whose primary purpose is the reformation of the offender. In the mid-nineteenth century this group resolved itself into two factions which, for convenience, might be called behaviourists and reformists. Behaviourists were not concerned about the processes by which an offender made his choices and some would have found the notion of moral capacity opaque, elusive and irrelevant. It mattered not what secrets were held in the offender's heart, but what he did. Whether punishment took the form of pain and deprivation or inducements (more usually these elements were combined), behaviour was the crucial test. Behaviourism accommodated itself to a deterrent regime of discomfort, deprivation and pain, as well as a positive training one. Its proponents (such as Lord Carnarvon) thought it particularly suitable to the 'low, brutish nature' of the armies of petty offenders that annually marched through the criminal institutions of mid-Victorian England.

Reformists, by contrast, were concerned with the offender's personality and moral choices, and wanted him to change his course of life by an act of will, because he had been brought to the realisation that this was the right thing to do. A true reformist avoided material inducements such as an abridgement of punishment or improvement in conditions. The test of reformation was the spirit in which the offender came to change. Inducements might encourage superficiality and hypocrisy, fatally blocking the offender's path to true self-fulfilment and change.

Of penal objectives, the oldest is incapacitation. In the past this was achieved by certain forms of corporal punishment (branding or mutilation), by imprisonment or by death. The intention was physically to hinder or prevent further offending. A missing limb, mutilated nose or ears, or prominent brand, restricted the possibilities of another offence. A prisoner in close confinement was unable to commit further crimes (except on his fellows or keepers). The death penalty was, of course, the ultimate form of prevention. Only incidentally in any of these forms of incapacitatory punishment would the offender's state of mind arise. It is true that some reformers sought repentance and thus redemption even on the gallows – a practice that continues in the United States and certain other countries that retain capital punishment. Even so, to those who place prevention at the top of their penal agenda, moral capacity and offender choice are little more than a distraction.

Retribution is that penal course which might most be expected to concentrate on the offender's moral capacity: how but with the attribute of culpability, may the retributive punishment of an offender be justified? Retribution, after all, looks backwards to the offence and the harm that has been done. It is true that a retributivist may concern himself with an offender's mental state in calculating culpability (and indeed, for many offences the modern sentencer is bound so to do). But a retributivist might approach harm in a more objective way, ignoring the offender's moral capacity. The test might simply be how much harm has been done – an objective examination of the crime itself and of its outcome. This exercise is not so different from the assessment of tortious damages in civil law, and providing a matrix for such calculations much preoccupies certain retributivists.

Many approaches to structured sentencing distinguish between offence and offender, and direct the sentencer separately to consider the aggravating and mitigating characteristics of each. It is possible to look only at the offence – personal or property – and to assess harm. This can be a difficult enough exercise, but when one turns to the offender, judgement becomes more complex, even haphazard, not least because status and mental state are unavoidable issues. Is this a mature person, one in a position of trust? Was the act impulsive, or protracted, repeated and deliberate? Was it for indulgent gain or pressing necessity? And how is one to weigh those several compulsions – drug or alcohol addiction or a mental illness or disturbance that falls short of insanity? Should we distinguish between the hardened and novice offender? Should repetition be treated as aggravating contumaciousness? Is it possible to combine the personal and the 'objective' in assessing harm and culpability: do we have a rational, consistent and defensible theory?

The classical school of jurisprudence

A number of these issues concerning free will and culpability crystallised in jurisprudential debates that were conducted between the mid-eighteenth and early twentieth centuries. Several thinkers consolidated and systematised their views into a set of ideas (never wholly unified) which came to be known as the classical school of jurisprudence. This essentially grew out of the Enlightenment. In reaction to the irrationalities and uncertainties of the law, and the many indefensible privileges and defective procedures of the *ancien régime*, Cesare Beccaria and other reformers sought clarity and certainty. That focus included the criminal offender, who was deemed to be fully responsible for his actions: each was supposed equal with all before the law. In theory, but to varying extents in practice, offender aggravation and mitigation and judicial discretion were minimised. While this might appear to be stern justice, it should be understood as part of the move towards those heightened standards of certainty and predictability that underpin modern legality.

This approach was more than comfortable to English and American lawyers, who in the jury, an independent judiciary, open and fair trials, oral procedure and strict rules of evidence saw all necessary protections for the accused. A conviction arrived at by such means, so jealous of the rights of the accused and asserting the even-handedness of the law, allowed confidence in the verdict and justified full punishment, irrespective of personal circumstances. This rigorous doctrine was buttressed by belief in free will: the culprit had made choices that – rational and calculating or not – were his responsibility alone. He might have made a stupid choice, might indeed be a stupid person, but neither was a saving grace. The ineptness, lack of skill, miscalculation or bad luck that had led to detection and trial in no way detracted from the evil intent, which was the core of the offence.

The criminologists

The history of criminology is largely the story of the attempted refutation and modification of classical jurisprudence, by shifting the attention from the crime to the criminal. Broadly speaking, these criticisms were grouped in two schools – the environmental and the hereditary – a version of the now endlessly ventilated nurture vs. nature debate. The nurture side included those social statisticians, social investigators and sociologists who perceived that crime is not distributed randomly throughout society, as one might expect were it simply the product of independent judgements and choices. Age, sex, parenting, occupation and domicile all proved to be powerful predictors of criminality.

Any survey of the literature of crime and punishment of the eighteenth century would show that the effects of a defective upbringing, ill-chosen companions and acquaintance with the criminal milieu were well understood. But anecdote can always be blunted or refuted by counter-anecdote. National statistics (however flawed we now understand them to be) possessed a wholly different order of authority. The publication of the first volume of French criminal statistics in 1827, a conspectus achieved later by other countries, significantly shifted the bounds within which debates were conducted, advanced scholarly investigation of criminality, and began to have an effect on policy. It bears emphasis that, from the outset, most of these analyses made no claims of individual prediction. In 1846 Lambert Quetelet, the Belgian pioneer of statistical criminology, dismissed such notions. One would not use a mortality table (even then well developed by insurance actuaries) to predict at what age a particular person might die: 'it would be still more absurd to use any [criminal statistics] tables to form conjectures as to his actions'.

It is one thing to map the regularities in criminality, another to explain them – to use social facts to fashion a theory that delineates causes and connections, and that attempts predictions. The theorists run from political economists and sociologists such as Marx and Durkheim to the numerous distinguished and adroit criminologists who published between the 1920s and the 1960s, principally in the United States. By the latter part of the twentieth century attempts to construct a general theory of crime had run into the sand or been abandoned in favour of explanations for crimes, or strategic retreats into various forms of relativism or subjectivism. But the regularities and correlations, integral to the methodology of social science, and contributing to the formation of social and criminal policy, convincingly undermined the doctrine of free choice, and to varying extents shifted culpability from the offender to his social circumstances. Salvation removed itself from the pulpit to the drawing-board of the social engineer. As popular education expanded, the redirection of blame became a device of personal exculpation and even comfort and justification to certain offenders: Quetelet's admonition had no place here.

Those who looked primarily to heredity and individual constitution to explain crime attacked from the other flank. Although he had forerunners, Cesare Lombroso was the first to draw systematically on Darwinian biology to examine the individual criminal and to propose a criminology. At the outset of his career, Lombroso claimed that some 70 per cent of offenders were 'born criminals', in addition to their breaches of the law displaying a range of physical features by which they could be identified. He subsequently reduced this proportion to 40 per cent or less. Agreeing that some criminals – those whose offences were occasional – were physically more or less normal, Lombroso nevertheless insisted on the centrality of individual and inherited impulses in crime. His disciple, Enrico Ferri, defended heritability against the arguments that social circumstances determined criminality. Not all who experienced need, disappointment, frustration or humiliation responded by committing a crime: in his particular reaction to such stimuli the offender reveals himself as abnormal.

I shall shortly turn to the new biology, but here note that Lombroso and his work have long since passed from the stage of serious contention. This was largely because of his mechanical approach, fanciful propositions about atavism, speculations about evolutionary throwbacks, and reliance upon physical stigmata as evidence. The whole notion that crime was in retreat before the ever-strengthening forces of civilisation had a certain plausibility as from the 1870s states took those early steps in social policy that seemed to moderate the excesses of unrestrained capitalism or unregulated urbanism. Civilisation cast its net over the teeming slums.

Although at first ameliorations, hope, discipline and regulation had an impact upon crime, it was not long-lasting. Crime, it seemed, was akin to a water-table and continually rose to the level of civilisation. In this sense, the criminal was as civilised as his judge or, as others would have it, both were products of civilisation. In the face of this evidence that the atavism of crime would not be bred out of existence, Lombroso's form of biological determinism withered into a curiosity. The creed of heritability, of constitutional abnormality in criminal explanation, passed to certain psychologists, psychoanalysts, psychiatrists and a section of the medical profession – and those social workers trained by them. Even as late as the 1960s the tautology that criminals, or certain types of criminals, *must* be constitutionally abnormal, *because* of the crime they had committed, had ceased to be widely defended, but could still be heard.

Penal and social action

What were the consequences of these theories? Social statisticians, sociologists and political economists, feeding their findings and analyses into practical politics, contrived remedial programmes from the social regularities of crime. Some of these projects were ambitious but specific – education, housing, temperance, public health, employment and structured leisure were all early and are continuing targets for ameliorative action. Simple equations of cause and effect, poverty and deprivation, leading to disorder and crime, have given way to more qualified and sophisticated (or at least complicated) explanations. The phenomenon of rising crime and disorder in the midst of a general and historically unparalleled material abundance has thwarted those who based their programmes on intuitive connections between deprivations and various 'social evils', including crime. Theories such as 'relative deprivation', 'alienation' 'anomie', 'labelling' and 'differential association' attempted to bridge the gap. The immense destruction of two world wars concentrated the hopes of humanity on reconstruction and a new order of social democracy, harmony and justice. Many of those hopes have been realised, but virtue has still not been enthroned. Greed, violence, pitilessness and savagery show little abatement and have acquired new forms. Yet despite this shifting but essentially unchanged moral topography, measures of social amelioration and control remain part of the manifestos of most political parties in the developed world. Hope of change – transformation – is constantly encouraged. 'New' denotes virtue and good, and blurs the boundaries between commercial and political organisations and transactions. It is true that utopias have been abandoned in the light of our bitter experience of totalitarianism, but the doctrine of improvement and human perfectibility retains its attractions and has multiplied its followers, having been domesticated and trivialised.

Those who based their criminology on individual characteristics had a more direct path to their criminal and penal policy. Start with the 'born criminal' and the social and legal response is obvious. Where heredity is the prime factor in crime, a person cannot be held responsible, and without responsibility there is no culpability and therefore no justifiable punishment. Yet something has to be done, or the state itself is ultimately threatened. Retribution is meaningless, deterrence irrelevant, reformation questionable. Only one course remains – social defence. The individual is subordinated to the needs of society; and a judicial finding of guilt and the measuring of responsibility take second place to an assessment of risk. Lengthy incarceration and more are certainly justified by this doctrine: Lombroso proposed that born murderers should be executed and sex-offenders castrated. There is no direct connection between Lombroso and Ferri and Nazi policies of social defence and 'cleansing', but such biological theories, and the cast of mind that accompanied them, all too easily transmute into extremist political thinking. Some biological theories propelled the pseudo-scientific policies of killing and sterilisation that followed Hitler's rise to power. Such was the attractiveness of the selective breeding of human beings as a solution to social ills that even countries with the rule of law and strong democratic traditions experimented with eugenics on a large scale. The United States (30,000 to 50,000 compulsory sterilisations 1906–50) took this path, as until the 1960s did Canada, Sweden and Switzerland. And such measures continue: since 1996 some 200,000 Peruvian Indians have been pressured into sterilisation by their government.

Britain never established programmes of compulsory sterilisation, although the 1914 Mental Deficiency Act, which allowed persons to be detained compulsorily in institutions was, *inter alia*, a measure to control fertility. Common-law jurisprudence has never been sympathetic to theories, especially those of a scientific character. Although this narrowness has had a number of side-effects (including the long-delayed development of criminology in England and a dogged resistance to research as a basis for criminal and penal policy), it was an effective barrier to eugenics as public policy. Yet it should not be imagined that the common law and English public policy were opposed to social defence as penal policy. It lacked a scientific basis, yet the social observation technique of researchers such as Henry Mayhew in the 1850s, and the professional observations of judges and lawyers, reinforced beliefs in the existence of 'the dangerous classes' or 'the criminal classes'. Even earlier, in his *Rationale of Punishment*, Jeremy Bentham had written of delinquents (a vexing group which eluded the calculus of felicity) as 'a peculiar race of beings, which require unremitting inspection': like idiots and lunatics they had to be kept under restraint – 'they cannot, without danger, be left to themselves'. Lord Carnarvon, a leading figure in penal reform circles in the 1860s, was much exercised by the habitual criminal as 'a distinct class, with a distinct calling'. Natural-life sentences should, he contended, be imposed upon chronic recidivists, to protect the community, and the frequency rather than the severity of offending was the trigger. Although the conservatism of English political and legal leaders prevented a direct insertion of Lombroso's ideas into public policy, the notion of the self-reproducing criminal class came within a hair's breadth of concepts such as evolutionary throwbacks.

Indeed, belief in a distinct criminal class, immovably malign and immoral in its way of life, plundering when at liberty and sustained by the community when in the workhouse or jail, reproducing itself and unresponsive to normal social and legal measures, gripped the minds of many penal reformers and politicians. The advent of reliable methods of identification – long-debated and torn between fingerprinting and Bertillon's anthropometric system – provided a surer basis for the introduction of special legislation to deal with the habitual offender. Declining levels of crime from the 1870s onward paradoxically cast the spotlight more brightly on recidivists, blinding commentators and politicians to the trivial nature of the crimes of many in this category. The 1908 Prevention of Crime Act, based on principles of social defence, provided for lengthy sentences of preventive detention.

This is not the place to review this legislation and its several 'improved' versions. In practice it was so unsatisfactory, so manifestly unjust, so prone to pick up the habitual petty offender, that it dwindled away in use even though the legislation persisted until the 1970s. It is worth noticing one of the many objections to its introduction. Hilaire Belloc, then a Liberal MP, condemned what he saw as the 1908 Act's broadly Lombrosan background and the breach it made between crime and punishment, between responsibility and just deserts: 'A more monstrous principle had never been put forward, certainly by

Parliaments of countries which boasted of a high civilization and a system of law.'

Belloc and others (including Winston Churchill) would almost certainly have similar reservations of principle concerning modern forms of preventive detention – the two- and three-time loser provisions that began to emerge in the US in the 1980s. Although now part of the English criminal apparatus – introduced as a populist measure – their use has so far been restricted by a cautious higher judiciary. Having made the demonstration, British politicians for the moment seem content to accept judicial moderation in this matter. The public appetite for measures of social defence, however, apparently remains unsatiated and will from time to time be triggered by hard cases and stimulated by ambitious politicians.

New directions

What is the current position of theories of social and biological determinism? The former have sometimes been portrayed as absolute forms of determinism – man entirely as the product of his social circumstances. A few, it is true, have cast their argument in that way, but almost invariably these have been political extremists or vulgarisers. Mao, for example, wrote of man being a blank page on which beautiful things might be written. Marx was careful to keep an escape hatch for individuals such as himself in his cog-and-flywheel description of the machinery of history. Statisticians and social scientists in general have opted for levels of determinism and prediction a good deal short of 100 per cent. These social theories of human behaviour might most aptly be called 'soft determinism': at their most slack they amount to little more than the standard plea in mitigation of the criminal courts. Certainly most leave room for the concepts of choice and moral capacity, however unhappy some proponents are with such leeway.

Biological explanations of crime have remained the preserve of a few researchers and writers and, in the last 60 or so years, have generated much hostility. In large part this has been a matter of guilt by association. The policies of Nazism, from the early murders of the 'life unfit for life' programmes, to industrially organised genocide, have for many researchers and writers irremediably tainted any biological explanations of human behaviour. Even where biological studies might have produced interesting and useful findings, there is unease about legitimising the general approach which, it is perhaps feared, might slip loose, to be applied to more perverse ends.

Especially incendiary have been theories that discuss the heritable aspects of temperament, personality, intelligence and behaviour, and which further seek to relate these to class, ethnicity and race. This sense of caution has been justified by the agendas of some researchers (and by the lack of precision in terms such as 'class' and 'race'), but when exercised generally amounts to taint by proclamation and results in an embargo which no rational person could defend. Wariness has been overdone and has all too often produced a moral enthusiasm and intolerance which has made it extremely difficult to conduct *any* discussion on such matters. There is of course a self-fulfilling twist to this. Interdictions, suspicion and hostility will discourage all but a few from venturing along this path of study – careers might all too easily be broken, and few made. Among those who nevertheless ignore the disincentives, it could therefore be expected that some might have a warped or malign political agenda. Periodical exposés of such, their circles and their maleficent political views, harden opinion against a biological research interest and discourage genuine researchers; and so on. (It is curious and indeed remarkable by contrast that the vast upheavals and experiments of Lenin, Stalin, Mao and Pol Pot, which caused the deaths of tens, possibly hundreds of millions, and brought misery to many millions more, have not quarantined social theories.)

It is not that biological studies of the human condition have ceased. With the exception of certain fundamentalist religious groups, there has been universal agreement that research into the heritable component of somatic illnesses is a worthy and benign endeavour; it certainly has been able to prosper and to deliver important results. In terms of funding, the calibre and prestige of its scientists and the degree of political and social support, this work is at the forefront of contemporary science and carries great hopes for the relief of human suffering. It has contributed hugely to the standard of living and high level of welfare of the developed countries, and elsewhere to the relief of poverty and suffering, and the prevention of disease and premature mortality.

Far different the reaction to studies that venture beyond the heritable factor in disease (a physical and 'objective' phenomenon) to investigations of heritability and behaviour. If pressed, all but a dogmatic few would agree that there is some heritable factor in temperament or broad character traits. There are strong differences as to the significance and discernibility of this factor. Even among those most receptive to ideas of heritability some might caution that, not least in apparently straightforward cases, it is difficult to disentangle environmental and heritable factors. Nearly all would agree that personalities do have an inherited component of some kind and that this affects behaviour. Yet agreeing, many would not shed disquiet. Some of this fretfulness may have been soothed by work on sex differences. While a valuable corrective was applied to the biological determinists by those who pointed to the learned and conditioned components in gender, some polemicists inevitably pushed their case too far. The identification and repudiation of this excess and a new self-confidence in certain feminist writing and analysis have paradoxically enabled us to take a more level-headed and unpolemical approach to the biology of sex differences.

Advances in biology – notably the recent completion of the map of the human genome and all the work that has begun to flow from that – may have changed the picture further. To the layman a DNA sequence is an 'objective' form of evidence. This has raised hopes, buoyed up by popularising reporting, that the gene for a particular pattern of be-haviour may or indeed has been found. Before going further, therefore, it would be as well briefly to sketch the current state of biological science in its approach to human traits.

This research falls into three broad areas – quantitative genetics, research on animals and molecular genetics. The first two are well established and their work has long been publicised, attracting only intermittent popular interest. Quantitative genetics deals with groups, rather than individuals, and attempts to distinguish between genetic and environmental elements in behavioural traits. These researchers frequently publish findings based on twins.

The second type of research is conducted via animals. This is in some ways more flexible and ambitious than either of the other two approaches and may, for example, involve selective breeding and direct genetic manipulation. It has clear limitations when one attempts to address inherited behavioural dispositions. Besides the physical and genetic differences between humans and animals (not as great as might be imagined), human behavioural traits are shaped by culture and are the transformational effects of self-consciousness.

Molecular genetics – a relative newcomer – seeks to identify and examine those variations in genes which affect outcomes in the individual. This is a difficult field of study, since the interaction of genes is complex and may be sequential. An effect may only occur where different and seemingly unrelated genetic structures and conditions are present. Some researchers have also suggested that the body learns to trigger genes in response to certain stimuli: this could further blur the nature/nurture boundary and, if true, greatly complicates analysis. It seems unlikely therefore that there is a simple gene-to-behaviour sequence – a 'mathematician's', 'painter's' or 'burglar's' gene. While some doubt that such patterns will ever be unravelled, others think it will be possible to pierce the complexity of several interacting genes and to identify with some precision genetically determined behaviours.

Finally, it must be said, all three types of research may supplement and inform each other, all will increasingly be propelled by the research arising from the mapping of the human genome; all are enriched by advances in computer sciences and sophisticated modelling. This is a powerful and growing field of study, rich with commercial potential and therefore likely to be driven forward with energy and investment. It will undoubtedly claim a prominent place in philosophical, political and policy debate.

In our times

Before moving to the last section of these observations I should like briefly to consider the state of penal policy. As a preface, let us agree that criminal policy and administration have become highly politicised over the last 30 years. The exact relationship between public opinion and party political contest always occasions debate, but that criminal policy is now central to party politics throughout the liberal democracies is beyond doubt, and that it becomes supercharged at times is a matter simply of observation. Crime and punishment are shown by one opinion poll after another to be in the top handful of electoral concerns.

I have alluded earlier to incapacitation and the time has come to return to this in a broader context. Economic achievements and social expectations are of some importance here. We in developed countries live in conditions of unparalleled affluence and material well-being. Nor is this static. Whatever the short-term fluctuations, we expect a generational rise in income, welfare and standards: suppliers of goods and services and political parties sell themselves on this basis. Whether all can benefit from the general enrichment and whether deprivation can ever be excised from an economy and society that prospers through competition, skilled employment and capital-intensive production, are matters central to modern politics. Alongside these sharply contested issues there are well-known social facts. Communities have fragmented, and many have vanished entirely. Individualism has become even more accentuated. We have long experienced a decline in the extended family, and it is not too hard to see that this trend will continue. But even the nuclear family is in decline. Divorce now ends two in three marriages in Britain, single-parent families are at an historic high, and social forecasters anticipate a continuing rise in single-person households.

With all the caveats that may be inserted concerning the reliability of statistics of reported crime, it is beyond dispute that crime has increased hugely in the last 50 years. Untangling all the different explanatory threads is bound to be difficult and controversial, but a number of factors come together in the decline of community. The break-up of old industrial towns, villages and areas is well documented. Much the same has happened to traditional working-class areas in cities. Communities exercise social control (which is one of the reasons they fit uneasily into or act as a cultural brake upon a society that emphasises change and competition). A stable set of values, securing the respect of others, being under scrutiny by persons to whom one is known and whose opinions one values, are all powerful restraints on behaviour, from public appearance, language and demeanour to criminal acts. There is tension and frequently conflict between conformity and innovation, stability and change, which public policy, rather than resolving, is more likely to exemplify. The crux is well recognised. Some penal approaches – communitarianism and restorative justice, for example – propose policies that would restore some element of community support and control within modern capitalism.

Whether it will be possible to reinsert community values and mechanisms into an individualised society so obviously and strongly antithetical to them is open to doubt. Certainly the present climate of despondency and cynicism about social action is not admirable, but some of the blame for this must be laid at the absurdly overreaching ambitions of the social determinists discussed earlier, and the simplistic, culturally shallow and frequently hubristic social engineers who attempted to give effect to the lessons of the determinist gospel. They found support in the politicians – naive to overweening – who cleared the way and provided the funding for generally well-meaning but frequently inhumane schemes. Some social action was possible and beneficial: the greater access to public services of all kinds, and the benefits thereof, are undoubtedly a part of our economic success and personal security and affluence. However, claims were made and expectations raised that could not be satisfied and that, indeed, produced contrary and negative outcomes. Promises were made of a social democracy and cohesiveness which now look threadbare. Fundamentally the social engineers have been discredited because of their failure to acknowledge the obstinate persistence of those human faults, sins and crimes, which are inseparable from the virtues which define them.

There are other problems which any practising politician would happily discuss. Public services and projects – leaving aside their claims and effectiveness – are always much more expensive than initially imagined. The reasons for this are involved, but at bottom relate to performance and control. Unlike the private sector, where poor performance is punished and ultimately corrected by market forces, public-sector enterprises operate in an uncertain disciplinary environment, have elaborate defence mechanisms and can prove impenetrable. And who is going to analyse, regulate and supervise them – another public-sector organisation? In the last few decades Western governments of all complexions have wrestled with these compelling issues.

One set of solutions has further undermined the strength of community in our lives. Searching for means of reducing the costs of public services, yet increasing reach, efficiency and effectiveness, governments have centralised control. This has taken many forms, but in Britain and certain other countries the outcomes have been similar – the vast bulk of taxation gathered into central government and the administration of local services essentially on an agency basis, whether by a public or private body. Consultation mechanisms are provided, but these mean little when tax collection is taken out of accountable local hands, together with ultimate executive authority. Without control, there is little incentive to participate, and community values, as measured perhaps by local political contest, are absorbed into more remote national standards. The citizen is taken further down the path of passivity.

All public services are affected by these considerations. What is the right amount of money to spend when efficiency is so hard to achieve and enforce and when financial demands (to expand access and variety and to improve quality) are virtually limitless? Government is charged precisely with this task – the allocation of resources and the efficient and proper spending of taxpayers' money. Just as the history of social engineering has produced a deep scepticism, there has also emerged a resistance to increased taxation. In part this is due to an apparent failure of many public services to respond to extra funding. Related to this, both as cause and effect, is the desire to retain for personal choice and disposal as much of one's income as possible. Many social democrats and public-sector lobbyists would argue that the retreat from universal public services is part of a destructive circle which must be broken: public dissatisfaction produces indifference or hostility to state-provided services and this, they would claim, leads to a fall in funding or a failure to keep abreast of demand. The consequence of this is a further decline in standards and a greater resort to privately funded services. The quality gap between the two sectors increases, taxpayers are even more unwilling to countenance higher taxes – and so on.

'What', you might ask 'does all this have to do with penal philosophy and politics?' Part of the answer is given by the prison populations of the developed countries. With some exceptions they are at historically high levels, both in gross numbers and by rate of imprisonment. Add those subject to direct penal control outside the prisons – electronic tagging and curfews as a bail condition, as a sentence of the court and as a form of early release from prison, and the numbers and rate increase further. Halfway houses (hostels), probation, parole and punishment in the community also swell the penal sector.

I have earlier given a sketch of the economic and social background to this expansion in state punishment, and that account can now be rounded off. In place of those traditional objectives of punishment – retribution, deterrence and reformation – penal policy has been switched to the track of extended incapacitation for particular sets of offences. These include crimes of violence and of a sexual nature, and recidivism in both. In the last two decades special laws and severe penalties have been brought in to deal with drug offences, especially production, trafficking and supply: very long terms of imprisonment are now being imposed. Early release on parole has been abolished in many jurisdictions, and where it is granted, much stricter surveillance and control measures are imposed. The 'tariff' that retributively links offence and punishment has been increased across the range of target offences. The political arguments justifying this increase have frequently been based not on harm done, but on the need to prevent future crimes. Retribution, in the sense of an attempt to calculate just deserts, is subordinated to incapacitation.

Nor will a reduction in reported crime (and certainly by reliable measures such as victim report surveys, most forms of crime have recently been static or even declining) prompt a move away from incapacitation. As noted, the late Victorians experienced a substantial reduction in crime rates, and the volume of all criminal-justice business diminished; prisons closed throughout Britain. (The US, with an expanding general population and substantial intake of immigrants, had a different history, but until the 1970s, it had a remarkably stable incarceration rate.) While more flexible means were developed to deal with minor offenders, the diminishing prison population focused greater political attention on those who appeared set on a life of crime. There is therefore no reason to imagine that if we succeed in reversing crime rates substantially, we shall reduce our demands for the long-term incapacitation of those that remain.

I have noted that penal policy has been animated by party political contest; what 30 years ago was a backwater of public policy is now undoubtedly in the turbulent midstream. This shift is sometimes taken as evidence that the increased punitive appetite of the citizenry has been stimulated by the knavish tricks of party politicians, playing on public anxieties – inflaming them, even – in order to steal a march on their opponents. While there some truth in this, it is not the whole truth. The relationship between public opinion and party politics is neither simple nor unipolar. Do politicians, Robespierre-like, spy where the public is headed, and rush to the front to lead it? Alternatively, do they use their dark arts to conjure up an issue that will advance their interests? They will do one or the other, or both from time to time. The content and tempo of public debate is substantially governed by professional politicians (in symbiosis with the media) but to prevail, issues must be rooted in some public interest – no matter the manner in which they are subsequently cultivated.

Punishment has ceased to be an elite topic, its forms and application reserved for judges and a small band of penal reformers and specialist academics. In Britain, as in many other countries, there has always been a hanging-and-flogging sector of public opinion, but the extremity and simplicity of its demands have confined it to the fringes of political influence. A recent phenomenon is the more reasoned criticism of the application of conventional punishments and demands for greater severity. This can been seen as part of the people and politicians equation discussed above, but it also denotes a decline in deference, greater popular scepticism about public institutions, and a diminution of the authority of traditional elites.

Through this haze, and whatever the detail of the clearer picture, we must acknowledge a substantial degree of public concern about crime, a hardening in attitudes about punishment, and a cloud of political anxiety hanging over all. Incapacitation is expensive. Prisons cost a lot to build and to run. Welfare costs for the prisoners' dependents and some loss of taxes add to the bill – yet the public is willing to pay it. In numerous elections they have voted for parties and politicians who promise to build their way out of crime; no party dares to venture too far from this gold standard. The medium- and long-term possibilities of social programmes evidently have far less appeal than the certainty and immediate satisfaction of taking convicted criminals off the streets.

Deus ex machina?

It is with these developments in mind that we must assess the penal application of molecular genetics. The penal course is already set for social defence. The public has sanctioned and is willing to pay for an increased use of extended incarceration, and for more intrusive and prolonged surveillance and control of those released into or punished in the community. There is, certainly, more variety in methods of dealing with less serious offenders and a greater willingness to innovate. Restorative justice schemes have been tried and are established, but are still in my view more talismanic than substantive. Some effective prison programmes have been developed to deal with particular aspects of criminality. Prisons and jails are far from being oubliettes and conditions and treatment are governed by civil- and human-rights law applied by more willing courts and activist lawyers. But even allowing for the innovations, the variety and the decency that the criminal and penal processes have achieved and to which they aspire, this is a scene in which risk overshadows all – laws emphasise it, sentences are built around it and techniques of penal assessment are constantly honed and improved to use the expensive resource of preventive imprisonment as efficiently as possible.

Although the terminology has a new ring about it, risk assessment has long been with us. The heavy sentences passed upon those deemed to be habitual offenders, whether under authority of statute or of judicial convention, have two roots. One was the reaction of the court to the supposed contumaciousness of the repeat offender; the other an assumption – part experience and part intuition – that the habitual offender would continue in his course. In either case severe punishment was justified, but in the latter it was for preventive purposes. I have touched on some of the flaws in repeat-offender legislation and cannot here give a blow-by-blow account of its history. In the early 1980s, when the United States was teetering on the edge of its vast penal expansion, there was much interest in 'selective incapacitation'. The notion was straightforward: use prison only or mainly for those who pose a serious risk and the resources thereby made available could give more protection (and reassurance) without extra cost.

The difficulty with this well-intentioned approach was the lack of a reliable test for criminal risk. Again, this story must be compressed in the telling. As measured by subsequent convictions, clinical assessment (that is, interview by a qualified psychologist or psychiatrist) proved next to useless: flipping a coin would have given equally good results. Ethically and fiscally this was unsatisfactory: one needs no very high standards of justice or economy to take issue with a decision to remove liberty on such a capricious and unreliable basis. Actuarially based testing raised a different problem – the one alluded to by Quetelet a century and a half ago. One cannot use mortality tables to predict the date at which an individual will die; one cannot use tables based on the criminal outcomes of a group of a thousand, or ten thousand, to predict whether an individual will re-offend. This uncertainty has not prevented those risk tables being used for classification and assignment within the prison system, and for parole decisions. Any 'false positives', the rationale might go, are regrettable for the individual, but overall (as for the insurance companies) risk will be accurately assessed and the public protected in the most economical way. As for the offender given a long preventive sentence, unnecessarily assigned to a high-security prison, or denied early release on parole, some advocates of the risk tables would argue that among the costs of committing a criminal offence is the chance that one may become subject to the unavoidably imperfect risk assessment and assignment mechanisms of the penal system. A defect becomes the instrument of retribution, as in the eighteenth century the supposed deterrence of *squalor carceris* justified the ruinous state of the prisons.

At first sight, the technology of genetics appears to offer a solution: individual justice and reliable public protection at the same time. As a forensic tool, DNA identification has made its dramatic appearance over the last 15 or so years. As it is refined and proved to be versatile in application, expectations continually rise. Notorious murders and other very serious crimes, where the most minute traces have been left, have been solved, to great public acclaim. Applying the new techniques to long dormant cases, police have obtained convictions for rapes, assaults, robberies and murders; at the same time a number of wrongfully convicted persons have been cleared unequivocally. Criminals confronted with DNA evidence have confessed to their offences; juries are impressed by its seeming omniscience. In Britain, all convicted adult offenders are now obliged to provide DNA specimens for a national data bank. Controversially, it is now routine practice that all persons charged with an offence must provide a specimen – whether or not their case goes to trial or results in a conviction. Britain's current Home Secretary thinks this is not enough and promises to legislate to empower the police to require a sample from any person they detain. In some official and political circles there is support for the notion of a comprehensive national data bank to which all citizens would be obliged to contribute DNA specimens. Opposition to this on civil liberties grounds is countered by the familiar argument of the authoritarian: 'innocent people have nothing to fear'. Notwithstanding the extreme intrusiveness of this measure, it seems to have a degree of political and media support, which would doubtless fuel a campaign in the wake of some revolting and heartbreaking crime.

The rights and wrongs of these proposals are not central to our discussion, but they are indicative of the ready acceptance of a sweeping application of DNA technology to the problems of crime. Let us assume that molecular genetics continues to develop at its current pace, and that predictive tests continue to attract research and development funding and marketing expertise. No matter what qualifications scientists may insert in any claims about the relationship between a particular genetic configuration and behaviour, politicians and the public are likely to accept correlations as a basis for decisions on individuals. Policy could thus minimise or disregard complications about genetic sequences, triggers, physiological 'learning' and control of certain genetic capacities – and of course the general complication of environment as a filter. The imperatives of risk prediction and control may well sweep all doubts and qualifications aside.

A final point: in the United States, and in various other countries, the penal process has become a focus for major commercial and industrial activity. This has arisen through an expansion of the traditional supply of goods and services to prisons, together with more recent arrangements such as the outsourcing of management and technical services, privately run prisons and jails and various other forms of privatisation. The profit opportunities of a US prison and jail population that exceeds two million, and a jail turnover of more than ten million persons a year, are readily apparent. All kinds of goods are supplied, from basic hygiene and food products to security equipment and sophisticated restraint devices (including Hannibal Lecter masks!); services range from medical, dental and educational to training and various forms of management assistance. It is a competitive arena in which new products and services are constantly sought. This group of development and supply companies may well be the first to introduce kits for the genetic testing of behavioural risk. Whatever teething troubles there may be – technical or legal – there will be enormous pressures to market the new devices. And whether developed in the penal field or elsewhere (the armed forces, education, social services or commercial employment services, for example), once in regular use, applications will multiply.

It seems likely therefore that in the not too distant future a criminal conviction for an offence of violence, arson and almost any sexual offence, could entail a genetic test either as part of a pre-sentence or parole report. It is also not unlikely that even to be arrested for certain offences could result in samples being taken and tested and the scores retained for retrieval or further testing in response to a number of contingencies, civil as well as criminal. Such tests will yield a risk score, and anything above the 50 per cent level – perhaps even less – could result in preventive penal measures being taken. In the present state of knowledge these scores, despite having a biological basis, will remain actuarial in relation to outcomes, based on correlations and probabilities: there does not appear in prospect a direct and certain step from genetic endowment to behaviour. (Though one cannot rule this out, especially where special, limited and uncomplicated behaviours or basic traits are involved.)

Decisions on the basis of the tests may involve prolonged detention if the offence before the court is deemed sufficiently serious in itself, is a 'trigger' instance of a potentially more serious offence (a concern even with certain minor charges), or is a repeat offence. With those merely arrested, a test could be a deciding factor in charges being brought, and if brought to trial might be offered in evidence, possibly during the fact-finding phase of trial, and if not then, at sentencing. The absence of a reference to a 'good' test score in court proceedings would inevitably lead courts to draw conclusions, even if a 'bad' score were not proffered by the prosecution. New British legislation allows at the judge's discretion previous convictions to be disclosed to the jury: genetic test scores may seem a small and irresistible step further. In addition:

- Employers, regulators and insurance companies may insist on these tests being administered to applicants for certain types of employment – access to children and the vulnerable, positions of trust and those involving certain types of stress. Test scores and profiles may eventually appear on CVs, and (as with silence in court) their absence would invite questions.

- As it develops, genetic therapy may be offered to certain offenders and implicitly or explicitly will be tied to sentence or release on parole.

These developments would have far-reaching effects on the criminal process and many other aspects of the way we live. Their potency derives from the fact that they apparently allow us to make judgements of a different level of certainty from those based on the circumstances surrounding a crime – 'situational or individual' – which currently form part of 'soft' criminological theory or court pleadings. Periodically stimulated by sensational and atrocious cases, they are particularly apt for political and media campaigning.

Mind and body

I do not wish to open the mind–body debate in any detail here, not least because it can have no conclusive outcome. I am happy for the purposes of argument to follow a fairly well-trodden path and to accept Kant's position that causality is a necessary condition for an organised and coherent experience. Consciousness remains a mystery, its irreducibility unaffected by long-established knowledge of the effects of pharmaco-logical and surgical interference with the brain. It is self-evident that our major social institutions, and the criminal process in particular, would be impossible without a general as well as a particular belief in free will and therefore moral agency. How, for example, should we evaluate love in its many forms – romantic, spousal, parental, familial, institutional, patriotic, religious – were we assured that its direction and intensity are wholly or largely an outcome of genetical endowment, or of social conditioning, or both? Does love become any the less important? Must we not set aside the implications of the automaton and insist on the myth of autonomy? Certainly we can be fierce in our resistance to such reductionism – not only in personal belief and affirmation, but also in our literature and art.

Of all the many myths by which we live, free choice may be the lubricant – the grace – that makes possible relations involving the concept of love. One could make similar observations for honour, achievement and integrity – and indeed many other cornerstones and keystones of our lives. In all of these most of us would oppose the reduction of virtue or other high and valued qualities to a mere reflex. And when it comes to the darker side of our lives, is the myth not equally important? When, more than 100 years ago, Samuel Butler satirised the determinists in his dystopian *Erewhon* ('suffering from a severe fit of immorality'), was he not making this point? In Butler's imagined society bad conduct was viewed much as illness is by us, and when it struck was similarly deplored but was 'nevertheless held to be the result of either pre-natal or post-natal misfortune'. Ill-luck, on the other hand, was considered an offence against society, and ill-health (as an extreme instance of ill-luck) was taken to be a crime and was severely punished. Butler's point is surely relevant to this discussion. The criminal and social institutions that we would need and construct were we to abandon the concepts of moral agency, guilt and desert, would almost certainly be illiberal, and also brutal, unrestrained, invasive, inhumane and ultimately and unavoidably tyrannical. To conduct ourselves as human beings we must first imagine ourselves as human beings, and that means endowing ourselves with the capacity to choose.

Sartre, among many other philosophers in the humanist tradition, has emphasised that choice is a defining part of the human condition. We cannot in our relations with others avoid it: that is 'bad faith'. In his philosophical notebooks Sartre put this in another way: 'morality is only possible if everyone is moral'. Christian theology is both based on and riven by the paradoxes of free will and choice: a man produced by the cosmic forces of a created universe cannot be a guilty man. Yet if this were accepted, much of Christian doctrine would be irrelevant: certainly the notions of original sin and redemption become even more opaque. One tradition seeks a way out of this difficulty through the supposed gift of free will from an omnipotent God; another by the even more elusive doctrine of salvation through grace. When questioned, all these explanations retreat into the inability of finite man to grasp the infinite. We are left with an endlessly unsatisfactory, never resolved, yet fundamental philosophical, theological and jurisprudential issue. It runs like a river of fire through all abstract thought about human existence and its investigation and attempted resolution have periodically had fierce (and sometimes bloody) political consequences.

The penal process and personal responsibility

The sociological studies of the nineteenth and twentieth centuries enabled us to map and better understand the regularities of criminal behaviour. For some offenders and those who deal with them, this provided constructive guidance, if only in a negative sense. But an important, unhelpful and possibly corrosive by-product should not be overlooked: criminology as rationalisation. We have noted that sex, age, social class, educational level, family stability and so forth are important predictors of many kinds of behaviour, but they are actuarial, not individual predictors. Degrees of freedom exist to varying extents in each case. That from much the same environments there could emerge very different courses of life was well understood, but often overlooked and even more often understudied. It could certainly be argued that the shift from group explanation to biographical rationalisation eventually (and not always through vulgarisation) diminished the standing of the criminological enterprise, and provided offenders with concepts and a vocabulary that destructively inoculated against acceptance of responsibility.

Marx, that great anatomist of historical inevitability, but also a full-time revolutionary, faced an apparent contradiction in his doctrine. Why was individual action necessary in the face of historical inevitability? He came up with a deft formulation: 'Men make history, but they do not always do so under circumstances of their own choosing.' But, the whiff of sophistry aside, is this aphorism not more appropriate to the ordinary human condition than to revolution, revolutionaries and grand historical junctures? We have choice forced upon us; our humanity is thus defined – our self-consciousness and moral agency. And yet we proceed in circumstances that are fraught with chance: of birth, of health, of upbringing, of social experience and economic advantage – and of course of genetic endowment, physical and mental ability and temperament. Life is complicated and the world seems unfair, sometimes heartbreakingly so. But it is precisely these exigencies that lend dignity and sometimes heroism to the human experience. Culture, as it has developed through the millennia, surely rests upon the response of the man, woman, group or whole people to unevenness, chance and choice. Art in its many forms, together with religion and philosophy, are given force by our hunger for the transcendent. We face pain, loss and annihilation with the consolation of creativity.

To help us appreciate this thicket of circumstance, and the part it plays in our lives, let us contemplate a more controlled environment. Imagine a time, perhaps already upon us, when affluent and informed parents, with consultant geneticist and embryologist to hand, choose intelligence, beauty or athleticism for the unborn (the unimplanted, to be exact). Could populist pressures to extend this boon to the population at large long be resisted? And if prohibited in one jurisdiction, would the service not be legally provided elsewhere, or indeed illegally? If too costly for those of average income, would a political opening not then be created? Not only would achievement be rendered meaningless, diversity limited or even extinguished: the very notion of civilisation would be threatened.

If this seems far-fetched, consider the following. Choices are already being made for the sex of the child, with potentially disastrous social consequences. In an agonising moral dilemma, but with the sanction of English courts, parents are now able to conceive and have the embryos searched for a genetic match for a living but ailing child whose condition can be addressed only by a genetically identical donor. Such hard cases will almost certainly smooth the way to genetically precise family planning, leaving only technical obstacles to be overcome. The implications for our concept of humanity can only be imagined. From the mass of problems and crisis in politics, genetic chance may come to be viewed as a safeguard of social cohesiveness, greater than we had ever appreciated, and its challenges, handicaps, imperfections and even tragedies the only basis of a humane freedom. This would indeed be another ironical full stop to the rationalism of the Enlightenment.

This is not, of course, to propose a blind acceptance of all social or genetical fate, a sort of neo-medievalism. Political, economic and social programmes will always have to be devised to curb the more extravagant swings and excesses of fortune. Ethics and doctrine apart, the stability and well-being of the majority, and privileges of an elite minority, ultimately depend on a consensus, and that on some form of social justice. There is no simple formula to resolve the ethical, political and personal dilemmas surrounding heritability and health. But for the most part these concerns (certainly as they have been addressed in the last century or so, in the liberal democracies) have arisen in connection with conditions of a social or physical nature so extreme that consensus is possible. The new biology and its emerging technologies, by contrast, offer choices so innovative, sweeping yet subtle and apparently attractive that their resolution must go straight to the centre of the unceasing debate about what it means to be human.

If, in spite of all the pressures and temptations, a sufficient degree of chance is to be allowed, cherished and protected in our lives, must we not accept the bitter with the sweet, the cankered with the wholesome? And that being so, the wheels of justice and the millstones of punishment will never cease to turn. The frail, unfortunate, selfish and wicked must continue to parade through our courts and penal institutions.

Bibliographical review

I am conscious that this is a discursive and wide-ranging piece. Each topic on which I touch has an extensive literature, especially the philosophical and scientific ones. What follows therefore is largely a set of starting points for further exploration.

In recent years there has been a new eruption of books and articles that attempt to place crime and punishment in a broader context and to discern underlying social, economic and political changes, which affect how we approach criminal policy. These essays tend to be speculative rather than empirical but provide valuable stimulation and questioning for all that. Prominent in this category are the books and essays of David Garland. *Punishment and Modern Society*, (Oxford: Oxford University Press, 1990) and *The Culture of Control* (Oxford: Oxford University Press, 2001) fairly comprehensively state his position. Addressing the nature of just punishment in a society where life chances may be said to be unevenly or maldistributed, Nicola Lacey's *State Punishment* (London: Routledge, 1988) presents a clear analysis and an explicit statement of her political values. At the other end of the political spectrum are the works of James Q. Wilson, particularly *Thinking About Crime* (New York: Basic Books, 1983, revised edition); see also Wilson's edited collection *Crime and Public Policy* (San Francisco: Institute for Contemporary Studies, 1983). Digby Anderson has also brought together and edited a useful collection of conservative-leaning essays in *This Will Hurt: The Restoration of Virtue and Civic Order* (London: The Social Affairs Unit, 1995).

There are a number of readers on the philosophy of punishment. One that I have found particularly useful over the years, both as a sourcebook and teaching aid, is Stanley E. Grupp (ed.) *Theories of Punishment* (Bloomington: Indiana University Press, 1971). This collection includes C.S. Lewis's inspirational and intentionally provocative 'The Humanitarian Theory of Punishment' as well as a measured critique and response from Norval Morris and Donald Buckle. Anthony Duff and David Garland (eds) have put together an excellent collection of sources in their *Reader on Punishment* (Oxford: Oxford University Press, 1994).

In a book now almost 40 years old, Leon Radzinowicz provides valuable insight into the transition from penal philosophy to policy over the last 250 years. This was his 1965 James Carpenter Lectures at Columbia University School of Law (*Ideology and Crime: A Study of Crime in its Social and Historical Context*. London: Heinemann, 1966). Cesare Beccaria's *Dei Delitti e delle Pene* (1764) has had a number of English translations, and is required reading for any student of penology. Cesare Lombroso's thinking is summarised in his *Crime: Its Causes and Remedies* (translated H.P. Horton. Boston: Little Brown, 1918). Versions of Enrico Ferri's several works are available in readers and reprints and provide a useful introduction to the biological school of deterministic criminology and its consequences for penal policy.

Turning to sentencing, Andrew Ashworth's *Sentencing and Criminal Justice* (London: Butterworths, 1995) is a clearly written account of how theories of punishment affect the structure and practice of sentencing. There is a helpful discussion of the move from rehabilitative and welfare-directed crime strategies to social defence and incapacitation in David Garland's *The Culture of Control* (see above). This has produced various commentaries and responses, including a recent empirical study by Carla Cesaroni and Anthony N. Doob 'The Decline in Support for Penal Welfarism', *British Journal of Criminology* (2003) 43, 434–441. Leon Radzinowicz and Roger Hood, writing before the current vast expansion in the incapacitatory use of imprisonment, nevertheless provide one important line of its genealogy in their essay, 'Incapacitating the Habitual Criminal: The English Experience', *Michigan Law Review*

(August 1980), 78, 8. As a closely related topic, I discuss English ideas about the criminal classes in my *English Local Prisons 1860–1900* (London: Routledge, 1995). For a contemporary account of the 'dangerous classes' and their near neighbours, see Henry Mayhew and John Binny, *The Criminal Prisons of London and Scenes of London Life* (London: Griffin, Bohn, 1862; republished by Frank Cass, 1968). Ask if there are not resonances with some modern studies and discussions.

The prison matters dealt with in this essay fall under various headings. On the distinction between behaviourists and reformists and the general context of imprisonment in early Victorian England, see my *History of English Prison Administration*, Vol. 1, 1750–1877 (London: Routledge and Kegan Paul, 1981). Michael Ignatieff also illuminates this important phase in penal history, although he confines himself to the penitentiary movement, in his *A Just Measure of Pain: The Penitentiary in the Industrial Revolution* (London: Macmillan, 1978). For Jeremy Bentham's still-stimulating views, see *The Rationale of Punishment* (London: R. Heward, 1830, and subsequent editions). Alfred Blumstein has for several decades been analysing the prevalence and expansion of imprisonment in the United States and is recognised as the pre-eminent authority in this field. With Allen Beck he gives an analysis of the growth in numbers in recent decades, 'Population Growth in U.S. Prisons, 1980–96' in Richard Frase and Michael Tonry (eds) *Prisons* (Chicago: Chicago University Press, 1999). For regular, if constantly depressing updates, website and hard copy, consult the Home Office in London and the Bureau of Justice Statistics, Washington, D.C. The Council of Europe also regularly publishes criminal and penal statistics. As with all similar comparative compilations, these need close and careful reading and (usually) a deal of qualification. For 'selective incapacitation', see Don Gottfredsen's essay in Stephen D. Gottfredsen and Seán McConville (eds) *American's Correctional Crisis* (Westport, CT: Greenwood, 1987).

Discussions of free will are of course to be found throughout philosophy, from the ancients to modern times and in almost all theology. I have referred here to Kant and to Sartre, both of whom discuss notions of autonomy and freedom and from different perspectives argue that we must accept the necessity of choice, if only from the practical point of view, to enable us to conduct our lives. Of Kant's work, see especially his *Critique of Pure Reason* (1787) and his *Critique of Practical Reason* (1788): these are available in various reprints and collected editions. Sartre's thinking about free will and morality evolved from a highly individualised to a more socially expressive philosophy: his 1947 *Cahiers pour une morale* are particularly significant. C. Howells (ed.) *The Cambridge Companion to Sartre* (Cambridge:

Cambridge University Press, 1992) is an excellent introduction to this complex philosopher. Karl Marx and Sigmund Freud set the scene for much twentieth-century discussion of free will and morality. Both authors were prolific and ambitiously comprehensive and there are many editions of their works. Although it has its critics (including some impressive modern scholars), Isaiah Berlin's *Karl Marx* (London: Thornton Butterworth, 1939) remains one of the very best introductions, to the man and his thoughts, not least because of Berlin's sophisticated strand of liberalism. Accounts of Freud and his teaching have similarly been subject to modern criticism – some of it fierce. Maurice MacMillan, *Freud Evaluated* (Cambridge, MA: MIT Press, 1990) is an outstanding and widely praised review of Freud and his critics.

The literature of modern biology, evolutionary and genetic, is in constant expansion. The most controversial recent work is Steven Pinker's excellently written polemic against social determinism, arguing the case for innate biologically transmitted differences: *The Blank State: The Modern Denial of Human Nature* (London: Allen Lane, 2002). Whatever one finally concludes about Pinker's ideas, the comprehensiveness, clarity, combativeness and liveliness of his book make it essential for anyone seeking to understand this subject. Two reviews (of the very many which the book attracted) are particularly trenchant. Simon Blackburn observes that 'Pinker seems to know everything ...' and then goes on to mount his counter-polemic ('Meet the Flinstones', *The New Republic,* 25 November 2002). H. Allen Orr is similarly sceptical but also helps us better to understand Pinker's approach ('Darwinian Storytelling', *New York Review of Books*, 27 February 2003).

Now almost a decade behind us, Charles Murray and Richard J. Herrnstein knocked over several hundred hornets' nests with their book *The Bell Curve* (London and New York: The Free Press, 1994). *The New Republic* published sections from the book and a selection of responses in its issue of 31 October 1994. This is a valuable symposium, marred only by the excesses of a few contributors. The importance of *The Bell Curve* was its attempt to deal with race, genes and IQ, and through the latter with crime. In some ways this might be seen as a modern but, it must be said, well thought-out version of Lombroso's approach to the 'born criminal'. The most comprehensive statement of sociobiology and evolutionary functionalism is Richard Dawkin's *The Selfish Gene* (New York: Oxford University Press, 1989). A critique of these approaches is robustly provided by Steven Rose in his *Lifelines: Biology Beyond Determinism* (London: Allen Lane, 1997).

On the moral and public policy issues arising from genetics – and a little bit of crystal-ball gazing – I was hugely impressed by the October

2002 report of the Nuffield Council on Bioethics, chaired by Bob Hepple (*Genetics and Human Behaviour*. London: Nuffield Council on Bioethics). The thoughtfulness of the ethical analysis and the clarity and authority with which developments in molecular genetics are considered, make this an essential starting point for anyone wishing to investigate the subject. Numerous books, essays and newspaper articles are devoted to the ethics of genetic science. We may expect a torrent of these as technology makes ever more choices possible. Sheila Greene makes some interesting and important points in her succinct essay, 'What Makes a Person a Person? The Limits and Limitations of Genetics', in Maureen Junker-Kenny (ed.) *Designing Life? Genetics, Procreation and Ethics* (Aldershot: Ashgate, 1999). (Other contributions to this useful volume are also well worth attention.)

It is all but impossible to see where scientific solutions to the ills and imperfections of mankind will lead us. That there have already been far-reaching innovations is beyond doubt and that more are immediately in train is clear. 'More' is the theme of Bill McKibben's cautionary (if not Jeremian) account of our pursuit of perfectibility in man through science. Do we know where we are going? Why are we going? And what shall we do when we get there? (*Enough: Staying Human in an Engineered Age*. New York: Times Books, 2003).

On the 50th anniversary of the discovery of the double helix, Matt Ridley sketches the development of modern genetics and interviews leading scientists, who discuss possible future developments and ethical issues ('DNA: The Future', *Cam*, 38 (2003), 22–24; see also his book, *Nature Via Nurture*. Glasgow: Harper Collins, 2003). There are far too many new scientific results appearing to attempt even a cursory overview, but a recent analysis of the literature is too intriguing to overlook. Marcus Munro, T.G. Clark and their colleagues analysed 79 studies carried out in 18 countries. One of their conclusions is that people who have a version of a specified chemical (dopamine D4 receptor) may be more likely to try dangerous activities. ('Genetic Polymorphisms and Personality in Healthy Adults: A Systematic Review and Meta-Analysis,' *Molecular Psychiatry* (2003), 8, 471–482). I suspect that there will be many such analyses in the near future, dealing with behavioural traits. The cat is already strolling among the pigeons.

Index